WHY MICHAEL COULDN'T HIT

WHY MICHAEL COULDN'T HIT

AND OTHER TALES OF THE NEUROLOGY OF SPORTS

HAROLD L. KLAWANS, M.D.

AVON BOOKS  NEW YORK

AVON BOOKS
A division of
The Hearst Corporation
1350 Avenue of the Americas
New York, New York 10019

Copyright © 1996 by Harold L. Klawans, M.D.
Front cover photograph by Corbis Bettman
Published by arrangement with W. H. Freeman and Company
Visit our website at **http://www.AvonBooks.com**
ISBN: 0-380-73041-3

The W. H. Freeman edition contains the following Library of Congress Cataloging in Publication Data:

Klawans, Harold L.
    Why Michael couldn't hit, and other tales of the neurology of sports / Harold Klawans.
        p.   cm.
    Includes bibliographical references and index.
    1. Neurophysiology. 2. Sports—Physiological aspects. 3. Nervous system—Diseases—Complications. I. Title.
RC1236.N47K53   1996   96-24097
362.1'968'0088796—dc20   CIP

First Avon Books Trade Printing: April 1998

AVON TRADEMARK REG. U.S. PAT. OFF. AND IN OTHER COUNTRIES, MARCA REGISTRADA, HECHO EN U.S.A.

Printed in the U.S.A.

OPM 10 9 8 7 6 5 4 3 2 1

To Barbara,

My best and most loving critic.

Contents

(The) Pregame Show

Why am I, a physician, writing a book about sports? More to the point, why am I writing a book about the neurology of the games we love so much? In part, a neurological analysis of sports flows naturally from the fact that all behavior has a neurological basis, whether it is that flaw in Ben Hogan's putting or in mine. But that is only a starting point.

I could offer the usual excuses for my decision. Like most Americans, I started playing sports long before I had to contemplate the reality that I would have to consider some other form of activity to make my way in the world. I also learned when I was quite young to watch others playing sports. Both of these processes, beginning as they did so early in my life, have left their marks. Although I have been a practicing neurologist for three decades, I remain addicted to the Chicago White Sox and the University of Michigan Wolverines and to the phenomenon of competition in sports. My wife once walked in on me unexpectedly in a hotel room to find me *in medias res* with a strange game on the TV. It was a snooker match. I could not name either of the players. Nor could I tell her how the game was scored. Nor who was winning. But I resisted when she tried to turn off the TV. It was the competition and the observation of that competition that mattered to me, not the score or the scoring system. Neurologists, first and foremost, are observers.

When I finally acquired the skills involved in the process of neurological observation, I realized that the neurologist in me enhanced my understanding of a world filled with supposedly nonneurological behaviors, including sports and the people who played them. Neurological observation and reasoning can explain aspects of sports that are otherwise inexplicable, even to those who play and teach those sports.

What does neurology have to do with Michael Jordan's inability to hit a baseball? Everything. Or with Ben Hogan blowing a putt in a Grand Slam tournament? Just as much. Can it explain why Muhammad Ali developed Parkinson's disease in 1984 while the man he knocked out ten years earlier, George Foreman, kept on fighting for another decade until he regained the heavyweight title? Of course it can.

What is it that gives neurologists this unique perspective?

In part, this outlook is the logical extension of the nature of neurologists. In comparison to other physicians, we are irregular at best, often asking what seems to be the wrong question, at the wrong time. An elderly woman falls. Her hip hurts. The doctor in the emergency room orders an X ray. The radiologist reads it and makes a diagnosis of a fractured hip. That is his job and his perspective. The anesthesiologist puts the woman to sleep. The orthopedic surgeon inserts a pin or a new joint. Later the internist makes a diagnosis of osteoporosis and, along with the endocrinologist, starts to treat her for that. All well and good so far: modern medicine at its very best. The neurologist, if he happens to be called in to see that patient, asks the one question that no one else has bothered to consider, "Why did she fall in the first place?"

The proper function of a neurologist often makes me think of an anecdote about the great twentieth-century philosopher Wittgenstein that Tom Stoppard told in his play *Jumpers*. "Meeting a friend in a corridor, Wittgenstein said: 'Tell me, why do people always say that it was natural for men to assume that the sun went around the earth rather than that the earth was rotating?' His friend said, 'Well, obviously it just looks as if the sun is going around the earth.' To which the philosopher replied, 'Well, what would it have looked like if it had looked as if the earth was rotating?'"

The answer is obvious. It would look the way it does look, for that is how it is and how it appears. It is formulating the question that is pivotal. Good neurologists are trained to do just that—formulate the good "wrong" question.

The question is not why Michael Jordan, despite his wonderful, if not incomparable, athletic skills, couldn't learn to hit. There is a far better and much more basic question that must first be answered: How does anyone learn to hit a speeding, spherical baseball with a cylindrical bat? How does the nervous system go about acquiring that skill? The brain was certainly never designed to hit baseballs. No physiological system was selected by our evolutionary descent specifically to perform that task.

Once that entire process is understood, with all of its built-in limitations, the question becomes why anyone ever even fantasized that M.J. could learn to hit major league pitching at the age of thirty-one.

Another element of the neurological perspective comes from the nature of those activities that neurologists have been trained to observe and understand. Neurologists are no longer merely documenters of severe deficits. Is the patient paralyzed or not? We have become students of behavior in a far broader sense, from walking, to talking, to reading, to all the subtle variations of these complex activities. To understand what we observe, we have become students of the evolution of these behaviors within the brain and life of each patient.

Is learning to hit a baseball so different from learning to play a violin? Or to play Nintendo? Or to speak a language?

It is the neurologist in me that first realized that the answer to these questions is a resounding "No!" Understanding that "No" enhanced my understanding of sports and the people who excelled in them as well as those who didn't. But it was a two-way street. That understanding also extended my knowledge of the brain and its function.

I have always maintained that the best teaching I ever had in neurology was as an undergraduate student at the University of Michigan. The teacher was a classical archeologist, Clark Hopkins, who had been in charge of the excavation of the Roman city Dura-Europos. He taught in the Department of Fine

Arts and the course was Hellenic and Hellenistic art. In this two-semester sequence, Professor Hopkins taught us to look at a Greek statue and see it as a whole and at the same time see all those details that would allow us to date it to within a decade or two: the position of the arms, the style of the hair, the folds of the garments.

That was how I learned to analyze disorders of the human gait, by applying those same hard-learned principles to neurology. I was able to see a patient walk and in the same glance see how he swung his arms, lifted his feet, moved his legs through his hips, and every other pertinent detail. Only later did I realize that what I learned by watching all those patients also brought with it a greater understanding of Greek sculpture.

Learning has applications that apply in all directions. That is the type of understanding I hope to be able to convey here, for this is not a book about the brains of athletes but one about the human brain and its ability to learn and adapt and modify itself. Athletic skills are merely one example of this process.

I have not treated Muhammad Ali or Primo Carnera or Ben Hogan, or any of the other famous athletes whose stories I relate here. I know what diseases most of these athletes had because they have been documented in medical journals or biographies. In other athletes, photographic or filmed records revealed evidence of their diseases.

In the 1983 movie *Max Dugan Returns*, the grandfather, played by Jason Robards, is a gangster who returns years later after having run out on his daughter. Max reads philosophy and hires Charlie Lau, who was at that time the White Sox batting coach and an expert on the philosophy of hitting, to teach his grandson how to hit a baseball. The climax of the Neil Simon screenplay revolves around the grandson's attempt to "hit one out for Wittgenstein." In the spirit of Max Dugan, this book was written for both the Wittgenstein enthusiast and the Michael Jordan fan in us all. And to answer the question of why some other Charlie Lau wasn't there when Michael Jordan needed him.

chapter 1

Why Michael Jordan Couldn't Hit a Baseball

HIS ANNOUNCEMENT STUNNED SPORTS FANS around the world: Basketball superstar Michael Jordan told us that he was going to retire from professional basketball. Not many other sports figures had turned their backs on sports at the top of their games, and most who had were boxers, world champion heavyweights like Gene Tunney and Rocky Marciano. But that was boxing, and this was basketball. M.J. had been living out the great American dream. How could he give it all up? The roars of the crowds? The adulation? The success?

Chicago fans were devastated. How could this be happening, and why? Michael was the greatest basketball player of his era and possibly of all time, right up there with Bill Russell and Julius Erving. Beyond that, Michael was certainly one of the most popular sports figures ever. He was a recognized superstar around the world. What made his retirement even harder to accept was that he was still in the prime of his career. Although no longer a kid—he was just over thirty—M.J. wasn't an old man, even in basketball terms. He had no lingering or recurring injuries. He had plenty of great years left in him, years that promised more National Basketball Association championships for the city of Chicago. Why would he retire?

In his retirement announcement, Michael Jordan gave the sports world two reasons for his premature departure. First, he had nothing left to prove—and in basketball terms that may well have been true. Jordan had been larger than life since he had been a college freshman. In his last game as a freshman, he had made a long jump shot in the final seconds to win the NCAA championship for coach Dean Smith and his North Carolina teammates. After leading the United States to a Gold Medal in the 1984 Olympics, he was drafted third by the Chicago Bulls in the 1984 NBA draft. All-star center Hakeem Olajuwon and the oft-injured Sam Bowie were drafted one and two. Jordan was named rookie of the year, playing shooting guard for the Chicago Bulls. Soon he became the perennial scoring champion, a perennial all-star, and one of the best defensive players in the league. For the previous three years before he quit basketball, he had been at the pinnacle of his game and had led the Bulls to a "three-peat," three consecutive NBA championships, a feat no team had accomplished since the almost mythical Boston Celtics, coached by Red Auerbach and led by Bill Russell. During those three seasons before his retirement, Michael had led the league in scoring all three times, giving him seven consecutive scoring titles. He was the league's most valuable player in the play-offs during all three of the Bulls' consecutive championships. Along the way he led the NBA "Dream Team" to the 1992 Olympic championship and thereby added a second Olympic Gold Medal to his collection of mementos.

Michael Jordan's other reason for his retirement echoed one excuse that Chicago sports fans had been asked to accept since 1920. That was the year the Black Sox scandal broke and eight players of the Chicago White Sox were accused of throwing the 1919 World Series to the Cincinnati Reds. One of the organizers of the plot, the star pitcher of the team, Eddie Cicotte, was asked why he had done it. His reply, "I did it for the wife and

Michael Jordan, tongue extended, elevating for another of his unstoppable jump shots. During his first full season back in the NBA (1995–1996), he led the league in scoring for an unprecedented eighth time and added a fadeaway jump shot to his repertoire.

kids." Michael echoed the same sentiments. He wanted to spend more time with his family. What could anyone say to that? Nothing.

Then a few months later there was another announcement, this one bringing joy to the hearts of Chicago fans. Michael Jordan was coming back to us. He was going to leave wife and family behind and come out of retirement, not to return to the Chicago Bulls but to become a professional baseball player. M.J. had signed a contract with the Chicago White Sox. True, it was a minor league contract, but to most fans that was a mere technicality. It would only be a matter of time until Jordan would be patrolling right field for the White Sox and leading another Chicago team on to glory. He could become the first man to be in both the Baseball Hall of Fame in Cooperstown and the Basketball Hall of Fame in Springfield, Massachusetts. That was what the local pundits were predicting. Considering his overall athletic skills and talents, it was only a matter of time and practice. The Chicago fan in me wanted that to be true.

Michael Jordan is a great athlete. There's no question about that. He was, at the time of his initial retirement (in the spring of 1993), the greatest athlete of his era, or darn close to it. But it was hard for me to join the accolades that pronounced him the greatest athlete of the century. He was a basketball player. Period. Others had been great athletes in more than just one game. Jim Thorpe, the great Native American athlete, had won both the decathlon and the pentathlon at the 1912 Olympics, an accomplishment never matched before or since. Then, after he was stripped of his medals for having played a couple of games of semipro baseball, he went on to play both major league baseball and professional football. Despite his unexcelled variety of athletic skills, Thorpe only managed a lifetime batting average of .252 in six seasons as a major leaguer. His best season was his last, 1919. That year he hit .327 in sixty games. But as soon as professional football beckoned him, he gave up baseball. In football he was a star people would and did pay money to see.

Michael Jordan had played basketball and only basketball, and because of that the neurologist in me knew he could never make the grade as a major league baseball player. We would never have the pleasure of watching him star for the White Sox or even for the Birmingham Barons, or whichever team the Sox picked out for him. For wherever he swung the bat, Michael Jordan would not be able to hit a baseball, at least not well enough to play competitively at a major league level.

That was a bet you could take to the bank. Not because Michael Jordan wasn't a great athlete, with both speed and quickness, or because he would get poor batting instruction. And certainly not because of any lack of effort on his part. He could be taught and could learn to play the field and run the bases with the best of them. No one would work harder to develop his own abilities. Unfortunately, hard work and dedication would not be the issues. His inability to hit would be the direct result of a neurological problem. It would not be due to any undiagnosed neurological malady but to the way in which his brain and ours have evolved to do what they do. His lack of hitting skill is part of his legacy as a member of the human race.

No matter how great a superstar he had become, no matter how superhuman the rest of his body seemed, his brain was still a human brain with all its attendant abilities and limitations. Hitting successfully is not a pure muscular skill, like pressing a couple of hundred pounds. Hitting is a visual-motor skill, and like all other skills it has to be learned. The brain has to learn how to recognize the spin and speed and direction of the ball as it leaves the pitcher's hand, and then to swing the bat at just the right speed and in precisely the proper location to hit the ball solidly as it crosses home plate. This is a tall order for anyone's brain. And the sad fact was that at age thirty-one, Michael Jordan's brain was just too old to acquire that skill.

How could that be? Thirty-one is young. People learn at ages far older than that. Hitting is not exactly nuclear science. And that is precisely why it can't be learned at such an ancient age.

To realize why this is so, it is necessary to try to understand the human brain and how it learns and acquires skills. The human brain did not just appear fully developed within our skulls. It evolved to get there. Our evolution, like that of every other species, began as a biological one. It was part of the process of classical Darwinian descent. But the evolution of we humans and how we live and function no longer consists of merely biological evolution but also includes social, cultural, and environmental changes. We have developed the ability to alter our environment to an extent that no other species can even approach. Hence, by changing and controlling our own environment, we have effected a second form of evolution, which guides and directs the brain's further functions. In other words, our brains have evolved the ability to guide and direct their own development.

While rarely looked at in that way, baseball is a prime example of such an environmental change, a change that can be fed into the developing brain and alter the way in which it develops and functions. Not even Abner Doubleday made that claim. American children grow up being exposed to baseball as a man-made environmental condition and learn how to hit baseballs with baseball bats. We do not all do that equally well, but we do it. We also learn how to dribble basketballs while for reasons unknown to us our French counterparts are raised in an environment deprived of baseballs but replete with soccer balls. These French kids acquire the skill to dribble that ball with their feet.

How does this difference come about? How does baseball as an environmental input act upon the brain? And why could that input not act on M.J.'s brain?

The increase in the size and complexity that characterizes the human brain has been achieved with remarkably little genetic change. There is an embarrassingly close similarity between our genetic makeup and that of the gorilla or the chimpanzee. More than that, the total amount of genetic information coded in the double helixes of DNA has remained fairly constant throughout all of mammalian evolution, from shrews to kangaroos to dolphins to us. It is thought that there are about one million genes. That number is pretty much the same in the mouse and in humans. It is divided up into different numbers of chromosomes in different species, but the total number of genes is relatively stable. In all humans it is, of course, identical, and the actual number of active genes is far less than one million. In fact, the number is closer to one-half that, since forty percent or more of all chromosomal DNA appears to be redundant and plays no active role in development.

The best estimates suggest that about ten thousand genes, which is one percent of the total gene pool (or approximately two percent of the active gene pool), play an active part in the design and construction of the brain and the rest of the nervous system. This is true for humans and chimpanzees and walruses and even pet gerbils.

For humans, this number seems to be woefully inadequate, especially when the size and complexity of the human brain are considered. It seems enough for a simple house cat, or maybe even a chimpanzee—but for us? The human brain is made up of 10^{10} nerve cells—that is ten billion cells—one cell for each dollar it would cost to build a couple of top-of-the-line nuclear submarines. Looked at in that way, ten thousand genes do not seem quite so inadequate. After all, the defense budget took only three or four hundred members of Congress to set it into place. And we all know how many of them are redundant (or at least seem that way).

There are, in addition, 10^{14} synapses, or active connections between nerve cells, where messages can be sent or interrupted. That is one hundred trillion, a number that dwarfs any projection of the national debt into insignificance. That is a number worthy of respect.

How can a mere ten thousand genes manage to control so many synapses? How can these relatively few genes do so much more for us than they do for other species? Remember that most of what they do for us is not that different. Any survey of comparative anatomy of the nervous systems of mammals supports that conclusion resoundingly. The major structures are all the same, whether the brain belongs to a sheep or a person; and so are most of the major pathways. The hardwiring is pretty much the same, far more similar than dissimilar.

Consider the optic nerves. They always start as outpouchings of the brain itself, beginning in the retinas of the universally paired sets of eyes. They then travel back toward the rest of the brain and decussate (or cross) partially in order to read the same geniculate bodies of the thalamus. There, pathways known as the optic radiations carry the visual images back to the occipital lobes. It is pretty much the same in every species.

This arrangement sends information from the right visual field (everything seen with either eye that is to the right of the middle when looking straight ahead) into the left visual cortex, an area known as the calcarine cortex of the occipital lobe. Analogously, images from the left visual field end up in the right calcarine cortex. This system has the same structure and function in all mammals. The same genes have done the same job and produced the same basic wiring diagram. It is this system that lets lions see which gnu is straying too far from the pack and that Chicago fans hoped would allow Michael Jordan to pick up the exact spin on a baseball as it leaves the pitcher's fingers. For it is learning within this pathway that is critical to the batter. Without it, he cannot hit a lick.

The baseball world is divided between right-handed hitters and left-handed hitters. But hitting (with the exception of one-armed Pete Gray, who played outfield for the St. Louis Browns during the last year of World War II) is a two-handed affair. Both hands grasp and swing the bat. Right-handed batters differ primarily from their left-handed counterparts not in the use of a dominant arm for hitting but on which side of the plate they stand. And how they look at the opposing pitchers. And, of course, pitchers do differ as to which hand releases the ball and where that release point is in relation to the vision of the batter.

It is the visual fields that differ with batting stance. The right-handed hitter stares out at the pitcher and must pick up the pitch coming out of his left visual field, if that pitcher is right-handed. But he must see the ball rotating out of the center of his vision and right visual field from a left-handed pitcher. This is undoubtedly why right-handers fare better against left-handed pitchers. They get a better look at the ball. This has a neurophysiological and neuroanatomical basis. There's nothing psychological about it. For the same reason left-handers see the baseballs coming at them from right-handed pitchers better and hit those pitches far better. Yet hitting is never easy, and as Yogi Berra put it, good pitching always beats good hitting. And vice versa.

The best example of our phylogenetic debt to other species in the design of the hardwiring of our brains is probably the entire process of decussation, or crossing, to the other side of the brain. The right brain directs the left arm. Why? It also feels sensation from the left side of the body: pain, touch, temperature, pressure, position sense. It sees to the left. Again, why? This all results from a crossed wiring diagram filled with decussations galore. But why? How did it get that way? Put most simply, it came about because the pineal eye of early amphibians had a lens.

On our long trip from amphioxus to human, one stage was the amphibians. Many amphibians developed a single extra eye in the top of the head. Although this eye was above the parietal lobes, and is sometimes called the *parietal eye,* because it served to transmit signals to the pineal area of the brain, it is more often called the *pineal eye.*

The pineal eye had a lens, and it is the lens that makes all the difference. If an object, say, some insect the amphibian would love to eat, moves from left to right, the image on the retina of the pineal eye also moves. If there were no lens, the image would move in the same direction. Since there is a lens, however, the image moves in the opposite direction, to the left. The fly is now on the right, but the image is on the left side of the pineal retina and the left half of the brain. And the amphibian still wants to eat that fly.

To eat it, he must catch it; to catch it, he must see it. So as the fly moves farther to the right, he must turn his eye by lowering the right side. A muscle on the right side of the head must pull that right lens down. But the sensation to trigger that movement is in the left brain. So the left brain has to send an impulse out along a nerve to that muscle on the other side of the skull—from left to right. That phenomenon is called decussation, or crossing of nerve fibers, and it all started with the amphibians.

If the hardwiring and the basic structure of the human brain are so similar to those of other species, why do our brains function so differently?

The complexity of our brain is not achieved just by our genetic heritage but also by what that heritage allows the brain to do. Our genetic coding allows the brain to grow and develop while interacting with the environment. It is, in essence, still growing and developing as it is learning. This interaction with the environment shapes and directs the brain's growth and development. No other species can make that statement.

Human infants are underdeveloped and helpless at birth and remain so for a long time. The human brain is far less developed at birth than were the brains of our newborn ancestors. We are born with an immature, almost embryonic brain that continues to grow and evolve in relation to its environment to a degree and for a duration of time that is unprecedented in any other species. How did that happen? And why?

The brains of most other species are fully formed by birth, whereas the brains of the primates continue to grow during a brief, early postnatal period. However, the brains of humans continue to grow at rapid fetal growth rates long after birth. This process extends for many years. The duration is different in different systems of the brain, and in some even continues into what we consider adult life. At birth, the human brain is only about one-quarter of its eventual adult size and weight. In other words, at least seventy-five percent of the brain develops after birth where environmental influences can help shape that development. It is during this prolonged period of dependency, of growth and development of the brain, that the brain is most plastic and thereby most susceptible to environmental influence. It is not just the ten thousand genes that figure out how all those synapses are to interact but the environment that helps write the software. It is during this period that most environmentally dependent skills are acquired by the brain.

This is one reason why it is almost impossible to discuss the inheritance of acquired skills, including such skills as language abilities or intelligence, as purely genetic issues. Nature determines the limits of what nurture can accomplish. That is an absolute. But at the same time nurture determines not only what nature can do but the way in which nature develops in order to do it. In so doing, nurture determines what we measure as nature. It is not because it was good politics that the Head Start program was the most successful aspect of Lyndon Johnson's Great Society. It was because it was good science.

The drawn-out period of brain development means the period of infantile and childhood dependency on adults lasts many years. This dependency is both a result of the lack of adult adaptive function by the brain and a sign that the process of acquiring adaptive skills is still proceeding. The ongoing brain-environment interactions build upon the plasticity of the still-developing brain, but this is not a process that goes on equally forever. The human brain is distinguished from the brains of other species by the postnatal capacity for learning and its apparent plasticity, but there are limits. There are critical periods, or windows of opportunity, for different types of learning. If a skill is not acquired during its critical period, then the acquisition of that skill in later life will be harder, if not impossible. Language has usually been our model for such skills, but no skill is more environmentally dependent than hitting a baseball. In other words, an adult who was deprived of exposure to baseball as an adolescent and tries to learn to hit a baseball would be much like an adult who had never been exposed to language trying to learn to speak at the age of twenty. To extend the analogy, hitting a major league change of pace is far more like trying to learn to read. Skills must be learned at the right time, if they are ever to be learned well.

We are not unique in this. Birds learn the specific songs that they will spend their lives singing by imitating the songs of other birds. In order to be able to do this, almost every species of bird must hear these songs quite early in life, in the first couple of months in fact. If the songs are not heard during this critical period, they are never learned. Birds deprived of this input remain songless. The one exception to this rule are canaries. It appears that each season canaries can learn new songs. It is almost as if they can recapture their youth. This annual rebirth of a critical period for learning is accompanied by an annual crop of new auditory neurons that makes the acquisition possible.

Would Michael Jordan be able to recapture his youth, or was he merely a human whose window of opportunity had come and gone? His superior athletic skills did not mean that he had a unique ability to regenerate new visual-motor neurons on an annual basis. His brain was no different from any other human brain. His unparalleled basketball skills were the results of talents he had acquired and developed long before his thirtieth birthday, at a time when his brain was still developing and was still capable of selecting such neurons and neuronal networks.

Human infants acquire a bewildering number of different skills as their brains mature. They learn to sit up, to stand, to crawl, to walk. None of these physical skills requires any teaching. None is even based on mimicry. A blind infant masters them all. It is as if the acquisition of these skills is hard-wired— built— into the nervous system.

The process is not the same for hitting. A child who is unfortunate enough to be born into an environment without baseball will never learn to swing a bat on his own. The acquisition of a particular athletic skill is analogous to the acquisition of particular songs by songbirds. The ability to acquire songs is there. It has been ingrained genetically into the brain. The specific song depends on the environment. So it is with hitting. It is just like our acquisition of language. The ability to learn language is genetically encoded in our brains. What language we will learn depends on exposure. So Americans learn English and how to swing a bat. The French learn French and how to kick a soccer ball.

Children do acquire language with very little assistance from anyone else. It is primarily self-taught, as long as a child is exposed to language. Our brains appear to be innately equipped with systems that are able to acquire language. But this innate capability is both governed and limited by the maturation of the brain.

Michael's concentration was there. So were his athletic conditioning and skills. Yet his strikeout to home-run ratio was over 30. Babe Ruth's for his entire career against major league pitching was under 2 (1,330 strikeouts compared to 714 career home runs). Hank Aaron's was also under 2 (1,383 strikeouts compared to 755 home runs). Neither Ruth nor Aaron, though, ever sank a jump shot against professional competition.

As the human brain matures and acquires specific self-taught hard-wired skills, it simultaneously passes through a succession of stages when language may be acquired. By age one, when the child can stand alone, she is capable of duplicating some syllables and understanding some words. Six months later she is creeping backward and downstairs and can walk forward. She now has a repertoire of anywhere from a few to fifty words, but they are used as single words, not phrases. By two years of age, she is running with numerous falls but nonetheless running, and now she uses short phrases; the babbling that had begun at about six months, when she began sitting up, disappears. And so it goes until age four, by which time language is well established. Hitting a baseball remains in the future. The physical skills a person can acquire are entirely constrained by hardwiring. They can only be learned when that wiring is completed and can be activated.

There is an attempt now to apply this type of stepwise approach to learning to hit by starting very young kids off hitting a stationary ball resting on an elongated tee. Whether this is educationally or even neurologically sound is unclear. Most baseball hitters are not exceptionally good at hitting golf balls. And hitting a stationary golf ball does not in any way prepare one to see and hit a baseball. They are far different neurological processes. Golf at its most basic depends primarily on maintaining a posture that allows the golfer to carry out a finely controlled skilled movement. Hitting a baseball is a visual-motor skill that is about recognizing where a baseball is going to be at a particular instant of time and then getting your bat there, posture be damned. They are not the same skill at all. Besides, the window of opportunity for hitting may not begin until later than the age of six or seven. Having a youngster at age five hitting off a tee could be like reading to a six-week-old baby—it could just be too early to matter at all.

The same stepwise learning occurs in the acquisition of language, with one other constraint. Just like the learning of bird songs by birds and learning how to hit a curveball, the acquisition of language requires environmental input. Infants acquire the language they hear. American children learn English, French children French, Arabian children Arabic, and so forth. No matter what the language, the process and the stages are pretty much the same. And no matter what culture the human infant is raised in, no matter what language he is exposed to, acquisition of language can only occur during a critical period of development. A critical period is a specific time interval in which an ability must be acquired if it is ever to be acquired at all. It is the entire window of opportunity. For language, that critical period, or window of opportunity, is estimated to end at about puberty.

But how do we know that there is a window of opportunity for language? The earliest evidence came from those few humans who had not been exposed to language until after this critical period had passed. Their hardware was never given the needed software. One of the first and most celebrated of such instances was that of the Wild Boy of Aveyron. This boy, who was given the name Victor, was found living alone in the woods near Aveyron, France, toward the end of the eighteenth century. He was thought to be about twelve years old when he was captured. At that time he could neither speak nor understand language. In fact, he had no understanding of the concept of using language for communication.

Professor Jean-Marc-Gaspard Itard, a physician who was interested in the study of human behavior, took charge of him. Itard had published the first case of what later became known as Tourette's syndrome. For over five years, Itard tried to teach Victor to speak, to get him to learn even the rudiments of language, but Victor was unable to acquire the skill. After years of effort, he was able to understand a number of words and phrases but had learned only a few utterances, such as milk (*"lait"*) and Oh God (*"O Dieu"*). These he often said incorrectly. The now tamed Wild Boy never came close to acquiring the use of language. His critical period for doing so had passed.

We do not have all of the details of Victor's case history. It is possible that he may have been mentally retarded or deaf. But neither need be true to explain Victor's failure to learn language. For Victor, no language exposure before puberty translated into no language ever. Does that mean that the failure to see a ball hurtling toward you during childhood will translate into an inability to ever pick up a bat and hit a ball? That's hard to believe. Especially based on one eighteenth-century French kid.

Other far better documented cases of children who were completely deprived of environmental language input make the same point. A girl who has been dubbed "Genie" is one of the most recent examples (1977). She had been isolated in a room and kept away from virtually all human contact from the time she was twenty months old and should already have been able to say a number of words and understand a great deal more. Her isolation was continued until she was thirteen and had passed puberty. This imprisonment was enforced by her father, who was obviously schizophrenic and who treated her like an animal, to the extent that he barked at her instead of talking to her.

When Genie was finally discovered and rescued from her isolation, she was totally without language. Like Victor, she could neither speak nor understand speech. Whatever she may have learned early in her life had been lost. It was at this point that language exposure and instruction were initiated. Genie did better than Victor. She did learn to comprehend language but her speech lagged far behind her comprehension and she never mastered even the rudiments of grammar. According to her mother, she had learned single words prior to her incarceration. This suggests that she was not retarded, but more significantly that during the critical period early in her life, she had already started to learn language. So perhaps she had an advantage over Victor in that the key element of her postpubertal learning of language was relearning. As a result, Genie was able to reattain at least a fair measure of comprehension. Overall, however, her level of achievement was poor.

If Victor is the right model for the study of critical periods of development, then Genie does more than bring us into the twentieth century. The acquisition process may not be entirely all or none. Genie did learn something. By analogy, she could learn to swing a bat. Perhaps she could play sixteen-inch softball. But she could not really hit successfully, and certainly not at a major league level. And that is what has to be kept in mind when looking at Michael Jordan's career switch. What M.J. wanted to do at age thirty-one was not just to be able to play pickup games of softball in the park on Sunday mornings. He wanted to play major league baseball. He wanted to hit against the best pitchers in the game. He didn't want to learn to say a few phrases; he wanted to learn how to perform Shakespeare in the same company with Olivier and Gielgud. Not a bad fantasy.

What is the neurophysiological basis of learning that underlies both language skills and the hitting of baseballs? How does the genetically encoded brain actually learn the specific language to which it becomes exposed, or learn the sport of its environment? There are two opposing theories. One is referred to as instructive or constructive, and the other is called selective. The older, standard view is the instructive view, in which networks of nerve cells are "instructed" by experience to form certain synapses, or pathways, which, once formed and reinforced, are retained. This could easily produce a neural network capable of learning language as a process and then learning new languages with increasing ease. In this view, the critical period would close when the network would no longer be able to reinforce pathways.

A selective process works in just the opposite way. All the pathways are there waiting to be used. If used, they are reinforced. If not, they atrophy and disappear forever. In other words, the brain "learns" by selecting from a preexisting, wide range of possible pathways. The critical period starts when the maturation of the pathways sets out the range of adaptations that can be chosen. Those that are not chosen are eventually eliminated by continued maturation. The end of the critical period represents the time at which unchosen networks are eliminated. You learn to speak one language by such closure and you can add on to that one language of information. If you don't, you can't. End of ball game.

The theory of a selective process is very attractive and seems more consistent with the acquisition of language, which is far more dependent on exposure and selection than on instruction. The child hears sounds and learns to select the same sounds as part of its language. Whichever model is right, and most cognitive scientists are leaning toward selection, that process is bound by a critical period. The parameters of this window of opportunity remain the same, whether the process is selective or constructive. The relative skills of American athletes in world competition have not improved in the last two decades, but today we can field a competitive soccer team. Why? Because kids in the United States now play soccer. We, too, can now dribble with our feet.

Stories like those of Victor and Genie can be argued to be nothing more than aberrations. Such children were deprived of far more than just speech; they were both socially and emotionally deprived. Are they the only evidence we have for a critical period for speech?

Of course not. Victor was merely the starting place. The best support for the concept of a critical period during which speech and language must be acquired comes from clinical neurology and what neurologists have learned by studying patients who have lost the ability to use language. They have what neurologists call aphasia. The term *aphasia* denotes an abnormality with the use of language, either understanding language, producing meaningful language, or both. These disorders of the symbolic use of language are differentiated from neurological problems of the motor skills required for producing sounds on the one hand and disorders of generalized loss of intellectual function on the other.

Neurologists are a peculiar breed, and we think about the brain in a strange way. We begin by studying the anatomy of the normal brain and then superimposing on this the areas of injury, or "lesions," that we identify in patients with strokes and other neurological diseases. Whatever function was lost by a patient with a stroke must have been the normal function of the injured area.

For example: a patient had a stroke. At autopsy his brain shows an area of destroyed brain tissue called *encephalomalacia*, a brain softening. In this case the softening was in the right occipital lobe. Clinically, neurological examination before death had revealed loss of vision in the left eye, that is, loss of his left visual field. Hence we infer that vision of the left visual field is the normal province of the right occipital lobe. This has been demonstrated to be a hard-wired process genetically built into the brain. It is a structural-functional reality that we share with other mammalian species. Visual imagery from the left visual field enters both eyes. That from the right eye stays on the same side of the brain and, by way of the right thalamus, gets to the visual cortex of the right occipital lobe. The images of the left half of the visual field that enter the left eye cross the midline (our old friend, hard-wired decussation), meet up with those mediated by the right eye in the thalamus, and then are relayed together to end up in the right visual cortex.

Once these neuroanatomical and clinical facts are known, the system is infallible. When the next patient comes with a history of visual loss, the knowledge can be used. Examination of this patient shows complete loss of vision in the left visual fields of both eyes. The localization of the lesion is obvious. This patient has a lesion in the right occipital lobe that is interrupting the function of that lobe.

This hard-wired system is also influenced by the environment, and there is a critical period during which this influence can be expressed. These conclusions come from the studies of David H. Hubel and Torsten N. Weisel, who shared the 1981 Nobel Prize for physiology or medicine for this work. The visual cortex of cats and monkeys, and it is assumed of humans, contains neurons that respond selectively to specific features of the environment such as color or orientation. This selectivity can then be manipulated by the environment. For example, if a kitten is reared in an environment made up entirely of vertical stripes, then the neurons that respond to visual-spatial orientation will learn to respond primarily to vertical lines as opposed to horizontal lines. This bias can only be acquired during a critical period of growth and is an example of a selective rather than an instructive process. In other words, the system could initially respond to either vertical or horizontal lines, but the exposure to vertical lines results in vertical bias. Experience serves to define or select neurophysiological function. This is a good model for the role of the environment in ever more complex learning such as acquisition of language and hitting a baseball.

Each time a young batter tries to see a pitch and hit it, certain cells are "selected" to see that pitch and start off that process. If no pitches are seen, then absolutely no selection is made. Players talk about picking up the rotation on the ball as it leaves the pitcher's hand. It is this rotational bias that must be selected. It cannot be selected at age six by hitting off a tee, or later in life when the time for selection is over.

Language, like hitting, must be selected to occur in the correct area of the brain at the correct time during the brain's development. What is known about aphasia can be summarized into a couple of general rules derived from neurological observations:

Rule 1. A lesion of only one hemisphere is needed to cause aphasia. Ergo, one hemisphere is dominant for speech. If a patient is aphasic, he has a lesion of the dominant hemisphere for speech. In right-handers the dominant hemisphere is all but invariably the left. So if a right-hander is aphasic, he has a problem in his left hemisphere. In left-handers the situation is not as clear, because in most left-handers the left hemisphere is dominant for speech.

Rule 2. Not all aphasias are identical. If a patient has more trouble speaking than understanding, the lesion is more toward the front of the dominant hemisphere. If the patient has more trouble understanding than speaking, the lesion is more toward the back of the hemisphere. All of the rest of the theorization is secondary and, in a way, mere commentary.

What does all of this have to do with Michael Jordan and the art of hitting? The study of aphasia proves that critical periods for learning particular skills are part and parcel of normal brain function and development.

While the selection of the left hemisphere as the dominant hemisphere for speech is fairly automatic, injury to the left side of the brain can force the opposite side to be selected. And this is done automatically, at least early in life. How long can this ability last?

Until puberty or thereabouts. Every neurologist knows this from personal experience in treating brain-injured patients. The commonest cause of this form of acquired aphasia is a stroke, and though strokes are relatively rare in childhood, they do occur. In children, they are often related to inflammation of one carotid artery supplying blood to one of the cerebral hemispheres. This results in a significant injury of that hemisphere and a contralateral in hemiplegia or infantile hemiplegia. If the dominant hemisphere for speech is involved, this also produces aphasia. So what happens to children with aphasia from such strokes?

If the infantile hemiplegia and aphasia occur at age three or four, speech becomes severely impaired, but after a short time is almost invariably fully reacquired. The ability to be selected to acquire speech had not yet been lost by the so-called minor hemisphere, which as a result is willing and able to become the dominant hemisphere for speech. This switching of dominance is carried out almost without skipping a beat. In fact, once recovery begins, these brain-injured children pass their language milestones at an accelerated rate until they catch up to their expected age-related capabilities. They then move on as if nothing had ever happened to them. However, the hemiplegia often remains as a serious deficit. Thanks to our evolution, the control of movement in the opposite half of the body is entirely hard-wired. No other area can be selected to take over.

But this plasticity does not go on forever. Most children fully recover speech as long as they were stricken with aphasia before the age of nine and as long as the disease process was a stroke or other lesion that involved only one hemisphere of the brain. Puberty is the turning point. By the age of fifteen or sixteen, the prognosis for recovery from aphasia is the same as that of adults.

Although recovery from aphasia is more difficult in adults, it is not impossible. Most recovery, if it occurs, occurs rapidly and represents neither adaptation nor relearning. Selection of new networks plays no role in this whatsoever. This recovery represents healing and "shrinkage" of the initial lesion. Such rapid recovery suggests that the initial loss was due to loss of function of areas of the brain that were partially injured but not permanently destroyed. The symptoms that are still there after a few weeks tend to be permanent.

Children who become aphasic between the age of nine and their mid-teens fall in between in their recoveries. They rarely fully reacquire speech but they recover more than adults do. So what does all of this mean? There is a critical period for the acquisition of speech, but this critical period is not an all-or-nothing phenomenon with a sharp cutoff. Up to age nine, the brain has areas on either hemisphere that can be selected to carry out all language functions. By age fifteen or sixteen this kind of recovery is no longer possible; the period for selectivity is over. In between there is a period of transition.

So much for the neurological data. The logic of neurology is not beyond reproach. It depends on the loss of function in an abnormal brain to imply normal function. M.J.'s brain was not abnormal, and certainly not in the area of visual-motor skills. He could hit a running jump shot with the best of them.

Support for the notion of a critical period for language is within the experience of almost every one of us. Just consider the struggles of normal brains to acquire new language skills. All of us are aware of the problems faced in learning a second language. What tourist hasn't returned from France amazed that four-year-old French children have mastered the skill of speaking French, complete with correct accents, a skill that has stumped the tourist most of his life. Second languages are far easier to acquire during childhood than during adolescence or adulthood. This situation is now being played out in classrooms across the United States, as it has been to some degree with each successive generation of immigrants to this country. The results will be no different for this generation, but this time the results have been far better studied. Learning has become a subject of research.

The acquisition of English by Chinese and Korean immigrants to the United States has been carefully tracked. And guess what? These children learned English quickly and correctly, with no accents at all, right up to the age of puberty. After puberty, the acquisition of English became harder. Between puberty and age seventeen it was moderately, but significantly, more difficult, and after that age it got even harder. Between puberty and seventeen, some accent usually remained. After seventeen, there was almost always a definite accent, and one that sounded foreign to anyone who learned English before puberty, including the immigrant's own family members. This should have been news to no one. It had been the experience of many American families for the last century or more. But it is always nice when science confirms everyday experience and tells us what we already knew.

Despite all the hurdles, people can and do learn a second language after puberty and even during adult life. Much of the population of Israel has. But it takes considerable effort, far more than it does prior to puberty. Furthermore, a second language learned after puberty is always that, a second language grafted onto the first rather than a natural language fully and easily acquired. It is disturbing that despite our continued educational experience of the inverse relationship between age and the acquisition of a second language—a relationship that must be within the experience of every teacher and school administrator—the teaching of a second language in our schools is almost always begun seriously only in high school, at precisely the time when the critical period has already passed and the learning of a second language has become increasingly difficulty.

Learning to hit may be difficult, but it is not as difficult as learning a language. It is a motor skill, visual-motor in fact, but still a nonverbal motor skill. But nonverbal motor skills also have critical periods. These windows of opportunity are well within the everyday experience of all of us. Since the explosion of Pac-Man on the American scene about two decades ago, such computer games have been proliferating. Computers themselves have become a part of the workplace and home life of many of us, and despite a late start, many of us have learned a variety of computer skills. Some of our contemporaries, beginning as adults, have become surprisingly proficient.

But give an adult computer pro a Nintendo, match her against an eight-year-old kid who can barely read the instructions, and see how well the adult does. Reading the instructions is scarcely a necessity for kids raised with computers. The games are visual and the rules are all pretty much the same and easily learned by visual-motor experience.

So what happens?

The kid wins—every time, day in, day out, year after year. The adult who first played such games as an adult can never catch up, and each year another crop of kids can and do beat him. Why? The adult computer pro was too old when he got started. In our terms, there is a critical period for acquiring this nonverbal visual-motor skill, and if you first start to learn it after that period you can never really master it.

The same is true of learning to hit a baseball. It is a fact of baseball life. Not one major league baseball player has ever learned to hit a baseball after the age of twenty-six and certainly not after the age of thirty. Michael Jordan was thirty-one when the 1994 baseball season started.

How can I be certain of this, and why was I, as a neurologist, one who knew it was true? I was certain because I was both a neurologist and a baseball buff. But I was not alone in my knowledge. Every major league baseball coach and manager knew it was true. They had just never thought about it in this way.

Every year there are pitchers, major league pitchers, good pitchers, sometimes even star pitchers, whose careers suddenly come to an end. There are a variety of causes. Sometimes it is tendonitis. Other times they develop what are called sore arms or dead arms. The exact process is not relevant; the result is functionally the same. Their fastballs are suddenly no longer as fast as they once were, and they can no longer get them past anyone. What happens to these pitchers? No one ever tries to convert them into hitters.

Why not? Such a conversion seems a natural option. Many still have contracts that must be paid off over the next two, three, or more years, contracts that may call for payments of several million dollars each year. Why not let them hit for a living? In high school, almost all of them did far more than pitch. On the days they didn't pitch, they played first base or shortstop or somewhere in the outfield, depending on their speed and fielding skills, and batted third or fourth in the lineup and starred as both the best pitcher and the best hitter on their teams. Then came decision time. To hit or not to hit. Or more specifically, to hit or to pitch, but never both. A choice had to be made and was made, usually by someone else, a college coach or more traditionally by the major league team that drafted the player out of high school and guided his minor league career.

The decision was made and the future major leaguer became a pitcher. He excelled and progressed. Eventually, he developed a sore arm. He had been a hitting star in high school, a mere eight to ten years ago. Not exactly another lifetime. Why not make him into a hitter once again? It can't be that hard.

It isn't hard, it's impossible. Hitting in high school is analogous to the few words that Genie acquired before she was locked away in that room. It is the right start but that start must be built on before it is too late. The sore-armed pitcher's ability to hit is like Genie's ability to talk; it is rudimentary at best, and rudimentary never makes it in the big leagues.

So each year big-league pitchers get sore arms that end their careers, and no one ever contemplates converting them into hitters because everyone involved in major league baseball knows it can't be done. The pitchers themselves know it. Their coaches know it, and the managers know it. Their general managers, the team owners, and even the fans know it.

And Michael Jordan was not a hitting star in high school. He played basketball in high school. What kind of chance did he have to learn to hit major league pitching? As the sports cliché goes, he had two chances: remote and none. The smart money was on none.

Yet whenever baseball fans have been confronted with this concept, they have been skeptical. Can their heroes all be that human? Is it really true that no one ever has learned to hit after the mid-twenties?

Then they all ask the same questions. What about Babe Ruth? Didn't he switch from being a pitcher to being a hitter when he was already well into his career? The fact is that he didn't. The Babe was probably the greatest baseball player of all time. He had both pitching and hitting records that stood for over thirty years. Not only did he hit sixty home runs in a single season and seven hundred fourteen in his career, he also had a lifetime batting average of .342. Only Ted Williams has managed to compile that high a lifetime average in the last fifty years, at .344. As a pitcher, the Babe won ninety-four games and lost only forty-six for a career winning percentage of .671. He won over twenty games in both 1916 and 1917. His record of consecutive shutout innings pitched in the 1918 World Series lasted longer than his record of most home runs in a season, before it was broken by Roger Maris's Yankee teammate, Hall of Famer Whitey Ford. Both records were broken the same year—1961. Maris hit his sixty-one home runs during the regular season, and Ford pitched his shutout innings during the World Series. The home-run record had been set in 1927; the pitching record in 1918.

In 1920, when the Babe hit fifty-four home runs, he actually hit more home runs than any *team* in either the American or the National League. The number two home-run hitter in the American League that year was fellow Hall of Famer George Sisler of the St. Louis Browns, who hit a career high of nineteen round-trippers. Only ten other American League players hit ten or more home runs that year, and two teams had no player who even managed to hit ten homers.

That season (1920), Ruth hit almost fifteen percent of all the home runs in the American League. For Maris to have accomplished a similar feat the year he broke Ruth's one-season home-run record (1961), he would have had to hit over two hundred home runs. Instead, he managed only sixty-one, which represented less than a measly four percent of league totals or, relatively speaking, only about one-fourth of the percentage that the Babe managed in a single season. Ain't statistics great? The Babe still holds several records, including lifetime slugging percentage and lifetime ratio of home runs per times at bat.

No question about it, he was great. But the Babe did not actually switch from pitching to hitting. Ruth's first full season in the major leagues was 1915, when he was twenty years old.

George Herman "Babe" Ruth late in his career. In his prime his athletic skills were never on a par with Michael Jordan's. His concentration was, and his ability to hit a baseball farther more frequently than anyone else remains unrivaled. In his last full season as a Yankee, when he was thirty-nine years old and managed to hit only twenty-two home runs, he struck out only sixty-three times for a ratio of less than 3.

He pitched in thirty-two games and had a record of eighteen wins and eight losses. That year he played in forty-two games, including ten in which he did not pitch but in which he did hit. He hit .315 and knocked out four home runs. The league leader in home runs that year was Braggo Roth, who hit only seven while splitting the season between the Chicago White Sox and the Cleveland Indians. In order to smack three more home runs, Roth came to bat over four times more than Ruth did. The next year, Ruth pitched in forty-four games and had a record of twenty-three wins and twelve losses. He hit in sixty-seven games, batting .272. In 1917, his third year in the majors, he was twenty-two years old and hit .325; and by the time he was twenty-three he pitched in only twenty games, compiling a record of thirteen and seven, but played in a total of ninety-five games. That year he hit .300 and led the league in home runs with eleven. He played in fewer than one hundred games and in fact played fewer games than anyone who ever led the league in home runs. The next year (1919), his last as a Boston Red Sox, he again led the league with an unprecedented twenty-nine round-trippers. The rest of his team managed only four that entire year. Alas, Babe Ruth did not start learning to hit at age twenty-three. By then he had been an accomplished major league hitter for three full seasons. He had never had to decide whether to hit or not to hit. He always hit. In 1919, the decision was made to pitch or not to pitch. He chose to hit.

There are two other players that true baseball aficionados suggest as having made a late-life transition from pitching to hitting. The first was Babe Ruth's one-time Boston Red Sox teammate Smokey Joe Wood. Wood came up as a pitcher and only batted in games he pitched. In 1912 he won thirty-four games and lost only five. During the season he won sixteen straight games and then won three games during the World Series. Not a bad season. In 1915, the year the Babe made the team, Smokey Joe won fifteen and lost only five, leading the American League in win-loss percentage and earned run average; but his arm caused him so much pain that season that he could no longer pitch. Three years later he made a comeback as an outfielder for the Cleveland Indians, and in 1921, in sixty-six games, he hit .366. Joe Wood was twenty-six when his arm gave out. Baseball lore traces Wood's bad arm back to the spring of 1913 when he slipped fielding a ground ball on wet grass and fractured the thumb on his right (pitching) hand. Wood always thought that was the root cause of his problem. He was not certain whether he also hurt his shoulder in the fall or whether he injured it by coming back too soon and putting an abnormal strain on the joint. There were no MRIs back then, and no one specialized in sports medicine. In either case, he wound up with shoulder pain whenever he pitched.

So you'd think Wood must have learned to hit a baseball after the window of opportunity was supposed to be closed. A nice try, but in his eight years as a major league pitcher, Wood averaged .241 as a batter. As a full-time hitter he averaged only some forty points higher. He may have further developed his skills as a hitter when he switched from full-time pitcher to full-time hitter, and he may well have perfected them then, but he already had these skills. The year (1912) he had won thirty-four games as a pitcher, he had hit .290.

The other candidate for the legend of learning to hit late is Francis "Lefty" O'Doul. True believers would have it that Lefty started unsuccessfully as a pitcher, returned to the minor leagues and became a position player, struggled to learn to hit, and finally reached the majors at age thirty-one as a bona fide slugger.

Unfortunately, it is not really true. Not in the way the legend would have you believe. O'Doul did make it as a hitter in the majors in 1928 at the age of thirty-one and then played seven full seasons, putting together a lifetime batting average of .349, an average topped only by Ty Cobb (.367), Rogers Hornsby (.358), and Shoeless Joe Jackson (.356). Not bad for an ex-pitcher. In 1929, playing for the Philadelphia Phillies, O'Doul led the National League in batting (.388) and set a National League record for hits in one season (.254) that still stands.

But, alas, he did not begin as a pitcher, per se. He started off his major league career in 1919 and in the first three seasons played in all forty games, but he pitched in only eleven of those games, playing outfield or pinch-hitting in the others. He returned to the minors when he was twenty-six, playing for the San Francisco Seals. His first year there, when he concentrated primarily on hitting, he just missed winning the Pacific Coast League batting title with an average of .392. Over the next three years, with pitching behind him, he averaged two hundred seventy hits a season.

So much for the legend. Lefty O'Doul was always a position player and in his mid-twenties, when he gave up pitching, immediately improved as a hitter. And he was in his mid-twenties, not his thirties. His late appearance in the majors was related to the structure and economics of baseball in the 1920s, not Lefty O'Doul's limitations as a hitter.

The reverse switch is far more common. Players who start out as position players have become successful pitchers even at the age of thirty, long after their careers began even. Hal Jeffcoat played center field for the Chicago Cubs for half a dozen seasons before he first started pitching at age thirty. He then pitched for six seasons in the majors, winning thirty-nine and losing thirty-seven. Jack Harshman hit forty-nine home runs in the minors one year but couldn't hit in the majors. He switched to pitching and made it to the big leagues for good at age twenty-seven, winning sixty-nine games over his nine-year career.

Then there is Bob Lemon. He made the majors in 1941 as an outfielder and third baseman, and became a pitcher in 1946 at the age of twenty-five. Lemon pitched his way into the Hall of Fame.

Baseball is statistics, and the glory of statistics is that they can lead to more statistics. Statistics galore. There is some information that can be gleaned directly from an analysis of baseball statistics that confirms that hitting skill is governed at least in part by a critical period. In 1994 Robert Schulz and a group of coworkers from the Department of Psychiatry and the Center for Urban and Social Research at the University of Pittsburgh studied the relationship between age and performance among baseball players. They analyzed the lifetime performance data of two hundred thirty-five major league hitters who were playing in the major leagues in 1965, to determine the age of peak hitting abilities and age-performance relationships. To no one's surprise, they found that performance in hitting improves rapidly after the age of nineteen and peaks around age twenty-seven. This is as true of Hall of Famers as it is of benchwarmers. In addition, the performance of the best hitters is better than that of less able players (judged by career totals) even at a very early age. This, too, is not surprising.

There were, however, a couple of interesting results. The primary difference between the best players and the others was that the performance of such elite players remained at peak level for more years and declined more slowly. One or two good years at the peak does not a Hall of Famer make. The biggest surprise was that hitting ability, as judged by performance and not promise of performance, improved very little after fifteen hundred at bats. And as all fans know from bitter experience, less able players never catch up to the better players, no matter how hard they work and how long they play. In other words, the gains derived from years of experience become marginal over time. And over those years, the brain ages. It takes four to six years for most players to acquire sufficient experience, or until they are somewhere around age twenty-six. There is no coincidence in that.

The case of Jim Thorpe is interesting here. As soon as he was stripped of his Olympic medals, Thorpe turned to baseball. It was virtually the only professional sport around. He started to play baseball seriously in 1913 when he was already twenty-six years old. He never even got his fifteen hundred appearances at bat in his six short seasons in the majors. It is possible that he may still have been learning in his last season, when at age thirty he had his best year and hit .327 in sixty games. We'll never know for sure. It could have been little more than the baseball equivalent of statistical scatter: a few more seeing-eye ground balls that made it into the outfield or a few more leg hits. Take away five of each and he would have hit about fifty points lower. Ten more hits doesn't prove that he learned how to hit. Only time and a few more seasons would have told. But he quit baseball and went back to running with a football.

So why do teams have all these batting coaches? Not to make players who are already in the big leagues better hitters. If that were the reason, the data suggest they should all look for new jobs. The primary role of batting coaches is to try to maintain peak performance and to slow decline, and give some supportive psychotherapy during the bad times.

Do batting instructors help? I know of no statistical theory that suggests that they do. Who was Shoeless Joe Jackson's hitting instructor? Or Babe Ruth's? Ted Williams's? Mostly their own brains during their windows of opportunity. And none of them ever became renowned for teaching his own skills to others.

Right-handed hitters hit left-handed pitchers better than right-handed pitchers, and vice versa, as noted above. Sometimes the differences are so great that players are platooned and only play against pitchers who pitch from the opposite side, so to speak. So why not make them into switch-hitters? That would give the batting coaches something to do. These players have made the big leagues. They already know how to hit. There are batting coaches around who can teach them how to hit. What's the big deal?

Training other neurons to see the ball is the big deal, and another series of experiments conducted by Hubel and Weisel explains why. Hitting is all visual-motor skill with an emphasis on the visual. Left-handed hitters see the ball with different brain cells than do right-handed hitters. They have trained different cells—selected different cells. To become a switch-hitter means that new cells must be self-taught to acquire those skills necessary to hit. Can this be done?

In the early 1980s, Hubel and Weisel studied the early development of cats and showed that most of the nerve cells in a cat's visual cortex can respond to light coming from either eye. These "binocular" cells make up some eighty percent of the cells in the normal visual cortex. The other twenty percent respond to only one eye and are "monocular" cells. However, this can all be changed. If one eye was sutured shut, almost all of the cells became monocular and even remained so later in life after the eye was opened. If the sutured eye was opened later in infancy and the other eye was then closed, the cells remained monocular but now they were monocular to the other eye. This is another example of plasticity in the nervous system, but plasticity with a time frame. The ability of the brain to select cells to perform a function is determined by the timing of the environmental exposure. Recruiting visual cells to respond to particular binocular cues can only be done if those cues are presented to those cells at the right time during the development of the brain. By the time players are trying to learn to hit in the majors it's too late to select new cells to take over the job.

Switch-hitters like Mickey Mantle are not born that way, but they usually get that way by early adolescence or so—at the latest.

Before you start feeling sorry for ball players and conceding that their limited careers justify their overblown salaries, you should ask yourself if they are unique. A number of researchers over the last seventy or more years have studied the age-related rise and fall of artistic, intellectual, and athletic performance. Age is a factor in all areas and the age-performance relationship is similar in all fields. Productivity in all these fields increases rapidly to a definite peak, after which there is a gradual decline. In artistic and scientific domains, productivity typically begins in the twenties, peaks in the thirties or early forties, and then begins to decline gradually.

But there are also differences among the general fields of endeavor. Productivity in mathematics, physics, and lyric poetry tends to peak some time in the late twenties. Novelists, philosophers, and historians peak in their late forties and early fifties. Those fields in which people peak earlier are typified by steeper declines than those in which they peak later and decline more gradually. This, too, is true of baseball. Pitchers, on the average, peak two years later and have careers that last two years longer than those of hitters.

Despite all of this, Michael Jordan was given his chance and he made the effort. He went to spring training with the White Sox and played in thirteen exhibition games. In twenty appearances at the plate, he managed to hit only three weak singles for an anemic batting average of .150. The White Sox then sent him to play for their Class Double A farm club, the Birmingham Barons. Class Triple A is the highest level in the minor leagues and is where the best minor league players and future prospects play. Double A Birmingham is one step below that. Michael Jordan played the full season for the Barons. His final batting average was a dismal .202. This was better than he had managed during spring training, but it was still the lowest batting average of any regular player in the entire Southern League, and many of Jordan's hits were leg hits based on his quickness and speed.

Outfielder Michael Jordan managed a grand total of only three home runs and struck out 28.4 percent of the time. In baseball terms, his strikeout average (.284) was higher than his batting average (.202). He was still fast. He stole thirty bases, fifth best in the league, but he was caught stealing eighteen times. His record the next winter in the instructional league was not much better. It was time to go back to basketball.

It had made about as much sense for Michael Jordan to try to learn to hit for the first time at age thirty-one as it would have for a sore-armed, thirty-year-old, left-handed pitcher to try to learn to pitch right-handed.

Absurd? Perhaps. But what is handedness other than an acquired nonverbal motor skill? About ninety percent of the population is right-handed. Those who are right-handed not only prefer to use the right hand but are far more skillful in the use of that hand for a wide variety of learned skilled activities, including writing, drawing, and, it goes without saying, throwing. This difference in function is not paralleled by any difference in structure, as the two hands and arms remain perfect mirrors of each other. Thus, handedness has no structural basis but is dependent entirely on brain function. Such right-handed preference is universal; it is characteristic of the entire family of humans.

Given that universal preference, why does some ten to twelve percent of the population come up left-handed, generation after generation? Some left-handers, of course, become so pathologically, or through disease. But was Babe Ruth a pathological left-hander? We should all have such brain damage!

Handedness is inherited, at least in part. The most attractive genetic theory was proposed by British psychologist Marian Annett in 1985. She proposed that genetic variations in handedness could be due to the function of a single gene, which can exist in either of two alternates, or alleles. The dominant allele produces a right shift in those who possess it. This would account for the fact that the distribution of handedness in this population is heavily biased toward right-handedness. Some tiny fraction of this population will be left-handed, due to environmental influences, but that factor is not enough to explain the ten percent incidence of left-handedness in the population as a whole.

The recessive allele does not cause left-handedness but results in an absence of any bias toward handedness, so either side can be selected to become dominant. This explains why the children of two left-handed parents are themselves equally divided into left- and right-handers, and also explains why left-handers show a very mixed pattern of asymmetry on other measures, such as eye dominance, footedness, and even fingerprints.

But when is handedness acquired? Quite early in life, it seems, and as expected, here, too, there is a window of opportunity. It is not as obvious as the critical period for speech but it is just as definite. Adults who have a stroke resulting in severe paralysis of their dominant right hand do learn to use their left hand for skills they previously performed with their right hands. They can learn to write, to use a fork, and to perform a wide variety of tasks. However, these tasks are never performed as skillfully as they were with the dominant right hand.

Although the studies haven't been as numerous as those for speech, the rules of recovery from hemiplegia (with switching of dominance for handedness) parallel those rules that apply to speech. The brain, as the basis of genetic inheritance and environmental input, selects a dominant hemisphere for handedness. If this hemisphere is injured early in life, the brain can select the opposite hemisphere and switch dominance. After puberty this becomes difficult and in adults it cannot be done. Abilities can be acquired by the noninjured hand and hemisphere but true skilled handedness cannot.

So a pitcher with a sore dominant arm cannot learn to pitch skillfully with his other arm. He is never even given the opportunity. He also cannot learn to hit and is not given the chance to do that, either.

Michael Jordan could not learn to hit but was given the chance. Why? That may have been a business decision. It certainly was not a neurological one. The Barons set a franchise attendance record in 1994: 467,867 people paid to see them play. The rest of the league also prospered as attendance swelled everywhere Michael and the Barons played.

But reality is reality. A batting average like Jordan's does not a major leaguer make. Michael Jordan summed it up in his second retirement statement: "As a thirty-two-year-old minor leaguer who lacks the benefit of valuable baseball experience during the past fifteen years, I am no longer comfortable that there is meaningful opportunity to continue my improvement at a satisfactory pace." The critical period had passed and even he recognized that fact. All that was left for him was to return to the NBA and be a superstar once again.

Michael's achievements following his return to the NBA demonstrated that he had lost none of his athletic skills. Clearly, whatever problems he had hitting could not be attributed to an overall decrement in his athletic abilities. He played briefly at the end of the 1994–1995 season, but his real comeback was staged during the 1995–1996 season. He once again led the NBA in scoring, and led the Chicago Bulls to the best single-season record in the history of the NBA (seventy-two wins and ten losses) and to the NBA championship. Along the way he picked up all three Most Valuable Player awards (All-Star game, regular season, and final series of the championship playoffs). Not bad for a guy who couldn't hit a baseball. Incidentally, this "triple crown" had been achieved only once before, when New York Knicks center Willis Reed was voted all three awards in 1970.

For those of us who have retained our personal fantasies of someday becoming superstars, the sad truth is that Jordan's window of opportunity may have been gone long before he was thirty. And, by analogy, so may have ours. There are no scientific studies of windows of opportunity in baseball players, but the appropriate studies have been done in violinists. Becoming an accomplished violinist requires motor skills that must be mastered by the brain. Instead of learning to recognize the spin on a speeding baseball and translate that into a muscular response, playing a violin consists of the brain learning to give rapid and complex directions to the fingers of both hands in response to visual or aural clues.

Scientific investigation of the process showed pretty much what professional musicians have always known. In order to become a violin virtuoso, a musician has to start playing before the age of thirteen. Not at fourteen, not at fifteen, but before the age of thirteen. That's a pretty slim window of opportunity.

How was that shown? Edward Taub of the University of Alabama at Birmingham, along with two colleagues from Germany, studied magnetic images of the brain in violinists. This technique shows which neuronal circuits are activated during a specific activity. They found that those fiddlers who started playing early in life (age thirteen or younger) activated larger and more complex circuits in their brains than those who started learning to play their instrument later in life. The magnetic images of those who had started at age three or four looked no different than those who started at eleven or twelve. After that things changed. The abrupt change occurred between the ages of twelve and thirteen. Those who hadn't started by thirteen never caught up. The circuits they activated were smaller, less complex, and more restricted. The time frame during which their brains could be guided to select those circuits had come and gone and left them forever without that ability.

No one wanted Michael Jordan to become a virtuoso violinist. Had he tried and failed, no one would have cared very much. At his age, though, what he had wanted to do was equally impossible. Because he was Michael, we hoped that he could do it. We should have known better. Perhaps, deep down in our hearts, we did.

chapter 2

Primo Carnera:
The Bigger They Are

THE HARDER THEY FALL, or so the cliché of heavyweight boxing teaches us. The latter half of that adage became the title of a 1956 Hollywood movie starring Humphrey Bogart and Rod Steiger. It turned out to be Bogart's last film appearance. The film was based on a book with the same title written a decade earlier by Budd Schulberg. After its publication, Schulberg became well known as both a novelist and a screenwriter. In 1954, he wrote the screenplay for the Academy Award–winning movie *On the Waterfront*. His novel *Waterfront* came out a year later. This was not only a landmark in social criticism for Hollywood but a major break with the tradition in which the book always came first.

The Harder They Fall was the story of a physically enormous, yet naive, young boxer whose career was taken over, manipulated, and finally destroyed by the mobsters who controlled the world of boxing. The influence of such characters in boxing was not new to Schulberg, who had long been both a fight fan and a critic of the fight scene and who remains both to this day. Crooked boxing is also part of the sordid background of *On the Waterfront*. In it, Marlon Brando plays a young boxer who took a dive and lost a fight he could easily have won. Brando's plaintive accusation remains one of film's most memorable and poignant sequences, "I could'a had some class. I could'a been a contender." It is interesting that this entire sequence raised no eyebrows among moviegoers. No one watching in 1954 was skeptical that a major boxing match to determine who would become the contender for the crown was fixed. That was accepted as one of the realities of the American boxing scene.

Like so much fiction, *The Harder They Fall* also had its source in real life. It was, for the most part, the rather thinly fictionalized story of an amiable Italian giant named Primo Carnera. Carnera had been on the winning side of those fixed fights and because of them he not only became a contender, he even became heavyweight champion of the world. He became far more than just a "somebody." Carnera was only the second non-American to wear that crown and was the first, and to this day the only, Italian ever to win it. "Da Preem," as he was affectionately called by New York's large Italian-American population, was a hero to Italians everywhere, from Il Duce, Benito Mussolini, himself, on down. He got far more than just his fifteen minutes of fame, and he owed it all to a collection of crooks and an untreated neurological disease. More, in fact, was owed to the latter, for it was his enormous, abnormal size that attracted the gangsters to him in the first place. Only rarely do people profit from having a disease, and Primo Carnera was one of those few who did. What is even more remarkable was that Da Preem's disease was a brain tumor.

Primo Carnera was born in Sequals, a small town in northern Italy, not far from Venice. His family had lived there for over a thousand years or more, having moved down from the Alps in the distant past. He was the first of six children and thereby received the name Primo. Only two of his siblings survived childhood, two brothers named Secundo and Severino. By the time Primo was sixteen years old, he measured six feet four inches in height, and by nineteen he was topping off at about six feet six inches. His exact final height has long been a matter of debate, but he was probably about six feet seven inches tall during his boxing career. Among heavyweight champions, only Jess Willard at six feet six inches was in his range.

Carnera did not come from a family of giants. No one else in the family had ever approached that height. He was an anomaly whose size came not from his genes but from his tumor and the hormone it produced.

Patients and physicians have learned to think of diseases as bad things that can only do harm. In the long run that is probably true; there is no known disease that increases life expectancy. But for a while at least, some diseases can actually be beneficial. One such disease can make the patient bigger, taller, stronger, capable of dominating a basketball court or a boxing ring. This disease is acromegaly.

Acromegaly was first described as a disease state in 1886 by a French neurologist named Pierre Marie. At that time Paris was the most renowned center for neurology in the world. That prominence had been brought about almost single-handedly by the remarkable achievements of one man, Jean Martin Charcot. Charcot held the world's first professorship in neurology. Marie was one of Charcot's most successful disciples and was able to delineate acromegaly and its manifestations by using the tools of observation and medical reasoning that he had learned from Charcot Marie even invented the term *acromegaly* to describe this "new" disease. The descriptive word that he devised was so appropriate that it stuck to the disorder, and Marie had to derive his historical status in one-third of an eponym for another disorder, Charcot-Marie-Tooth disease, which he described in conjunction with another doctor and with his mentor.

Acromegaly was not a new disease, however. Most so-called new diseases are not really new; rather, they are newly described diseases. Diseases become described for the first time because medical knowledge or technology has developed to the point where differentiation of that particular disorder becomes possible. The few exceptions to this general rule are occasional infectious and toxic diseases. The former owe their newness to a genetic change in the causative virus or microbe, whereas the latter have usually appeared as the result of the evolution of technology that has devised a new toxic chemical and let it out into the environment.

Acromegaly undoubtedly had been around for a long time. It's just that before Pierre Marie no one had known enough to differentiate it from other illnesses. There has long been speculation that various famous giants of ancient history, such as Goliath, were acromegalic giants. There is, however, no proof that Goliath had acromegaly or any other specific diseases, as we have neither clinical descriptions of him, contemporary portraits, nor an autopsy report.

The word *acromegaly* itself comes from two Greek words: *akron*, which means "extremity" or "extreme," and *megale*, which means "great." Marie applied his new word to patients who manifested great growth of the distal, or extreme, ends of their body parts. To this day, the word is used to define this now well-known clinical disorder characterized by enlargement of the extremities, especially the hands and feet, as well as the nose and jaw. Acromegaly does not merely increase the amount of normal growth; it causes a specific pattern of growth at the ends of the bones, which results in the peculiar body features that characterize patients with the disease. Thus, experienced clinicians can diagnose the disease merely by seeing a patient. While his size was extraordinary and he towered over everyone, it was the nature of his uncontrolled growth and the effect on his proportions and physiognomy that make the diagnosis of acromegaly in Primo Carnera so easy.

His arm span was seven feet, about half a foot longer than his height. It is, however, the face that makes the diagnosis. All acromegalics have the same facial features. One facial bone, the mandible, or jawbone, continues to grow the most. The lower face and jaw begin to jut forward (prognathism). The skin becomes increasingly thickened. Normal folds are smoothed out. The nose becomes thickened and enlarged, as do the lips. The bony ridge above the eyes, the supraorbital ridge, grows and becomes more prominent. The entire face loses its subtle

Primo Carnera at the time of his arrival in America. Note his acromegalic features, including a long face with prolonged jaw (prognathism), coarse facial features, big feet, and big hands. His overt slowness cannot be appreciated in this photograph, nor his overall lack of boxing talent.

individuality and becomes the face of an acromegalic, the face of Primo Carnera.

Marie not only characterized the clinical manifestations of acromegaly but also showed that the disease was caused by a tumor of the pituitary gland, a very small gland that rests in the skull just below the brain. The pituitary is often called the master gland, for in conjunction with the hypothalamus, the part of the brain just above it, it controls the function of many of the other endocrine glands spread throughout the body.

For instance, the pituitary produces thyroid stimulating hormone (TSH), which controls the function of the thyroid gland. The thyroid gland in response to TSH produces thyroid hormone, thyroxin, which controls the metabolism of the body. No TSH means no thyroxin, which in turn means an abnormally low rate of metabolism. The pituitary also puts out adrenocorticotrophic hormone (ACTH), which controls the cortex of the adrenal gland. These two adrenal glands in turn produce the body's various steroid hormones, which perform a variety of functions throughout the body. A master gland among master glands, the pituitary also produces the hormone that controls growth. This hormone is called, simply enough, the growth hormone or human growth hormone. Marie did not know all of this endocrinology. Human growth hormone had not yet been isolated. He just recognized what was happening to his patients.

All of the extraordinary overgrowth of bone and the connective tissue of the skin and subcutaneous tissues that characterizes acromegaly is the result of excessive production of growth hormone by a pituitary tumor. If Primo Carnera had acromegaly, then he had to have had a tumor in his pituitary gland. An autopsy is not needed to prove it.

If the tumor becomes active and begins secreting excessive amounts of growth hormone before the age at which the growth centers of the long bones of the arms and legs become joined, the bones grow enormously in all their dimensions. This process results in gigantism, not just acromegaly. The patient becomes tall, thick, and heavy, a veritable giant. This syndrome is called pituitary gigantism. Primo Carnera's tumor became active during adolescence, before his growth centers closed, and he became a giant of a man.

If the disorder begins after these growth centers of the bones have united, the overgrowth is confined to the ends of the bones, producing acromegaly. If the tumor begins before closure of the growth centers and continues its active production afterward, the patient manifests both gigantism and acromegaly. This combination of pituitary gigantism and acromegaly was first described by another of Charcot's students, Henri Meige. It is this combined condition that pituitary giants develop. Although closure of the growth centers does not stop the pattern of uncontrolled production of excessive growth hormone, it does alter the way in which the body can respond. The long bones can't grow much longer. Primo Carnera stopped getting taller in his late teens, like other members of his family. He just stopped at a different altitude. This is where acromegaly gets superimposed upon gigantism: The acro-parts—hands, fingers, feet, toes—continue to grow.

So acromegalic gigantism made Primo Carnera big enough to help him become heavyweight champion of the world. Not on his own, of course. To succeed in boxing, this good-natured giant needed all the help he could get. Carnera received a number of nicknames throughout his career. These included such tags as Man Mountain, the Ambling Alp, and the Gorgonzola Tower. The Ambling Alp and Old Satchel Feet, another nickname, both implied his well-known lack of foot speed. Foot speed of some degree is usually thought of as one of the essentials of a great boxer. It was only the nickname Da Preem, however, that caught the essence of this amiable giant, so loved by Italians everywhere.

Da Preem was not a born boxer; nor did he start his career at an early age, when training might have been more effective in teaching him the basic skills and reflex responses needed to survive in the ring. He became a professional boxer almost by accident. It was 1928 and Carnera, who was then only twenty-one years old, was working for peanuts in a traveling carnival as "Juan the Unbeatable Spaniard." Under this alias he would fight all comers, which at times amounted to ten or more bouts each day against local toughs and would-be pugilists. He was far more a sideshow freak than a serious pugilist. Sideshow freaks are often the products of diseases, including the most famous sideshow "freak" of them all, the Elephant Man, who had neurofibromatosis, a hereditary neurological disease characterized by multiple tumors of the nervous systems.

Carnera's big break came while the carnival was working its way through the small towns of the Bordeaux region of France. There he was spotted by a retired fighter named Paul Journée. Journée had once been the heavyweight champion of France and was a disciple of Leon Seé. Seé was one of the major figures in French boxing both as a manager and promoter. He had managed nine French champions; Journée was one of them. After seeing Carnera, Journée signed him to a contract as a professional boxer, began to teach him some of the rudiments of boxing, and then sent him on to Leon Seé. It was Leon Seé who launched Carnera on a career made up of equal parts of fixed fights and public relations.

According to Seé's own book, *Le Mystère Carnera*, his young protégé fought four fights in 1924 and won all four of them, three by knockouts and one by a decision. According to the same source, all four of the fights were fixed or as Seé so quaintly referred to them, *"combat arrangé"*—combats arranged, fixed fights. "Mischievous fights" is what they were called years later in Carnera's obituaries.

All the time, Primo was trying to learn his trade. At the beginning he lacked any real punch, he had no acceleration in his fists and no killer instinct. This combination of deficiencies did not bode well for the survival of a heavyweight. Over time he did improve but not as much as his large size had promised. His arms were too long for his body. The mechanical advantage was not with him. He would never become a great puncher.

How could this mountain of a man not have the proverbial strength of a giant? How could his punches not be as devastating as any in the history of boxing? The relative lack of strength (force) in the punches thrown by Primo Carnera was the direct result of the laws of physics and the peculiar nature and geometry of his prodigious size.

It is common knowledge that adolescents who go through a sudden extraordinary growth spurt often "outgrow their strength." This relative weakness is caused by the rapid and massive increase in the inertia of their distal limbs, due to lengthening of these limbs without a corresponding increase in the mass of the muscles that move them. Another factor is that growth of a long bone, especially at its very end, can also change the relative location of the muscle attachments to that bone. As the end of the bone lengthens, the muscle attachment "moves" away from the end of the bone, thus decreasing its mechanical advantage.

How do normal adolescents catch up with their strength? The filling out of their muscles is one way; but a more significant factor is that the brain learns to direct movements in a far more efficient way. That, of course, is what our brains are designed to do. They not only shape our responses to the external environment but also the responses that we make to any changes in the dimensions of our bodies, our internal environment. The ability of the brain to acquire this new information, like its ability to learn how to hit a baseball, is governed by a window of opportunity. In this instance, it is not the environment that is sending clues to the brain as much as it is the individual's own body.

The brain has almost as many of its systems tied up in receiving feedback from itself as it does in receiving feedback from the outside world. If a person is going to pick a berry, he not only needs to see that berry and know where it is in space, he also needs to know where his hand and fingers are. This is done unconsciously, without looking. This proprioceptive system is constantly monitoring our body parts and their motions. The information that they send to the brain is as much a factor in modifying the brain's structure and function as the input from the eyes and ears. The body, after all, is the most important part of the world to which the growing brain must adapt. The brain of the growing adolescent learns to change the body's movements so that they depend on lower levels of acceleration to accomplish a task. Most tasks that can be done with faster movements requiring greater acceleration can also be done with slower movements, and also with movements that require displacement over a shorter space. All of this requires no formal teaching. It is part of the normal adjustment of the brain to the changes it encounters. It is not pure muscle strength that is changed but the nature of what the muscles are asked to do.

In boxing, unfortunately, such natural solutions are not ideal. Punches must be thrown. They must be thrown at the chin, head, torso, or arms of the other boxer, none of which is going to comply by coming closer. Shortening the distance of the punch is one solution, but it also decreases the acceleration and the effect of that punch. That helps the opponent far more than the puncher.

The other alternative is increasing the strength of the involved muscles. This is the solution of every "strong" forward in the National Basketball Association. Usable strength in a boxer would depend not only on pure strength but also on learning to get his body behind a punch. This is what boxers can be taught, and this is where Leon Seé and Primo's other managers came in. They taught Carnera how to box.

But Primo Carnera was not a normal adolescent who had merely "outgrown his strength." He was an acromegalic giant, and the nature of the growth in the disease placed him at even greater disadvantages than the average gangling teenager. What he had to overcome was the enormous inertia of his enlarged body, and overcoming that inertia would never be easy. Inertia, in physical terms, means the tendency of a body at rest to stay at rest. And Carnera, because of the nature of his disease, had inertia of gargantuan proportions.

Carnera's acromegaly defined the degree of his inertia. The moment (degree) of inertia depends on both the mass of the object to be moved (Da Preem's fist) and the distance of that object from the axis (Da Preem's body). Extreme size plus inertia compounded the problem for Carnera as a boxer. His fists got bigger.

How big do the fists of an acromegalic get? Too big. The best example of this may be the Roman Emperor Maximinus who ruled from A.D. 235 to A.D. 238. Maximinus had acromegaly. His coin portraiture shows the telltale signs: the jutting, prognathic mandible, the distinct supraorbital ridge, the enlarged nose. Maximinus was a Thracian, who first gained prominence and a commission in the Roman army because of his athletic skills as a wrestler. Wrestling depends primarily on low acceleration movements. Body hugs require almost no acceleration. Maximinus, like Primo Carnera, was a giant. He had giant hands. According to the ancient historians, he wore his wife's bracelets as rings. That's precisely what acromegaly produces, enormous hands with thick fingers and thickened, dense bones. It means hands that are enlarged and heavy. And more mass means more inertia.

How much more? Back to basic physics. Inertia is resistance to acceleration. Without effort, Carnera's fist is destined not to move. So how much effort must be exerted to throw a punch? All other things being equal, the linear acceleration caused by a force is indirectly proportional to the mass of the object being moved. The greater the mass, the less the acceleration. Like his historic predecessor, Maximinus, Primo Carnera's fists were massive, probably twice normal. That means that the same force would cause only one-half the acceleration. That translates into a punch that is very easy to avoid.

But this is not linear acceleration with the force being applied at the base of the wrist. This is the movement of the entire limb. Here is where Carnera's disproportionately long reach became a factor. The force of a punch is generated far from the object of the punch. Carnera's reach made this far, very far. And the resistance to acceleration, what physicists call the moment of inertia, is not just directly related to the distance, it is directly related to the fifth power of the distance.

What did all that mean to Carnera? His arms were ten percent too long. When you are dealing with a fifth power, that adds up. Or, more correctly, that multiplies up, just like compound interest. 1.1^5 means $1.1 \times 1.1 \times 1.1 \times 1.1. \times 1.1$. That comes out to be 1.61, meaning that the inertia of Carnera's arms was increased by 1.61 times. And that's a big deal, just like compound interest, but compound interest without withholding. No taxes, just principle plus interest year after year.

So what does that all mean for the Gorgonzola Tower? Back to Newton and basic physics: $F = M \times A$—force equals mass times acceleration. Had it all been just mass times linear acceleration, Da Preem's punches would have been slower but would have had the same force as any other boxer with the same "strength." The mass of his fist was twice normal and the acceleration would have been halved. The resulting force would be just the same. Slow, but powerful.

Here is where 1.1^5 comes in. Carnera's mass was doubled but the acceleration was decreased. Not to one-half but to one-third, since inertia had increased by 1.61 times. The force of his blows would be only two-thirds that of another man with the same strength and normal reach. This is still enough to do one heck of a lot of harm, for the average haymaker probably delivers a force of about one-half of ten. A third of a ten would still do far more than smart.

The problem is the resultant lack of speed of the punch. There is ordinarily very little time between the extension of the elbow to throw a jab and the moment of peak contact. Slowing that punch down to one-third of the speed at which it should be traveling markedly decreases the likelihood of ever delivering that haymaker—unless, of course, the fight is fixed. That is the physics and reality of the life and times of Primo Carnera.

The fist of an acromegalic giant throwing a roundhouse punch may be compared to one of those wrecking balls used to demolish unwanted buildings. The fist with its dense bones has enormous mass, just like that ball, and it is far away from the source of its movements, in this case the muscles of the shoulder joint. The moments of inertia of both the ball and the fist are enormous. Once set into motion, however, that ball can do a lot of harm. It always wins. The buildings always come crumbling down. Why couldn't it be like that for Da Preem?

Unfortunately, opposing boxers, unlike unwanted buildings, have a tendency to move around.

His last fight of 1928 was fought against a black South American named Epifanio Islas. Islas, like most of Carnera's opponents, was paid to take a dive. His was scheduled for the fifth round and would give Carnera a string of successive knockouts. The punch that Carnera threw lacked both force and acceleration and even credibility. So did Islas's flop to the canvas. The referee became enraged. He apparently believed that boxing matches were supposed to be on the up-and-up. He ordered Islas to get up and continue fighting. Islas followed the ref's orders, but somehow still managed to fight poorly enough to allow Carnera to win on points, a rare accomplishment for the young giant.

In 1929, Carnera fought a dozen fights. Most were fixed and resulted in a series of knockout victories for the Ambling Alp. Primo lost two fights that were not "arranged," but he was improving as a boxer. He was no longer a fairground sideshow attraction and was becoming a center ring attraction. And the biggest center ring for boxing was the United States, the heart of heavyweight boxing. More to the point, it was the heart of money to be made in boxing, home of the million-dollar gate. Who cared if gangsters controlled much of the American boxing world?

Not Leon Seé. Considering what he had to sell, it was all the better. It was time for the Ambling Alp to sail off to the New World.

Once Carnera and Leon Seé landed in New York, the goal was to get a fair deal. Fair did not mean honest, of course. It meant an arrangement that would parlay Carnera's size and ancestry into a successful career. No one could know just how successful that career would be. The big fights (the championship fights) were, for the most part, not completely arranged beforehand. If the reader detects any skepticism here, it is not without reason. In an atmosphere in which sideshow entertainers became challengers, there should be skepticism that the big fights were all legitimate. As Scarface Al Capone, the most famous of all Chicagoans before the advent of Michael Jordan, said of Chicago in that era, "Nobody's on the legit."

It was an interregnum in boxing. Gene Tunney had taken the title from Jack Dempsey, defended it, and then retired. There was no heavyweight champion and no one knew what would happen. What happened, in retrospect, was a series of not very good champions each having only a brief moment of glory until the next champion who was really worthy of that title took the crown. That, it turns out, was Joe Louis, the first black champion since Jack Johnson. The interregnum was much like boxing in the post–Mike Tyson era. If Buster Douglas and an aged anachronism like George Foreman can win it all, why not an acromegalic peasant from northern Italy?

The "fair" deal was arranged with American promoter Walter Friedman. The deal included a well-promoted debut followed by a well-planned series of victories, all accompanied by as much publicity as could be garnered. The public relations campaign was so successful that Carnera was a celebrity before he ever entered a ring in the United States. Rumors of his size and strength preceded him. He was said to be six feet ten inches, a giant among giants. A behemoth of unimagined strength with punches to match.

New York did not merely dominate the sports world, it *was* the American sports world in the twenties. It was also the source of most sports publicity in the United States. And, in that era before Joe DiMaggio, it was a city with a huge Italian population in need of a hero. Yankee second baseman Tony Lazzeri was good, but there had been better second basemen playing for the New York Giants in the twenties (Rogers Hornsby and Frankie Frisch). The Italian community took one look at Carnera, and it was love at first sight, Da Preem as folk hero.

Carnera was young, only twenty-two years old. His skills as a boxer were still limited at best. It was up to Walter Friedman to set the course of a successful career, but he could not do this by himself. He enlisted the two men who would exert the most influence on Carnera's future, William "Big Bill" Duffy and Owney "the Killer" Madden. Madden had been an associate of such stalwarts as Legs Diamond and Dutch Schultz. Madden owned a chain of speakeasies and his hobby was managing crooked boxers. What more could a boxer ask for?

Carnera's first fight was with Big Boy Peterson. Peterson was said to be about six feet five, but all statistics from that era deserve a certain degree of skepticism. It was billed as a battle of giants, to be fought in Madison Square Garden. Not a bad place for a debut. Carnera won by a knockout in the first round. Peterson had been paid to cave in as soon as one of Carnera's slow, right-hand uppercuts found its way to his jaw, the proverbial wrecker's ball at work. On a moving target, sure; but not one that moved very much. The crowd, many of them Italian-Americans, went wild. A KO in the first round. The legend of Primo Carnera, the Ambling Alp, was underway in the United States.

It had been a triumph of *"combat arrangé."* No one got hurt, certainly not Big Boy Peterson. Primo was on his way, and Owney the Killer and Big Bill Duffy made a few dollars out of it. Everybody won.

What followed was a series of early round knockouts against a range of nonentities such as Cowboy Owens, Farmer Lodge, and Bearcat Wright. There were over a dozen such fights with an occasional "sincere" bout scattered in here and there. His bout against Leon Chavalier in Oakland, California, which he won by a technical knockout, was said to be "on the legit," as was Carnera's loss to Jim Maloney in Boston. The latter was a real fight against a legitimate opponent, and Carnera fought for ten rounds before losing the decision. He was learning how to box.

His increasing competence as a fighter became more apparent the next year. He fought several legitimate fights. He went fifteen rounds with future heavyweight champ Jack Sharkey and lost the decision. Not bad for an ex-carnival showman. Even the press had been impressed. The sportswriters had, in general, been skeptical of Carnera and his "accomplishments," but the Sharkey fight changed that. An editorial in the New York *Daily Express* summed it all up:

Heavyweight boxing badly needed such a fight.... The world had grown skeptical of men of their bulk really hitting one another or of any fight going fifteen rounds. But Sharkey and Carnera ... battered one another ferociously, mercilessly, with all the punishment-taking pluck of the old-time bruisers, for fifteen gruelling rounds. Sharkey won, but as an exhibition of physical vigore and gameness the honors were even. It is now possible to speak of heavyweight prize-fighting without a yawn.

Carnera had learned his trade. In his next fight, he took a ten-round decision from another legitimate fighter, King Levinsky, who later fought Joe Louis in a championship fight. But the charade also continued. Over one stretch Carnera won a dozen straight fights by early round knockouts. All, at least by Seé's record, had been fixed. It was now the moment for real prime time, but there was only one drawback: Max Schmeling, the German heavyweight, had won the championship. It would be difficult to sell a fight between a German champion and an Italian contender to an American audience, even in New York.

Lady Luck stepped in. Sharkey took the crown from Schmeling. This may well have been more than a matter of luck. Sharkey won the decision but was the far more beaten and battered of the two. No matter, the result was what Carnera and his managers needed. The heavyweight champion was once again an American. The time was ripe. All Carnera and his managers had to do was make Carnera into the most logical contender.

That would take some doing. In order to contend for the championship, he had to defeat one of the other real contenders. These included Max Baer, Stanley Poreda, and Ernie Schaaf. Carnera fought Schaaf, with the winner set to fight Sharkey for the title.

The fight started slowly and then decelerated. It was an exercise in boredom with more hugging than the usual honeymoon. Then, in the thirteenth round, Schaaf took a couple of right uppercuts to his chin. They were not remarkable blows, just typical, slow-moving Carnera uppercuts with plenty of mass but very little acceleration. By this time the target had also slowed down. Carnera's fist and Schaaf's jaw met again, and Schaaf hit the mat.

He was out. He stayed down for the entire count. Carnera had won and would fight Sharkey for the championship.

Schaaf never woke up. He died five days later of a cerebral hemorrhage. The average fast uppercut lands with the force of half a ton, and Carnera's with two-thirds of that. One-third of a ton on a chin is still enough to kill someone, especially if that someone's brain is not normal to start with, and Schaaf's wasn't. He had recently been knocked out by Max Baer. Baer's faster than average fists landed with far more than average force and had produced a hemorrhage in Schaaf's brain. Carnera's uppercuts caused it to rebleed.

When the New York State Athletic Commission, ignoring the autopsy findings, the physics of boxing, and all logic, banned Primo Carnera from boxing as a heavyweight, a new class of fighting was born. It was called the dreadnought class after the superbattleships of the early part of the century. This class would be for fighters over six feet two and weighing over two hundred forty pounds. Carnera was just too big and too strong for ordinary heavyweights, the commission concluded. Big he was; strong, in boxing terms, he wasn't.

That ruling meant Carnera could not fight Sharkey in New York. Sharkey would have to defend his title there against Max Baer, and only Baer wanted that. Baer was a great fighter. His punches had caused the real problem. A guy could really get hurt fighting him.

What to do? There was money in a Sharkey-Carnera fight. The NYAC decided its rules about the dreadnought class didn't count in title fights. If the championship was on the line, dreadnoughts could fight heavyweights. Who ever said money didn't talk?

The fight was scheduled. The public relations machines went to work. Even the sportswriters jumped in. The immortal Damon Runyon, whose characters were the basis for that classic American musical comedy *Guys and Dolls*, realized that Carnera was not an instinctive fighter but suggested that when a giant of Carnera's size and weight "is merely shoving a ham of a hand encased in leather against a human object, that object is apt to be damaged."

Physics notwithstanding, when the fight was fought the object was damaged. Carnera defeated Sharkey by a knockout in the sixth round. Primo Carnera was now the heavyweight champion of the world. He was a hero to Italians everywhere. Il Duce gave him a private audience in the Palazzo Venezia. Carnera had reached a pinnacle never reached before or since by an Italian boxer, although Italian-American Rocky Marciano later became a far more deserving champion.

The Man Mountain's reign lasted only one year. He defeated Sharkey in June 1933. The next June he fought a real boxer, Max Baer. In between, he made his first movie for MGM, a boxing epic entitled *The Prizefighter and the Lady* featuring Primo Carnera and Max Baer as the boxers and Myrna Loy as the lady. *The Prizefighter and the Lady* is all but forgotten today, and rightly so. The script called for the fictional world champion, played by the actual heavyweight champion, Primo Carnera, to be defeated by a California wonderboy played by Max Baer, in fact, the California wonderboy of boxing. Carnera balked at the plot; the champion should win, at least, as long as he was the champ. In fixed fights he always won, and what was this, if not just another variety of fixed fights? Carnera finally gave in as long as got he paid more than the contender. After all, it was just a movie.

Life, however, imitates the movies. Baer fought Carnera for the championship in June 1934. It was no contest. Baer destroyed Carnera and became heavyweight champion of the world.

The fight had been carried back to Italy by shortwave radio and Italians throughout the country listened. But not Il Duce. He was too busy preparing for his first meeting with fellow dictator Adolf Hitler. Il Duce should have spent a quiet evening at home listening to the radio. What Baer did to Carnera, the Allies eventually did to Italy.

Baer's reign was also short. He was far more interested in the secondary gratifications that came with being champion than in working to retain his title. The interregnum continued. Baer lost the title to Jim Braddock. This gave Carnera another shot at the title. All he had to do was beat one other contender, a young black kid out of Detroit named Joe Louis. But that was far more difficult than it sounded. The fight was about as even a match as was Italy's invasion of Abyssinia. Louis battered Carnera senseless for six rounds until the ex-champ's corner threw in the towel. The interregnum would come to an end when Louis beat Braddock in his next fight and captured the crown.

When Louis saw Carnera in the ring, he was struck by the Italian's feet and is said to have commented that with feet like that Carnera could cover a lot of grapes. No foot covers a larger area than the foot of an acromegalic. It would have been far better for Carnera if his feet could have covered a bit more distance with a bit more speed. Alas, those attributes do not come from excessive growth hormone output.

For Primo Carnera, ex-heavyweight champion of the world, it was all downhill from there. He fought off and on for the next decade or so but he never again fought for the championship. He was never again a contender. His life as a somebody in the world of boxing was over. In his career he had fought one hundred and one fights and had won eighty-nine, including seventy-one by knockouts. There was probably even an occasional legitimate knockout or two among them.

Carnera returned to Italy and lived quietly in Sequals throughout World War II. Once the war was over, he realized that he still had to make a living and that he had two assets to help him accomplish that. He was still the Man Mountain and he had been heavyweight champion of the world. It was time for show business again, this time in two different forms, movies and wrestling. He was successful in both. He had small parts in such films as *Mighty Joe Young*, *Casanova's Big Night* (one of Bob Hope's less successful ventures), *On the Waterfront*, *Prince Valiant*, and others, though he was never much of an actor. He made most of his income as a wrestler, and he made a pretty good living out of it, too.

Most sports fans look down on wrestling as mere entertainment. The matches are exhibitions, not contests. They are right, on both counts, but the entertainers are usually paid and don't have their brains injured by the nature of what they do. Old wrestlers are neither stumblebums nor beggars. The same cannot be said of old boxers. Last year I heard an interview on National Public Radio with the son of another wrestler of that same era. The wrestler was a Native American (really a Native Canadian) who had wrestled under the name of Chief Don Eagle, complete with Indian headdress and war dances. His son looked back fondly on his father's career as an "entertainer." The father had been a college graduate who made a good living as a wrestler and supported his family quite well through the wrestling business. The son was, at that time, the assistant conductor of the Toronto Symphony Orchestra. Very few sons of boxers look back fondly on their father's careers.

Carnera ended his own movie career by an ill-conceived lawsuit. *The Harder They Fall* was obviously the story of his life. Hollywood had made a movie of his life, called it fiction, and paid him nothing for the rights.

The movie certainly followed the outline of Carnera's career. The boxing roles in this film were played by two former heavyweight champions: Jersey Joe Walcott, who had been the champ for one year in the fifties—between Ezzard Charles and Rocky Marciano—and Primo Carnera's old adversary, Max Baer. The role of Toro Moreno, the giant "Argentine" fighter, was played by Mike Lane. The star roles were filled by Humphrey Bogart and Rod Steiger. Steiger played a shady, mob-controlled promoter; and Bogart was an ex-sportswriter who now worked for him. The film revolves around the upward career of Toro Moreno. This was a succession of fixed fights that lead up to a real bout against a top contender who had recently been beaten into submission by none other than Max Baer. Needless to say, Toro's punches precipitate the brain hemorrhage that kills his opponent. This was called fiction, and fiction it was.

Carnera sued, even though he was a public figure and every detail of his life used in the movie was public record. Even the fact that a fighter had died after a fight with him. He certainly could not claim invasion of privacy, any more than the descendants of Huey Long could for *All the King's Men*. Nor, looking at his record, could he claim either slander or defamation of character. The judge agreed and threw out his suit. Carnera, by becoming Da Preem, had forfeited any right to privacy.

Why had he sued? Bad advice from his lawyer? Or was it just too much to watch Max Baer get paid for an appearance in Carnera's life story and Carnera not receive a red cent?

His lawyers, at least, should have known better. Once he filed suit, his Hollywood career was over. He made a few more films in England and Rome. One of these, Carol Reed's *A Kid for Two Farthings*, is even occasionally remembered today. Carnera also continued to wrestle. Of his public careers it was wrestling for which he was best suited. He could not act well enough to make a career of it, nor did he have the strength needed to be a boxer. Wrestling was perfect. He made enough money to retire and return eventually to his native Italy.

Carnera died in Sequals at the age of sixty. The cause of his death is variously ascribed to either cirrhosis of the liver or cancer, as if the two need be mutually exclusive. American sports fans have all learned from the recent death of baseball great Mickey Mantle that the two conditions can go hand in hand. Primary cancer of the liver almost always occurs in a background of severe cirrhosis, usually secondary to chronic alcohol abuse. That was the way it was with Mickey Mantle and Primo Carnera. Joe DiMaggio, the man who replaced Carnera in the hearts of New York's Italian-Americans and was replaced in center field by Mickey Mantle, outlived them both.

Primo Carnera remains one of those few athletes who owed his entire career to a brain tumor. If he had not had a growth hormone–secreting tumor of the pituitary gland, he would never have had pituitary gigantism. Without that extraordinary height and physique he would have stayed in Sequals and would never have ventured as far as Bordeaux as a sideshow boxer in a traveling carnival. He would never have become a boxer, a wrestler, or a motion picture actor. And he certainly would never have become the only Italian ever to win the heavyweight boxing championship of the world.

His tumor had to have been fairly quiescent for his entire adult life. That happens at times. The tumor just stops growing and stops producing growth hormone. Why this happens is unclear. The tumor may outgrow its blood supply and in a sense commit suicide. Or the cells may lose the ability to make growth hormone. This is a specialized function and most tumors of the pituitary cannot do it.

If a pituitary tumor continues to grow, it eventually destroys the optic nerves, resulting in blindness. Continued growth also frequently leads to further endocrinological problems, including impotence. A succession of seductresses, lovers, and finally a wife and children are evidence against this for Carnera. Had his tumor continued to produce growth hormone his acromegalic facial features would have become more and more pronounced. One look at photographs of him shows that this did not happen.

The peasant from northern Italy had a tumor that did all it could do to help him and then quietly stopped growing and went out of the business of producing hormones. Unfortunately, most patients are not that lucky.

For the last three seasons, NBA fans have been able to observe another pituitary giant attempt to perfect his athletic skills. He is seven-foot seven-inch Georghe Muresan, who plays center for the Washington Bullets. In 1993, Muresan had surgery on his pituitary for removal of the tumor that had been causing his excessive growth. The primary effect of the excessive growth

Center Georghe Muresan sporting number 77 to remind fans of his height, as if they needed any reminding. Muresan had his best year in 1995–1996, increasing his scoring and rebounding. Unfortunately, he was not able to increase his speed, and he remained the slowest player in the league. His facial features, like Carnera's, are typically acromegalic.

hormone production was a classic example of pituitary gigantism, but Muresan's size nineteen sneakers and facial physiognomy show that he also has some of the cardinal features of acromegaly. Muresan's tumor, much like Primo Carnera's, had become active fairly early in his life. Activity before closure of the long bones is a requirement for true gigantism. By the time Georghe was ten he was taller than anyone else in his family, and when he was fourteen he was already six feet nine. That's two inches taller than Primo Carnera's final height.

With his surgery and radiation therapy over, Muresan played for the Bullets during the 1994–1995 season and started most of the team's games, averaging ten points along with almost seven rebounds and close to two blocked shots per game. By the season's end, he was clearly learning some of the skills needed to play NBA basketball, although he still lacked speed and quickness. Muresan grew up in Transylvania, a region of Romania better known as the ancestral home of the Dracula family than for the height of its basketball players. Muresan grew while Ceauşescu was still the dictator of Romania. There are few other places in the Western world where his extraordinary growth would not have resulted in medical evaluation long before he reached seven feet seven. It is too early to tell how much he may have benefited from medical neglect. His eventual basketball achievements and his future medical history will be part of the answer.

chapter 3

The First Overtime: Sudden Death

I CAN STILL CONJURE UP THE IMAGE of Big Julie as easily as I can that of the Nike of Samothrace or the Rosetta stone. This is not too surprising since Julie was the first of my high school friends to die. I last saw him when we were both still in high school. That was before I had ever heard of either of those ageless monuments of the ancient world, much less actually seen them. His real name was Jules, and his parents were careful to always call him that. To us, he was Big Julie.

Big Julie was the first person about whom I ever made a correct diagnosis based solely upon visual observations, without anyone's help. The diagnosis was based on no laboratory data. I have never seen any such data. It was not based on a complete physical examination, as I had never examined Big Julie. He was never my patient. He died before I ever made the diagnosis.

We went to different high schools together on the South Side of Chicago, "together" because we were members of the same youth club, and we played basketball together week in and week out for much of the year. He was six feet seven inches tall, if not taller. To the rest of us, he seemed huge. The next tallest player on our team was eight inches shorter. Julie never liked his nickname. It reminded him of the gambler in *Guys and Dolls*, Big Julie from Cicero, Illinois. Our Big Julie was far from a flashy gambler. He was a serious student who went directly from high school to the University of Chicago. We all knew, even way back then, that one could not get much more serious than that.

Our Big Julie was also the tallest player in our entire league. Not the best, just the tallest. If there ever was anyone who defined the term *gangling* it was Big Julie. Not only had he outgrown his strength, he had left it so far behind that it seemed destined never to catch up. His arms were like the branches of some untrimmed shrub. They were too long and too damn thin. Yet at the same time they were not as long as they should have been for someone that tall. His trunk was too short for his legs, or was it his thin legs that were too long for his trunk? For any trunk? His feet were flat, too. Quickness was not one of his attributes. His arms were so thin that he had no upper body strength at all. Fighting for rebounds was not part of his game. Looking back, none of us had very much upper body strength. Those were the days before training with weights. Hell, we never trained at all. We just played basketball because we liked to get together and play. Big Julie played as poorly as the rest of us, he was just bigger. And his glasses were thicker.

I was still in my residency when my mother called me. I could tell from the sound of her voice that she was upset. "What's wrong?" I asked, fearing the worst.

"It's Jules," she replied. She never called him Julie, much less Big Julie. She and Big Julie's mother had known each other since childhood. They were cousins, although I never knew the lineage or the genetics of the relationship. "He died," she said.

And I saw him in my visual memory. Tall, thin, gangling, peculiarly proportioned, wearing his coke-bottle glasses, trying to make a short, two-handed set shot over an opponent almost a foot shorter. He missed that shot in my memory and suddenly I knew what had happened to him. "He had an aneurysm, didn't he?"

"Yes," she said softly.

"A dissecting aneurysm of his aorta," I concluded, perhaps a bit too triumphantly. I had let my pleasure at my diagnostic acumen get the best of me.

"How did you know that?" my mother asked.

"I didn't. It just had to be that. He had to have had Marfan's syndrome. I can see him. His size. His everything. Him. That's what he had. That is how they die all of a sudden. Of ruptured aneurysms of the aorta."

Aneurysms are abnormal widenings or dilatations of a blood vessel, usually an artery. I began to explain aneurysms to my mother. Then I realized I was being a clinician and a teacher when what she needed was a loving son who was still alive and well. I stopped teaching.

She asked me if I would go to the funeral with her. I said that I would. It was the least I could do for her and for an old teammate.

Marfan's syndrome is a hereditary disease and it is rare. About one out of twenty thousand people has it. It's named after the French pediatrician Antoine Bernard-Jean Marfan, who first described it in 1896. The original patient was a five-year-old boy who had long, thin extremities. Shades of Big Julie.

Excessive height is one hallmark of the disorder. People with Marfan's also often have high, arched palates. These factors do not cause any problems, but at times act as a diagnostic clue. Eye problems are even more common and include severe near-sightedness and lens problems. At times, the disease causes the chest to appear to be caved in, a condition known as pectus excavatum. But excessive height is the most prominent hallmark of the disease.

The patient is far too tall, taller than any other members of his family except for those with the same defect. It is not just ordinary excess of height, either. Marfan patients would never pass for Michael Jordan. Their limbs are too long, especially their legs. Lower body length is disproportionally greater than upper body length. Many medical authorities now believe that good old Abe Lincoln had Marfan's syndrome before Marfan described it. Why not? It's hereditary. Marfan did not describe the first spontaneous mutation on that gene.

Although they are symptoms, extreme height and pecu-liar physiognomy are not what make Marfan's a disease. It is classified as a disease of the connective tissue, those tissues that hold everything together. In Marfan's, it is collagen, one of the key ingredients of connective tissue, that is defective. As a result, many parts of the anatomy just don't grow right or function correctly.

The connective tissue is abnormal because of an abnormal gene hiding out on the thirteenth chromosome. This is one of the genes that is responsible for the production of collagen. It is another example of the all too familiar story of a genetic disease. Basically, abnormal DNA occurs in the gene, producing abnormal RNA, and causing an abnormal result. In this instance, it is abnormal collagen. The abnormal collagen then begets abnormal tissues.

Collagen is everywhere. It is the fibrous tissue that is found in bones, in joints, in the connective tissues that bind bones and joints and muscles, in the eyes, in the heart, and in the blood vessels. In Marfan's, the collagen and the connective tissue that make up the aorta are abnormal. As a result, the wall of the aorta becomes weaker and weaker, less able to withstand stress. With time the aorta dilates and then tears, and aortic blood under high arterial pressure rushes into the wall and cuts or dissects its way through it. This is a true medical emergency, one which is usually fatal despite the best efforts of cardiovascular surgeons. Big Julie's aorta had torn and his arterial blood had dissected its way through much of his aorta. He died on the operating room table with three of Chicago's finest cardiovascular surgeons doing their best to save him.

Some individuals with Marfan's syndrome have both extraordinary height and athletic skills to go with it. Some patients have had significant success in basketball, and even more in volleyball, where their long, thin fingers are less of a disadvantage. Such athletes at times have become stars, at least in part because of their disease. Flo Hyman was one such athlete. She played volleyball for the U.S. team that won the Silver Medal in the 1984 Olympics. She died when her aorta gave out during a volleyball game.

What should be done with an athlete who has Marfan's syndrome? Should Flo Hyman have been allowed to play volleyball and kill herself as the pounding of her own heart sent her blood dissecting into her weakened aorta? Or should she have been protected from herself and never been given the opportunity to win a Silver Medal in the Olympics? She died playing volleyball. It was just too risky. Yet she lived through the Olympics and was just as likely to have died in bed some night.

Those are the two sides of the issue, and there is no final answer. Physicians do have the obligation to examine athletes and to make the correct diagnosis. Once that is done, the patient-athlete has the right to be given all the available information and then make his or her own informed decision. Big Julie was in a study hall studying statistics when his aneurysm ruptured.

chapter 4

The Seventh-Inning Stretch: Michael Jordan and Wayne Gretzky

AS SOON AS MICHAEL JORDAN announced his ambition to play baseball, it was suggested that two of his physical attributes would all but assure his ultimate success. The first was his speed. Speed is certainly beneficial, but in baseball even speed has its limitations.

In the late 1960s, Charles Finley, owner of the Oakland Athletics, signed "the world's fastest human," sprinter Allan Lewis, to a major league contract. The "Panamanian Express" was twenty-six years old at the time and was the fastest sprinter in the world. Once in a major league uniform he became a pinch runner for the Athletics, and for six years he ran and ran and ran. Even in the World Series. Like Michael Jordan, he never learned to hit. Lewis was later replaced by another dash man, Herb Washington. When Washington was signed he started working on his swing, but after five days of spring training, he realized that he would never get to do anything but run. In his two years in the major leagues, he played in over one hundred games and never once came to bat.

The other attribute that was stressed in Michael's favor was his height. He is six feet six inches tall. While that is not considered tall by NBA standards, even for a guard, it is tall for a major league baseball player. In the ninety-six seasons of the modern baseball era, only three truly successful major league hitters were ever that tall: Frank Howard, Dave Winfield, and Dave Kingman.

Howard was six feet seven and had been a center for Ohio State University's basketball team. He played in the majors for sixteen seasons and led the American League in home runs twice. Dave Winfield was exactly Michael's height and had played college basketball at the University of Minnesota. His major league career lasted more than twenty years and included a stretch of twelve straight seasons during which he was chosen to play on the American League All-Star team. Kingman was also six feet six, and in his sixteen-year career he managed to hit four hundred forty-six home runs and twice led the National League in home runs. His lifetime batting average (.236) was unimpressive, even for sluggers, and his lifetime strikeout average (.272) was the highest ever recorded. (The brief career of six-foot-seven-inch Walt Bond hardly qualifies as truly successful. He stayed in the majors for only six seasons and was a regular in only two of them.)

The relative paucity of tall baseball players suggests that height may actually be a disadvantage in attempting to hit a baseball. A tall player has a larger strike zone. His visual-motor system must project the bat over a larger area. Besides, many more opposing pitchers can get a low pitch over to a hitter whose strike zone starts that high off the ground. This may also be compounded by the fact that height is not a simple measurement that is proportioned equally in all individuals. Blacks have relatively less of their height above the pubic bone than do whites. In whites, the average ratio of the length of the lower body (distance from the pubic bone to the floor) to the length of the upper (distance from the pubic bone to the top of the head) is 1.08; in blacks the ratio is 1.17. That means that the average black player at the same height has relatively longer legs than his white counterpart.

Whether this makes a difference in athletic performance has never been investigated. It may well be important in certain events in track. A longer stride could easily make the difference in short races. It might also be a factor in relative jumping ability. A basketball forward leaping for a rebound does not leap with his back muscles. A longer trunk is a disadvantage in jumping, while longer legs are a definite advantage.

In baseball, longer legs might actually hurt. At the same height, the average black would have a greater distance from his waist to his knees. This translates into a bigger strike zone and a greater area that the bat must cover, with much of that distance at the farthest reaches of the strike zone. Despite the fact that baseball has a mania for statistics, no one has ever collected data on this ratio in major league players and analyzed it to see if it does make a difference.

You'd think that those great power hitters who have hit baseballs out of sight had to have been big men. Hitting a baseball that far must be related to the size and strength of the hitters. But it's not so clear-cut a case. Hitting a round ball is never that simple, no matter what the size of the ball, or, in golf, the shape of the club.

In golf, increasing the distance the golf ball is hit is easily accomplished, at least in theory. It's all in the equipment. In order to increase the length of a drive, the golfer merely uses a longer club. It's a simple matter of applied physics. As long as the swing remains constant, admittedly an unwarranted assumption, the radius of the arc increases in direct proportion to the length of the club. That increase in the distance traveled by the head of the club increases the speed of the head of the club as long as the swing is no slower. The increased speed of the head imparts greater force to the ball. Since the inertia of the ball is a constant—one of the few constants in the physics of golf—the ball having been hit with greater force travels farther. Simple physics.

Those diabolical forces that have designed golf and its equipment could not leave well enough alone. Two more variables have been thrown into the equation. The first of these is the weight of the head of the club. More weight means greater mass. Greater mass means even more force. Since the era of Isaac Newton, force has been the product of mass and acceleration. If—and that's a big if—the acceleration of the swing is the same, then more mass produces more force, which translates directly into more distance. John Daly watch out.

That greater mass is not without its drawbacks, however. The greater mass means a greater moment of inertia of the head of the club. This is not a simple direct product but one that is related to the fifth power of the distance. The fifth power! Isn't physics fun! Increased resistance to the fifth power of the distance translates into a swing that is harder to initiate, harder to control, and far less reliable. If, for example, a club's length is increased by ten percent, then the resistance of the head is increased to the fifth power of 1.1. That is like getting ten percent interest each year without any withholding. By the end of five years or five powers the resistance has increased by over sixty percent. No wonder you cannot hit with that damn driver. John Daly can relax. It's time for a shorter club with a lighter head. Back to an iron. That is why golfers like Jack Nicklaus can go through an entire tournament and never once take their driver out of the bag.

These facts of the physics of golf raise questions about the way golf is played and taught. Why anyone over thirty who is starting to play golf is taught to use any club other than an iron for the first year or two is a question that golf pros cannot answer. The greater length of the woods and their greater mass produce a level of resistance to initiating and controlling the swing that cannot be compensated for by their slight advantage in force. None of the pros who teach golf started to play after they were fifteen.

In baseball it is so much simpler. The length and weight of baseball bats vary over a far narrower range. The moment of inertia among bats is fairly constant. Any one batter always uses the same bat. All the batter has to do to hit out a long one is to extend (that is, straighten out) his arms. That extension increases the radius of the arc of his swing. Greater acceleration plus more force at impact equals home run. Nothing could be more simple. Pure applied physics. A tall man with longer arms would have the advantage of an even longer arc, but with just one disadvantage: an increase in the moment of inertia to the fifth power of the length of the radius.

So how tall are sluggers?

They have to be big and tall enough to initiate a swing through the strike zone with enough speed to hit the ball, But how tall is tall? How tall is too tall? An examination of the height of the fourteen players who hit five hundred or more home runs during their major league careers, and the twelve players who have accounted for all nineteen times a player hit fifty or more home runs in one year, reveals that the average height of these sluggers is just over six feet. That does not exactly make them Goliaths. Roger Maris, who hit sixty-one home runs in 1961, and Mickey Mantle, who hit fifty-four the same year, stood six feet and five feet eleven inches, respectively. Mel Ott, who for over two decades held the record for career home runs in the National League, was only five feet nine inches. And the shortest slugger of them all, Hack Wilson, at five feet six inches, still holds the National League record for most home runs in a season, fifty-six. That same year, 1930, he set a record for runs batted in, with one hundred ninety, another record that still stands. Size, obviously, is not the key to hitting home runs.

How much time do batters have to get their arms extended in order to hit a pitch out of the park? A good fastball travels from the pitcher's hand to the plate in about forty-one-thousandths of a second. Thousandths of a second are better known in scientific circles as milliseconds. An average swing takes about twenty-eight milliseconds. That leaves a decision time of only thirteen milliseconds from the time the ball leaves the pitcher's hand. The best hitters have faster swings, so they have two or three more milliseconds to make a decision. But even for the best of hitters, the inertia of the bat most be overcome. The bat must also be accelerated to be in the right location at precisely the right time with precisely the right speed in less than thirty milliseconds. Start the swing a couple of milliseconds too soon and you look like a sucker. A couple of milliseconds too late and the ball is already in the catcher's mitt. That leaves very little margin for error.

Batters are admonished by fans and coaches alike to keep their eyes on the ball, but that simply cannot be done. The human eye cannot track anywhere near quickly enough to do that. No one sees the ball hit his bat, not even Ted Williams, the last man to hit a ball safely four out of every ten times he went to the plate.*

Baseball players are bigger and stronger than ever, but are they taller? In 1950, the Minneapolis Lakers won the first NBA crown. The average height of the Lakers' starting five was six feet four inches. When Michael Jordan led the Bulls to the first of their three championships forty-one years later, the Bulls' starters averaged six feet seven and a half inches, or about three and a half inches taller on average than those on that earlier team. That same year, 1991, the Minnesota Twins won the World Series. The average height of their starting lineup was only one inch taller than the lineup had been for the 1950 Yankees, who were on the second lap of their unprecedented "five-peat" in the World Series. That much taller baseball players have not gotten. In comparison to basketball players, baseball players are actually becoming shorter.

Greater height, on the other hand, is not a disadvantage for pitchers. In fact, it is a distinct advantage. The elevation of the pitching mound is designed to give a height advantage to all pitchers. Randy Johnson, the American League strikeout king, is six feet ten inches tall. Onetime National League strikeout king

---

*None of this applies to Babe Ruth. He used the heaviest bat of any major league slugger, one that was clearly so heavy that its moment of inertia was so great no one could possibly have used it successfully to hit major league fastballs. The Babe was blissfully ignorant of physics.

J. R. Richard was six-eight, and the one player to star simultaneously in both the NBA and major league baseball was a six-eight pitcher named Gene Conley. He was a forward for the legendary Boston Celtics and he pitched for the Boston Braves (who later moved to become the Milwaukee Braves), before going on to Philadelphia and the Boston Red Sox. He pitched in three All-Star games and one World Series in an eleven-year pitching career. While for most years Conley concentrated on one sport or the other, and either pitched or played strong forward, there were several years when he did both. He pitched in the 1959 All-Star game as a representative of the Milwaukee Braves and that winter he played forward for the Celtics. He was their sixth man when they defeated St. Louis to win the NBA championship.*

Danny Ainge, a six-foot-four-inch guard, also played both major league baseball and NBA basketball, but not simultaneously. He worked his way through college playing second base in the major leagues while playing college basketball. Once his college days were over, he became a full-time NBA player. Just think of poor Jim Thorpe. He was stripped of his Olympic Gold Medals for playing a couple of games of semipro baseball. Danny Ainge could play major league baseball and college basketball at the same time. Our notions of what an amateur should be have certainly evolved over the years. No wonder college athletes don't quite understand the rules of amateurism.

Looking back on Michael Jordan's transition, few sportswriters remarked on Michael's quickness or his terrific reflexes as great advantages in his baseball career. But what are the reflexes of an athlete? Like every other neurologist in the world,

*One other two-sport star should be mentioned, even though he never played in either of the major leagues or the NBA. That is the immortal Reece "Goose" Tatum. For decades he was the center for the Harlem Globetrotters and entertained sports fans around the world. That was the mid-1940s and the NBA then was all white. No blacks were allowed to play. Each season the best team in the NBA, the winner of their playoffs, would play the Globetrotters in order to make some money. And often the Globetrotters would win. I remember going to the Chicago Stadium in 1948 and watching Goose Tatum and the Globetrotters beat George Mikan and the Minneapolis Lakers. Basketball was not the only segregated sport in those days, nor the only sport at which Goose excelled. He played baseball for the Indianapolis Clowns in the Negro Leagues, and in 1947, Jackie Robinson's rookie year with the Brooklyn Dodgers, Goose was good enough to play in the Negro Leagues' East-West All-Star game

I spend an inordinate amount of my professional time tapping on other people's knees. We do so because this process supplies information about the functional state of the individual's nervous system. Each tap is a test of a specific reflex. These simple reflexes are an integral part of the way the nervous system works. They have come down, or up, to us from distant ancestors with far simpler nervous systems, and they have arrived in essentially unaltered forms. Reflexes are present in everyone and their characteristics are always the same, characteristics inherited by and hard-wired into the human nervous system. They are the purest example of the way the nervous system responds to an external stimulus. Each reflex is an expression of the automatic, inherent activity of the cells of the nervous system and so are not under conscious control.

Each nervous cell in the nervous system acts on an "all-or-none" principle, like a binary switch. A cell can either fire and send an electrical impulse flowing down its membrane, or not do so. There is no other choice. In a reflex, the appropriate external stimulus causes a specific neuron to fire, and this neuron in turn triggers a predetermined pathway of successive cell discharges from other predetermined neurons. The last of these transmits the signal to an effector cell. That can be either a muscle cell, which then contracts, or a glandular cell, which then releases its secretion. Those are the only choices for final output: either a muscle contraction of the type that neurologists love or a secretion of the type that made Pavlov and his dogs so famous. In either process there are not very many cells in these pathways, often only two or three.

The knee jerk, or patellar reflex, is a tendon-stretch reflex. The tap of the hammer on the patellar tendon causes a sudden stretch of that tendon. The stretch is the appropriate stimulus for specialized stretch receptors located in the nerves that supply the tendon. The sudden stretch activates the receptors and their sensory nerve fires, sending an electrical impulse up toward the spinal cord. In the spinal cord, this sensory nerve communicates with a motor nerve that innervates the muscle that causes the knee to extend or kick out. The electrical impulse in the sensory nerve releases enough neurotransmitter to cause the motor nerve to fire. It fires, relaying the impulse to the motor end plate, which causes the muscle to contract and the leg to kick.

The patellar reflex is a pathway starting with the stretch receptor then traveling up the sensory nerve to reach the motor nerve and then the muscle fiber. How can such a simple system, designed to maintain the level of stretch of muscles during continuous activity, tell anyone very much about the functional state of the nervous system? First and foremost, this reflex should always be present. Sometimes an individual has lost this reflex, meaning the reflex arc must have been interrupted. One or more components of that arc must be injured or diseased.

The reflex can also be more vigorous than normal, an increased reflex. How can that happen? These relays can either fire or not. All or none, not all or more. This happens because the nervous system is not as simple as its individual components. The sensory nerve of the patellar reflex does not synapse directly upon the motor nerve. It synapses with an interneuron, a neuron that only functions as a go-between. This go-between is regulated by fibers coming down to it from the brain. If there were no control from above this interneuron would relay the stretch input to every cell it could reach, producing a maximal reflex. That would make the control of stretch very erratic. This reflex is there for a purpose that long antedated the discovery of the reflex hammer. Stretch reflexes allow the muscles to retain needed tone as they change length. This is a process that must be carried out smoothly. In order for this to happen, the brain automatically dampens this response and prevents excessive responses that would disrupt the original movement. This, too, was developed by far simpler nervous systems and handed down to humans. If the ability of the brain to inhibit this reflex is interrupted, the reflex acts as if it is increased. In reality, it has been released from the normal level of inhibition forced upon it by the brain.

So one tap does tell a great deal. It can tell if there is disease in the arc itself that interrupts the reflex arc or disease in the brain or spinal cord that releases the arc into a state of hyperactivity.

Not all reflexes are that simple, however, and not all reflexes in humans are as uniform as the knee jerk. Remember, the human brain is unique in the degree of its postnatal growth and development. During such development the environment influences how the brain develops. Some people learn skills that others never even know can be learned. Some acquired reflexes have developed as a direct result of the way a particular developing nervous system interacts with its environment.

Reflexes have different degrees of complexity. A neurologist examines a patient. He scratches the right side of the patient's abdomen with a safety pin. The umbilicus is reflexly pulled toward the site of the scratch mark. The neurologist now scratches the left side, leaving the same mark but eliciting no response from the umbilicus. What does this all mean? Was there an interruption of a reflex arc on the left by disease in the nerves to and from the abdominal wall? Or release of a hyperactive response on the right?

Neither. This is not a simple reflex organized at the level of the spinal cord and then kept in check by the brain. It is a reflex that is centered in the brain. The painful scratch causes a sensory discharge that travels to the spinal cord, then is relayed to the brain where it generates the response that eventually reaches the muscles of the abdominal wall, which contract and displace the umbilicus. This is a multisynaptic reflex of the brain itself. The absent reflex on the left means that the arc has been broken, but that the injury has occurred in the brain or spinal cord.

The most important reflexes for complex motor activities are more like the abdominal reflexes. They involve more than one or two neurons, and they are centered in the brain, not the spinal cord. Hitting, in part, depends on this type of complex, multisynaptic reflex response. A ball is seen and the bat is set into motion without any conscious thought on the part of the batter. It is a complex reflex. The conscious decision is whether to suppress the reflex or not. Whether *not* to swing, not whether to swing. The pitcher winds up, and as soon as he releases the ball, the bat starts to move. Then the swing is interrupted or not. Pitchers take full advantage of this reflex arc by attempting to subvert it. Those who can, change the location of their release point. Sometimes they pitch overhead, then suddenly drop their arm down to a lower point. The batter may not see the release and the reflex is never triggered. He is caught with his bat on his shoulder.

It is no coincidence that the one major league player to have been killed as a result of having been hit in the head by a pitch, Ray Chapman, was struck by a submarine pitch thrown by Carl Mays. A submarine pitch is one that is released around the pitcher's waist. Most pitches are released above the shoulder and the hitting motion in the batter is started by the visual cells that "see" those pitches. Due to the complex pathways of the nervous system, these cells are located in the lower half of the visual cortex. A submarine pitch is seen by cells in the upper half, cells that have not learned to trigger any reflexes at all. Ray Chapman never really saw the pitch that hit him.

The role of such acquired reflexes is not unique to baseball. It is also the main principle in a number of other sports. One of these is hockey. The most important difference between a great hockey scorer and an average scorer is not the speed of the puck as the player sends it toward the goal. It is not even the overall accuracy of the shot. It is how quickly the player can get his shot off, how quickly he can pull the trigger.

Those reflexes can't really be reflexes in a neurological sense. But why not? Shooting a hockey puck is a complex, acquired behavior, just like hitting a baseball. The major difference is in the stimulus that triggers the response. Wayne Gretzky, "the Great Gretzky," is the greatest hockey scorer of all time. He may be both the Babe Ruth and the Michael Jordan of hockey all rolled into one. In his career he has set more scoring records than most other players have scored goals. He holds career records for total points scored (the sum of goals plus assists) and for assists. He has led the National Hockey League in goals scored five times, in assists twelve times, and in scoring (total

points) eleven times. In one five-year stretch, he had four seasons in each of which he amassed over two hundred total
points. His scoring ability can't just be because his reflexes are
faster than anyone else's.

Or can it? William Tatton is a neurologist who has studied
what are called long loop reflexes. These are motor responses to
sensory stimuli, which involve long loops of neurons in the
brain. This research was performed at the University of British
Columbia, and one of the subjects studied was Wayne Gretzky.
(Who else would a Canadian study but the greatest hockey
player around.) Gretzky had the fastest long loop reflex arcs of
anyone Bill Tatton had ever studied in his laboratory. That
is why Gretzky has no trouble pulling the trigger. Certainly
Gretzky has a hard, fast shot. Certainly he has an accurate shot.
So do lots of other hockey players. But it takes "the Great One"
less time from the instant he perceives the stimulus (an open
corner of the net) until his shot has been fired, until his long
loop reflexes have sent the puck off toward that goal.*

That same mechanism occurs within the brains of batters.
And it is the same in all batters, whether they are batting in
baseball or in cricket. No one taught them how to hit. No one
taught Babe Ruth to hit. In turn, Babe Ruth taught no one else
how to hit. That was beyond him. He had no idea why others
did not have the same reflex capabilities that he did. So where
did the Babe's skill come from? In part it was hereditary. Hitting
clearly has a hereditary bias. The number of family dynasties
of hitters is growing each year—the Bondses, the Griffeys,
the Alous, the Alomars.

*According to Bill Tatton, Gretzky has one other physical-neurological attribute that
undoubtedly contributes to his extraordinary success. Gretzky claims that he never turns
his head in order to make a pass. In fact, he never looks at the players on his wings before
passing the puck to them. What Gretzky is reporting is a much greater than average
ability to perceive motion far from his center of vision, and that this motion is sufficient
to trigger his passing skills. Most of us spend our lives moving our eyes in order to keep
objects within the center of our visual field where visual acuity and color discrimination
are greatest. Perception of motion, however, is maximal outside of this area and these
moving images are relayed from the retina to those visual cells that Hubel and Weisel
studied. These visual cells and their distribution are under hereditary control; but
without the proper stimulation during the appropriate window of opportunity they
will never develop to their maximal capability. Gretzky had this physical skill and
developed it.

In part, the acquisition of these complex reflexes is nature, but the inherited natural ability must be nurtured early in life before the window of opportunity is lost forever.

But what about Michael Jordan's long loop reflexes? They are probably far quicker than the average basketball player's and even than the average baseball hitter's, but a reflex depends on the reflex arc. Input leading to output. Michael's input from the visual cortex had never been exposed to the right stimulus at the right time to become a successful hitter. It never made the correct connections with the right output. His arc was not broken; it never existed.

chapter 5

The Bantam:
Ben Hogan

BIOGRAPHICAL SKETCHES OF BANTAM BEN HOGAN often seem to resemble medical case histories more than sports stories, yet they invariably fall short in both arenas, especially from the viewpoint of a neurologist. Ben Hogan was one of the men who helped to put professional golf on the map and into the newsreels, to make it an essential part of the world's sports scene, to get golf its share of the world's sports marketplace. Pound for pound, he may have been the greatest golfer in the history of the game.

I can still see him in those black and white newsreels; Ben Hogan competed and triumphed before we watched the thrill of victory and the agony of defeat in glorious color. I can still see him standing on a windswept green, surveying that green, calculating the break down to the millimeter, measuring his putt, addressing the ball. The crowd is hushed. Hogan moves his putter slowly back toward his right foot. He smoothly, almost imperceptibly, stops its motion and then with that same calculated smoothness begins to glide his putter forward. Deftly, ever so deftly. The consummate professional. Suddenly his hand jerks and the putter goes off line. It accelerates ever so slightly. The ball bounces off the putter and streaks to the left of the hole, ending up four feet beyond the target. Ben Hogan had blown not only the putt but the championship as well. The pressure had got to him. That's my image and that's what I remember.

But what is the real story of "the Wee Ice Mon," as the Scots called him, in part in fondness and in part in awe of his cold, withdrawn behavior on the course?* Hogan was born in a small town in Texas in 1912. When he was ten years old his father, who had been the village blacksmith, died. The family moved to Fort Worth, and Ben began to caddie at the local country club for sixty-five cents a round in order to help support the family. This was his introduction to the game of golf. It was an introduction that went well, even though it was awkward at first. Ben was left-handed, and the only golf clubs he could borrow were right-handed. So he learned to play right-handed. He learned so quickly that when he was fifteen and had been swinging right-handed golf clubs for only three years, he won the club's Christmas tournament for the caddies. It would be right-handed golf as a way of life from then on.

Hitting from the wrong side may have been an advantage for Ben. Today golf teachers often stress the importance of the usually nondominant or nonlead arm and hand in taking over during the swing. This may be more natural for a left-hander swinging in a right-handed way. The golf swing, like the baseball swing, is, after all, not a one-handed activity.

Like every other successful professional golfer, Hogan started out young. Gene Litler is often considered to be the odd man out in this regard because he didn't start playing golf until he was fifteen. It seems that hitting a golf ball, like hitting a baseball, is an acquired skill that has a window of opportunity—a time frame during the development and maturation of the brain when it must be learned if it is ever to be truly perfected. But Alistair Cooke, renowned English observer of all things American, first learned to swing a golf club at the age of fifty-seven. Cooke has

---

*Hogan, by the way, hated the nickname Bantam Ben. He liked to point out that he was five feet nine inches tall and weighed in at one hundred sixty-two pounds. Had he been a boxer he would have fought in the same class as middleweight champion Sugar Ray Robinson, often thought to have been the greatest boxer ever, or light-heavyweight champion (and later heavyweight contender) Archie Moore. The heavyweight classification in boxing starts at one hundred seventy-five pounds, a mere twelve pounds more than Hogan carried. In sports, as in much of life, perception is often far more significant than reality. Hogan at one sixty-two was a bantam or "wee." Did anyone ever call Sugar Ray wee?

never made the pro tour to be sure or even the senior tour, but at least, according to his own words, he was once able to get a thirty-nine on the back nine. He clearly had learned something about hitting a golf ball.

What is learned when golf is learned? When the ability to hit a golf ball with a golf club is acquired? What part of the brain is involved in that learning process? Is there a strict window of opportunity, an all-or-none chance to hit a two-hundred-and-fifty-yard drive and keep it on the fairway, or is there merely a window of maximal opportunity that fades into an ability to acquire lesser levels of skill as time goes on?

Hogan turned pro in 1931, when he was only nineteen. It was not the best of times in America to start off any kind of a career. The Great Depression was in full swing. Life was not easy for anyone who had to work for a living, and the world of pro golf was no exception. The winnings were slim, the sponsors few and far between, and endorsements rare. In the late twenties Babe Ruth had demanded a contract that paid him more than the president of the United States. When asked by reporters if he thought he deserved more than the president, the Babe supposedly replied, "I had a better year than he did."

In 1931 President Hoover had an even worse year. The Babe had a good year, leading the American League in home runs for the last time in his career with forty-six. Things were so bad around the country that America's only professional basketball league, the American Basketball League, stopped scheduling games and went into hibernation.

It was in this climate that Ben Hogan turned pro. His timing could not have been worse. Nor his hook. Needless to say, success did not come easily or quickly. He had no support, no endorsement money behind him. All he had was his own will and desire, his terrible hook, and one hundred dollars in cash. The money ran out in a month, and a dollar lasted a lot longer in those days. Hogan went back home to work on his shots, on his swing, on his grip, on every single aspect of the way he hit a golf ball. Day in and day out he worked at playing golf. Two years later he tried once again to make it as a pro. Hoover was no longer president. Roosevelt had told the nation that the only thing we had to fear was fear itself. Few people seem to have been convinced that fear of fear was the only problem. The Great Depression was still with us and even Babe Ruth was having a bad year. So did Ben Hogan. He was better, and his hook was less of a problem, but he was still not good enough to make a living playing golf.

He had now made two attempts to become a touring professional golfer and all he had to show for it were two failures. Perhaps the gods of golf were trying to tell him something. He was twenty-one. It was time to think of his future.

He did precisely that and came to the same conclusion he had in 1931: his future was golf. He still had an all-consuming desire to make it as a pro and he translated that desire into a will to improve his caliber of play in order to win. That will manifested itself as an intensity of concentration and work ethic that few have matched and none have exceeded. Ben went back to work on his game, on every facet of every shot, and work he did. He learned to concentrate on golf in a way that excluded any and all outside distractions.

The American poet Donald Hall has written that absorbedness is the paradise of work; such absorbedness is a form of unsurpassed contentment. If this is true, then Ben Hogan must have found his own vision of a paradise on earth, for no one was ever more absorbed in what he did. Hogan's absorption became part of his personality. On the course, he concentrated one hundred percent on his own game. He was not just taciturn, he was downright noncommunicative. He rarely said anything to anyone. His closest golf companion, fellow professional Jimmy Demaret, denied that Hogan refused to talk to him on the course. According to Demaret, Hogan talked to him on every single green they had ever played together. As they approached their golf balls, Hogan would turn to Demaret and say, "You're away."

Back home he worked on his game, day in, day out. He worked on his hook, on his swing, on his grip. He taught himself to overcome his hook, to defeat it. How? By learning to change the posture of his wrists during his backswing, to pronate

Ben Hogan teeing off. His long game, which depended on a different motor program than his putting, was never bothered by the dystonia that ended his pro career.

his wrists as he swung. Most golfers today are taught to begin with their wrists pronated, closing the **V** formed by their two forearms. Hogan had no local golf pro to teach him and could not stop at his corner video store for an instructional tape. Learning a new posture for his hands during his backswing makes it all sound so easy, but learning to perform acts with new postures is never an easy task for the brain.

The control of movement in humans, as in every other mammal, depends on the coordination of three separate but intertwined motor systems of the brain and the spinal cord. The first and most easily understood is the pyramidal system. Intuitively it seems to be the most important system, since it is this system that is injured in most severe strokes. Those strokes leave a person paralyzed on the opposite side of the body. A stroke on the right side of the brain causes paralysis of the lower part of the left side of the face, the entire left arm, and the entire left leg. Following recovery, the patient learns to walk again, but can't walk normally. The left arm and leg are stiff. The left leg cannot be flexed at the knee or the hip and remains extended. Without flexion at the knee and hip, the foot remains on the ground. Some new movement must be performed to get the foot off the ground in order to propel the leg forward. What working muscles remain? Those that swing the leg out and around. More correctly, the control of these muscles remains. Activating these muscles causes the leg to be swung away from the body. In doing this the foot is lifted from the ground and the leg moves forward. Neurologically this is known as circumduction, with the foot being led around the hip instead of being lifted off the ground. The left arm, in distinct contrast to the left leg, is held in a flexed posture, bent at the elbow and wrist. Fine movements are lost by the hand and fingers. This is the classic description of a left hemiplegia caused by a stroke involving the right pyramidal, or corticospinal, tract, the pathway that goes directly from the cerebral cortex to the motor cells in the spinal cord.

That is what happens when the pyramidal tract is destroyed. Remember that neurologists usually assume that whatever function is lost when a structure is injured represents the primary function of that structure when it is not injured, with some exceptions. Hence we believe that the healthy corticospinal tract, the pyramidal tract, directs movement. It carries messages from the cortex of our brain to the motor neurons. It tells the spinal cord neurons when to perform a specific movement and precisely what to do in order to carry out that task: take a step, lift the leg, bend both the hip and the knee.

It's the same in taking a swing at a baseball, for example. What could be easier? Nothing. Motorically, the swing is a simple task. The pyramidal tract can direct that movement in anyone. It's hitting the ball that is difficult. Ask Michael Jordan. Hitting does not depend very much on the swing, per se. That's why hitters have so many different types of swings. Hitting really depends on visual-motor coordination, in which an image is recognized in the visual system of the cerebral cortex. This cortical system learns what that image means and then generates a message to the pyramidal system to take that specific swing to get the bat to the right place at precisely the right time. The task is no longer quite so simple, but the output still depends primarily on the pyramidal tract.

Primarily, not exclusively. The three systems all work together—all the time. There is no isolation in the nervous system. Nothing works by itself. That is why the concept that the normal function of a part of the brain can be inferred by noting what is lost or left when that structure is injured can never be completely correct. The pyramidal system works only because other systems do their job in a coordinated fashion. Without that there would be no hitting. There would not even be any walking.

The second motor system that must and does cooperate in all purposeful movements is the cerebellar system, housed in the cerebellum, at the back of the brain. Unlike the corticospinal pathway, however, this system does not function consciously. We cannot turn it on or off. We cannot tell it what to do or when to do it. It does what it does whenever we tell any muscle to do anything, even when we aren't consciously directing any movement at all. It works whenever we move or chose not to move. But what does it do? The cerebellar system provides synergy and coordination, the minute, precise coordination of muscles to carry out any and all movements and postures.

This is the system that goes first when alcohol hits the brain. The police test for it by making you touch your finger to your nose. If you've been drinking, you understand the command and you can initiate the movement. You just can't keep all those muscles coordinated. Instead of coming straight to your nose, your hand jerks and darts, first in one direction then in another. Nothing smooth about that. And walking along a straight line? Forget it. And forget turning a steering wheel the number of degrees needed to negotiate that curve in the road. Even holding the wheel in place requires coordination, synergy. Those muscles that would tend to pull the wheel to the right must be synergized by those that would do the opposite. Without synergy, first one group would assert itself, then the other. A jerk to the right; then the left. Across the median line. Into oncoming traffic. Time for a designated driver.

If you are going to swing that bat at that ninety-six-mile-an-hour fastball, every muscle in your body must be coordinated to make that swing into a smooth, continuous effort, not some herky-jerky miss. That is what the cerebellum does. It balances the degree of stimulation and relaxation in all those pairs of muscles that must contract and relax in order to carry out the order relayed by the visual cortex to the cortical motor (pyramidal) system. All well and good. The ball has been seen and recognized. No mean feat that. The swing has been initiated by the pyramidal system and then synergized, or coordinated, by the cerebellum. Home run every time, right?

Golf should be even easier. No curveballs to differentiate from fastballs. No change of pace pitches. The ball is just sitting on the tee or the grass, or sometimes the sand, waiting to be hit. And its location will not change. It will be just where you think it is. Nothing could be easier: stand there, see the ball, measure the distance. Send out that message, and let the pyramidal system and the cerebellar system do their stuff, right?

If only that were true. There are, however, three systems to interact, not two. What does the third system do? What's left for it to do? The cortex has done its job. It has chosen the club and lined up the shot, measured the distance from your body to the ball, and taken a practice swing. And now it sends out its final order. The cerebellum is there to do its stuff automatically, without thinking about it. That's what cerebellums do.

So what is required of that third system? It creates and maintains postures. In order to swing successfully and hit that ball, the posture of the body must be rigorously controlled, and controlled as finely as the voluntary movement that is called the swing. In fact, more rigorously controlled. You never thought about that. That's the key. You don't need to think about the changes that your body must go through to allow those active muscles to do their thing and propel that ball down the fairway.

Without the smooth, unthinking coordination of posture, no one could ever hit either a golf ball or a baseball. You think about swinging the bat, reflexively in part, but volitionally. If you think you have made a mistake, you hold up, even though it's not easy. The cerebellum has relaxed those muscles you have to activate in order to stop your swing, but give it a try anyway. Often, you can stop the swing *in medias res*, so to speak. Swingus interruptus. It can be done. That is all under voluntary control. But what happened to your feet and your hips? You never thought about them. They must have done something. After all, you didn't fall flat on your face.

Here's another example. You are standing, waiting in a line to buy your ticket for today's baseball game. The person in front of you moves up and it's time for you to move. Come on feet, do your stuff. The cortex recognizes the signal and sends its message. So what is the first thing your body must do? Lift up your right foot? Take a step? Right? Wrong. First you must stop pushing down on your right foot. While you were standing in that line, both feet were supporting your body. Unless you do something about that, you can never lift up your right foot. You must first shift the posture of your body so that all of the weight is now on the left foot. You never thought of that, never had to think of it. That's the real hooker here. You never think of that and no one teaches you that—ever! As a baby you learned how to do it all by yourself, just like every other infant since the dawn of time and even before that.

That's precisely what the third motor system, the so-called extrapyramidal system, does. It got its name not because it was extra and perhaps not needed but because, unlike the cortical motor system that travels from the brain to the spinal cord through a structure in the brain stem called the pyramid, the extrapyramidal system gets from the brain to the spinal cord without passing through the pyramid. It goes outside the pyramid. It is extrapyramidal.

No matter what the activity, all three systems must participate. That's the way the nervous system does things. The relative roles of these systems are different in different sports. Learning to hit a baseball has a prominent visual motor–cortical motor component. In learning to hit at a major league level this component is critical. It is what scientists and statisticians would call the limiting step. Without it, nothing else matters. In tennis, coordination matters most, and the postural control is secondary. Think of all the shots made on the run. Is that why softball players and golfers drink beer while playing golf or baseball, but never during their tennis matches?

What component, then, is primary in golf? Posture. It may not be everything, but it makes everything else possible. Learning to control your posture unconsciously in order to initiate and coordinate the exact swing you want to take is the basis of golf. Without it, the rest goes for naught. And that control must become automatic. You can't think about it while you're trying to hit out of the rough over a clump of trees to the right of a sand trap. Postural control must be there in order to carry out your swing. Like a kid learning to shift weight in order to walk, weight must be shifted to hit a golf ball in the right way at precisely the right time—without a hint of conscious thought.

Control of posture is what Ben Hogan learned during those years of concentrated absorbedness in the study of his own swing. Not just control of the degree of pronation of his wrists during his backswing, but control of every facet of his posture during every type of swing in his entire repertoire of shots. Did he learn all that in three years? No, it is a process constantly being learned. The extrapyramidal system continually adjusts to new situations. That is how humans survive. It is not all or none. Golfers start early, but they often mature slowly. Their window of opportunity does not depend on the cortex, and stretches out over a greater part of their life spans.

Ben went back to the tour in 1936. His game had improved but he still had a long way to go. He qualified for the National Open for the first time, but failed to survive the thirty-six-hole cut. He kept working. Slowly but surely his game improved. After many lean years, he finally won his first tournament in 1940. He was twenty-eight years old and getting better. Very few hitters in baseball hit better after the age of twenty-eight. Ted Williams was twenty-three when he hit .406 in 1941, the last major leaguer to hit over four hundred. Hogan's first win came in the North and South Open at Pinehurst, North Carolina, and by the end of the year, he had won three more titles and tied for fourth in the U.S. Open. It was a big year. He led the professional tour in both earnings ($10,656) and lowest average score.

Hogan continued his winning ways until World War II interrupted his career. In the middle of the 1942 pro tour he became a lieutenant in the Army Air Corps. His duty lasted the duration of the war and he didn't get back to playing professional golf until the 1946 season. The big winners of the tour then were Byron Nelson and Slamming Sammy Snead. Could Hogan come back? Would it even be called a comeback? He had yet to win a major championship, but that didn't take long. He won the Professional Golfers Association championship in August 1946 by defeating Ed "Porky" Oliver in a thirty-six-hole final, by a score of six and four. The PGA championship was then a match play tournament with scoring depending on the number of holes won by each golfer in head-to-head competition. Hogan won by having won six more holes than Porky had with only four holes left to be played. From then on he was at the top of his game, which meant that he was the best in the business.

Hogan was thirty-four and approaching his peak. Not one great hitter in the history of baseball had peaked at that age, though a couple had peaked at age thirty-two. The first was Bill Terry, the last National Leaguer to hit .400. Terry hit .401 in 1930 at the age of thirty-two. True, Babe Ruth was also thirty-two years old when he hit sixty home runs in 1927. Maris was twenty-seven when he hit sixty-one in 1961. Rogers Hornsby was twenty-eight when he hit .424 in 1924, the highest batting average ever attained for a single season. Lefty O'Doul has always been considered to be a late bloomer. He made it to the majors in 1928 when he was thirty-one, but O'Doul had his best season the very next year at age thirty-two.

Then came 1949 and the medical case history that is the focal point of every other study of the life and accomplishments of Ben Hogan. Ben was driving along Highway 80 on his way home to Fort Worth from Phoenix. His wife, Valerie, was in the front seat beside him. They were in a hurry to get home, to take a break from the grind of the tour and get some work done on their house. It was early and the road was thick with morning haze and fog. From out of nowhere came a huge transcontinental bus hurtling toward their car. There was nothing Ben could do to prevent the collision. He flung himself in front of his wife to shield her from injury. This was before seat belts were introduced, to say nothing of air bags.

Hogan's heroic dive worked; Valerie Hogan got only a few minor scrapes and bruises. Unfortunately, things did not turn out so well for Ben. He had fractured his pelvis in two places, had a broken collarbone, a broken right ankle, and a couple of broken ribs. But he was alive. Soon after, though, he developed a life-threatening thrombosis of the deep veins in his legs.

The scenario was a common one at that time. He had suffered a severe injury followed by prolonged confinement in the days before pinning of bones and early mobilization were common practice. Prolonged immobility is by definition associated with stasis of blood in those immobile and damaged limbs. That means that blood flow slows down, especially in the deep veins of the hips and legs. I warned you that his history always reminded me of a clinical study. Stasis of blood in these big vessels can easily lead to a clot, or thrombus. And once formed, blood clots often do not just stay in place. Parts of the thrombus have a nasty tendency to break off, then travel. When this happens, the passive thrombus gets a new name and becomes an active embolus. The process is called embolism; a blood clot forms in one part of the body and then travels to some other part of the body. When it goes to the lungs it is called an embolism and can lead to sudden death. This is the scenario in which such embolisms commonly occur. In Hogan's day, all too often this scenario became a litany: injury, immobility, stasis, thrombosis, embolism, sudden death. Today we decrease the occurrence of thrombosis and embolism by treating immobilized patients with anticoagulants to prevent the formation of blood clots. Anticoagulants, like seat belts and air bags, were yet to come.

There was only one thing for the physicians to do: surgery to tie off the veins as they came out of Ben Hogan's legs and before they got to his heart. For this is the path of a pulmonary embolism, starting in the deep leg veins, breaking off and entering the abdominal veins, up through the heart to the lungs. Surgeons performed a two-hour procedure to tie off his inferior vena cava, the large vein of the abdomen, and thus prevent blood clots from traveling from his legs to his lungs. It worked. He survived. But would he play golf again?

This was also an era that knew very little about rehabilitation, or physiatry. Sports medicine as a specialty hardly existed. That lack of knowledge was prevalent among both sports fans and physicians alike.

Some doctors doubted that Ben Hogan would ever walk again, and the general belief was that he would never again play competitive golf. Why not? He had a lot of broken bones, to be sure, but bones heal. What mattered most was that his nervous system was uninjured. None of his three motor control systems had been injured in the least, not his pyramidal tract, his cerebellum, or his extrapyramidal system. His legs were weaker certainly. Their strength might never be what it had once been, but so what? The key in golf is the control of posture. That was what had to be regained, and if anyone had the tenacity to regain such a learned skill, it was Ben Hogan. Absorbedness was his middle name.

Regain it he did, with a vengeance, sooner and better than anyone expected. In mid-January 1950, he came back. He started at the Los Angeles Open at the Riviera Golf Club. He had won there in 1948 with a then record two seventy-six. He started off slowly, with a seventy-three on the first day. Then he put it all back together: sixty-nine on the second day, sixty-nine on the third day (in the rain), and sixty-nine on the last day to tie Sam Snead for first. Snead won the play-off the next day, another day marred by rain. But no matter, there was no rain on Ben Hogan. He was back. He had relearned all he needed to know about the postural control of his shrunken and battered legs. His extrapyramidal system had faced the test and triumphed. So had his indomitable will. It was only a matter of time until major championships would be won. And won they were.

Hogan won the U.S. Open in 1950, 1951, and 1953, and he tied for first in 1955, but lost the eighteen-hole play-off to Jack Fleck. Ben also took the Masters championship in 1951 and 1953. He tied for first in 1954, but lost the play-off to Sam Snead.

Hogan won the British Open in 1953, the only time he ever played in this tournament. That year the British Open was played at Carnoustie, Scotland. Hogan's victory there is one of golf's true legends. It was a typical Scottish links course—hard, craggy, pockmarked. It had traps so deep they made you understand why they are sometimes called bunkers. It had greens that Hogan compared unfavorably to putty. And the weather made the rain on the Riviera course seem like a gentle spray from a garden hose. It was cold, windy, and rainy: it was Scotland in the summer. What could be better for a game of golf?

In Scotland the ball was different, too. They used one that was smaller in diameter than the American ball. Today, the British and Scottish courses haven't changed, nor has the weather, but the ball has. They now use the American ball.

Hogan got to Scotland two weeks early. He walked the course. He played the course. He figured out what he had to do to win. Or, rather, not to lose. For he knew that something Gene Litler had once said was right. It wasn't great shots that won, but keeping the mistakes as small as possible. Ben was always one to keep the mistakes small and few.

The Wee Ice Mon won by four strokes. He had now done what no one else had ever done before or since: he had won the first three legs of the Grand Slam: the U.S. Open, the Masters, and the British Open, in the same year. All that was left was the PGA. Unfortunately, his travel plans went haywire and he never even got there. In his absence, Walter Burkemo beat Felice Torza to win the PGA.

Three Grand Slam titles in the same year. Hogan had peaked at age forty-one. Ruth hung up his spikes at forty. Williams played until he was forty-two and did hit .316 that year and even managed to hit a home run in his last time at bat. He certainly did not peak at that age. Even that legend of baseball longevity, Pete Rose, who holds the record for most hits in a career, only hit .260 after the age of forty-one, and hit only two home runs in his last four years in the majors. Cobb finished a bit stronger, hitting .323 in 1928 at the age of forty-one, but this was over forty points below his lifetime average.

For most storytellers, the medical aspects of the life of Ben Hogan end at Carnoustie. It is the perfect ending to a heroic story: Ben Hogan as the comeback kid, triumphing over adversity. It sells books. Hogan's victory seemed complete. He was at the top of the golfing world. He had been rehabilitated from his injury to a degree that no one could have predicted. This, however, is not the end. This is where the real medical story begins. What had come before was normal physiology. What was about to come next was abnormal physiology, and abnormal physiology is what medicine and neurology are all about.

It was in the U.S. Open at Rochester that Hogan's abnormal physiology first reared its ugly head in public. This is the scene that I remember. All Hogan needed were two pars on the last two holes to tie Dr. Cary Middlecoff, the golfing dentist, for first place. A par and a birdie, and the Open was his. He lined up a thirty-inch putt for par on the seventy-first hole. Then he froze. His hands wouldn't do what he wanted them to do. He backed off and tried again. His hands jerked. He blew the putt and lost the Open.

That was the beginning of the end. Hogan said that his nerves were shot. "It isn't the legs that go first," he said. "It's the nerves."

Nerves? In the Wee Ice Mon, of all people. How could that be? Even Ben Hogan himself thought that was what had happened to him. His nerves had gone first. The pressure had finally got to him. But had it been the pressure? Had the great pro choked, as we would now so indelicately put it?

No, it was not the pressure at all. It had not been his nerves, at least not in the way that he meant. It was all in his head, but in the same sense that a stroke happens in the head. What had happened to Hogan was a neurological problem, an example of altered physiology of the nervous system and the brain, producing unwanted, abnormal behavior. It was as neurological as the circumduction caused by a stroke or the shuffling of Parkinson's disease.

What precisely had happened on that putt on the seventy-first hole in his battle to tie Cary Middlecoff? There was no question about the pressure. Hogan lined up his putt. He held his posture just right, hardly thinking about it. He calculated the distance. His hands held their posture, keeping the putter in line. Then his hands moved back just the right distance. The brain maintained a posture and superimposed on that posture a finely controlled movement. Then a short circuit occurred, the posture went haywire, and a finger pulled away from the club. Hogan felt it and pulled back. He tried again but the same thing happened. This time he couldn't stop his swing. His posture had been changed when his finger straightened out, seemingly all by itself. Without that controlled posture, the angle of the club became all wrong even though the controlled fine movement for distance was perfect. The ball went three feet, just the right distance when you want to be certain that a thirty-inch putt goes into the hole. As Yogi Berra put it, "Ninety percent of putts that are too short don't go into the hole." If not even more.

Hogan's finger had not really moved on its own. Fingers can't do that, not even the fingers of great athletes. His finger moved because his brain had directed it to move, to pull off the club. It had been his nerves, to be certain, the nerves in his brain. Not as a psychological breakdown, but as a neurological condition. What had happened to the incomparable Ben Hogan is informally called the "yips." That's right, the same "yips" that plague so many Sunday afternoon duffers. Well, the condition is not restricted to the ranks of gross amateurs. The yips can and do affect such consummate professionals as Ben Hogan and, it is said, even his archrival, Slamming Sammy Snead. The yips are not the result of choking; they are a neurological disorder. It wasn't Ben's nerves that were undermining him, it was his brain. Those same structures that had combined to learn the postures of golf were now in revolt. They could no longer maintain that perfect posture to allow that finely controlled, superimposed movement that is putting. Enough was enough. His extrapyramidal system broke down and sent out the wrong signal. The posture of his finger changed. Once the posture changed, the willed movement resulted in the wrong action—and a win for Cary Middlecoff.

A change in posture, an abnormal movement. Neurologists classify the yips as a form of dystonia, like the tremor in Parkinson's, or one of the tics in Tourette's syndrome, or a choreatic jerk in Huntington's chorea. They sure as heck sound neurological, and in fact they are.

The dystonias are a group of little-understood and often unrecognized neurological maladies. Patients with dystonias are often accused of malingering, of being hysterical, or even of "choking" under pressure. Even the term itself contributes to the misunderstanding. From its linguistic roots, *dys* indicates "abnormality" and *tonia* "tone," or abnormal tone of the muscles. But its actual meaning has been expanded.

The word *dystonia* was coined by the German neurologist Hermann Oppenheim in a 1911 paper in which he described a previously undiagnosed neurological disease characterized by contorted postures of the limbs and the body. He gave this hereditary disorder, which he observed in children and adolescents, a latinized, descriptive name, *dystonia musculorum deformans*, "abnormal tone of the muscles leading to deformities." But which came first, the contortion or the posture, the abnormal tone of the muscles, or the movement?

Today we have a far different concept of both this disease and what causes its characteristics. It is the movement that comes first. True, the movements are often seen only when a patient tries to maintain a specific posture. When the patient moves into that posture, initially there may well be nothing amiss. Hogan lines up his putt. All is well. Only after he continues to maintain his posture does the abnormal movement begin. The muscles that are maintaining the posture receive an unconscious direction to alter that posture. It just *seems* as if the movement comes first.

Dystonia, then, is characterized not by altered muscle tone but by abnormal movements. So what should we call those movements? We already had a time-honored term to describe such patients. What to do? That was easy, pervert the meaning of the term, a phenomenon that happens in medicine all the time. Thomas Sydenham used the term *chorea* to describe patients with Sydenham's chorea because the patients had dancelike gaits. The same for Huntington and Huntington's chorea. Then neurologists realized that it was not the gait that made the diseases but the diseases that made the gait. What seemed to be the primary abnormality of these choreatic disorders was the random, isolated, purposeless movements. Ergo *chorea*, derived from the Greek word for the singers and dancers of Greek theater, came to stand for a class of abnormal movements. Not all patients with Huntington's chorea immediately display such movements, so the name was changed from Huntington's chorea to Huntington's disease. George Huntington had no idea that *chorea* meant a type of movement. How could he? The change in the meaning of the word came about long after he had died. But why quibble?

The same transition took place with *dystonia*, which has come to denote a group of abnormal, involuntary movements with specific characteristics. Unlike the rhythmic, to-and-fro movements of a parkinsonian tremor, however, dystonic movements are without any rhythm. They are sudden pulls or jerks that move part of a limb into an untoward position and keep it there. That is how neurologists recognize them and differentiate them from tics or chorea or any other type of movement. These movements maintain a posture. What choice do they have? Not much.

Actually, it is not that they maintain a posture so much as that they change the posture the patient is trying to maintain into a new, unwanted posture.

An unwanted posture is bad enough, but other character-istics of dystonia are even worse for people like Ben Hogan and his fellow golfers. Unlike the tremor of Parkinson's, dystonic movements do not occur at rest and disappear with effort. Just the opposite. It is maintaining a posture and then carrying out a controlled movement on top of that willed posture that brings on the abnormal movement. In other words, it happens at the worst time, just when the patient is attempting to control both movements and posture as finely as possible. Hogan was not just lining up that fateful putt. He was beginning to exert force, to superimpose a directed movement upon that posture. And it was not just another putt, but the one that mattered the most. Then it happened. At just the worst time. On the seventy-first hole. Not on the practice green. Not when there was no pressure. No won-der Hogan felt his nerves were shot.

The dystonias encompass a range of movements and diseases that vary from the severely debilitating and life-threatening to others that seem more like annoyances. Dystonia musculorum deformans often results in severe deformity and can lead to both severe disability and death. Now that's a real disease. But the yips? After all, how can poor putting really constitute a disease? Much less choking in the big one? Then why couldn't missed free throws be a disease? One that becomes epidemic in fourth quarters?

The yips are one of the dystonias that appear to be far more like annoyances than a disease. They are a form of occupational dystonia. The occupational dystonias are a diverse set of abnormal movements that occur primarily during the postures and movements related to a person's occupation. It is not really the occupation that is key here, but the type of movement and posture involved.

What varieties of occupational dystonias are there? The most common is probably writer's cramp, in which the act of writing brings out an altered posture that inhibits the ability to write. But the occupational dystonias cover a wide range of activities, from those of professional violinists to those of golfers. In all of these conditions the brain sends out the wrong message, causing sudden uncontrolled movements and new unwanted postures.

What is it that ties all of these occupational dystonias together? Writing, playing the violin, and putting are quite similar from a physiological perspective, as are all of the activities that bring out occupational dystonias. They all are characterized by being actions in which a very finely controlled movement is superimposed on a rigorously controlled and maintained posture. Take handwriting as an example. The same fingers that hold the pen in place must maintain that posture and simultaneously move the pen to form precisely the right letters. The brain learns to do this, though it is not something the brain was designed specifically to do. Written language is an artifact of the last three or four thousand years of civilization. Writing as a physical skill has no particular reproductive advantage, and even if it did, selection doesn't work quickly enough to favor brains that can write faster or with greater fluidity for longer periods of time. For a while in Western Europe, such individuals were all monks who were supposed to be at a reproductive disability. And literary skills were certainly not advantageous in Stalinist Russia. No matter, these are recent irrelevancies from a genetic perspective.

Dystonia brought on by writing occurs during a form of movement that the human brain did not develop specifically in order to master. Remember, all of the movements that bring on occupational dystonias show controlled movement superimposed on controlled postures. The dystonia of a violinist does not involve his or her bowing hand but the hand with which the violinist supports and positions the instrument while fingering the strings. Spurred by maintaining ever changing posture, shifting position and pressure, and expressing tremolo, all at the same time. Superimposing these postures one after the other for hour after hour.

Did the descent of humanity select for activities with such stringent requirements? No way. No more than it selected for putting. For hunting, perhaps. But the only hunting activity that has been around long enough to have played a role in selection would have been throwing, and in that activity the maintenance of posture is not expressed in the same muscles that throw the stone.

So what happens in the brain? We do not yet have an answer. As far as we know the brains of patients with dystonias look normal when examined under a conventional microscope after the patient has died. All that means is that there is no anatomic abnormality; no particular group of cells has been injured, no collection of neurons has died. They can just no longer do what is demanded of them. Why is that? The answer may well be that they weren't designed to perform like that in the first place, and after years of performing above and beyond the call of duty and function, they eventually no longer can do it. That's when dystonia rears its head, or more characteristically, rears a finger or a thumb.

So a brain is not built to write for hours. But writer's cramp doesn't just come on after hours of writing. It usually starts that way, and once it develops as a condition, it starts as soon as the writer picks up a pen. Because the nervous system learns the dystonias, in a way. We don't normally think of learning in this way, but what is learning? Motorically, learning is gaining the ability to carry out a performed activity more easily, more quickly, or more automatically. We strive to learn to control our movements and postures more and more finely. That is why bad habits learned early tend to get ingrained. And why such short circuits, once they occur, tend to occur earlier and earlier. In a way, the extrapyramidal system has learned a new posture. It learns to get into that posture more and more easily. Consequently, the violinist can only practice a few bars, the secretary can only pick up her pen, the golfer wants to take that putter and throw it away. Can you blame him?

So why do yips only interrupt putting? Why not driving? Why not chipping? Why just putting? More than any other stroke in golf, putting consists of maintaining a relatively fixed posture, and at the same time superimposing on this posture, on the same muscles that are maintaining the posture, a delicately controlled movement. Few human tasks combine these two, usually separate, types of motor control tasks. The golfer with yips can drive away with a fluid swing to his heart's content. It's all in his head—in the extrapyramidal system of his brain.

Can anything be done about this? Or is it time to give up the game?

The ability of the extrapyramidal system to maintain the appropriate postures is dependent on all of the inputs it receives. Take Parkinson's disease as an example. Often a patient with Parkinson's can walk through a room without much problem, but as he gets to the doorway that all changes. His strides become shorter, shuffling occurs, the posture changes. The body becomes more stooped, more flexed. More parkinsonian. The gait comes to a grinding halt. Once through that doorway the process rapidly reverses itself. The patient stands up straighter, the strides become longer, the shuffling disappears.

Why did that all of that happen? Why will it happen again at the next doorway? The doorway was wide enough for two people to walk through. The patient saw that. He knew that, consciously. But only the corticospinal, the good old pyramidal system, is under direct conscious control. All three motor systems receive visual input and all three respond to that input. In two of them, this response is beyond conscious control. Visual input to the extrapyramidal motor system changes output. This should come as no surprise. All input changes output. Not just the input normally associated with posture. In Parkinson's disease, visual inputs to the extrapyramidal system can bring out abnormality. It is the extrapyramidal system that controls posture in Parkinson's disease and in writing and in putting.

Can visual inputs also bring on a "return to normalcy"? Back to Parkinson's disease. The patient is shuffling. He can hardly lift his feet. They are glued to the floor. Draw a line over the floor and he steps over it. Draw a series of lines and he steps over them all. One right after the other. All the way through the doorway. Changing visual input into the extrapyramidal system can make things better, at least in Parkinson's disease.

Does this also apply to dystonias? You bet it does. This has been described best in spasmodic torticollis. *Torticollis* means "turning of the neck." Spasmodic torticollis is a form of dystonia made up of abnormal twisting movements of the neck brought out every time the patient tries to maintain a posture of the neck. A golfer with the yips can give up putting. He can give up golf. Life will go on. But it's pretty hard for a patient with spasmodic torticollis to give up sitting and standing and walking.

Most patients feel normal when lying in bed. As soon as they sit up, or as soon as the extrapyramidal system is called upon to do something, the pulling and contortion begin. It didn't start that way. At first the torticollis only occurred after holding their heads in place for a long time; sitting and typing for hours at a time. Then it started to become symptomatic at other times, in other situations, like driving in heavy traffic for an hour. From there things just got worse. Less and less was needed to bring out the movements. Less stress and less time. Soon, sitting in a restaurant became a problem. Then just trying to stand up. Just like writer's cramp and the yips. What's a body to do?

You've got to have a gimmick, a gesture or a sensory trick. Not every patient has one of these, but many do. These gestures are maneuvers that fool the brain. They aren't planned that way, but that is what they do. They change the brain's game plan by altering the information that is being sent to it for processing. They are not discovered by any logical process of deduction or elimination. They come about by serendipity. The patient rubs his ear. The torticollis straightens out. He holds his ear and it straightens out again. Eureka! The gesture has been discovered. Except there was no hunt and no shout of discovery. The patient finds the gesture by luck and performs it almost without thinking about it. Give the brain a new input and it may well give you a new output, an output without the unwanted dystonias. The range of such gestures is broad, from simple ones such as touching the chin to far more complicated alterations of input such as draping a purse around the neck while driving. Even wearing a heavy turban can be a gesture, in a neurological sense, since it changes the sensory information being relayed unconsciously to the brain.

These gestures often work. Not always and not forever, but often and for a meaningful period of time. Consciously or even unconsciously, many patients with dystonias have learned that their dystonias can often be influenced by tricking the brain.

Can such gestures help putting? Sometimes. But there are two problems. Putting involves both hands, so the common gesture of changing sensory input by touching yourself somewhere with one hand is out. Putting also poses a far finer problem in motor control than merely holding an upright posture. Golf is far more like trying to write; you have to be able to control a fine movement. Still, changing the input is the first thing to try. How? By adding weight to the putter. The brain is now dealing with a new type of postural control. Buying a new putter might work. A long putter like the one President Bush used is more like a pendulum than a golf club, and with that pendulum the tasks are not distributed equally. The top hand does only one thing. It holds the pendulum in place, providing postural control. The lower hand sets the pendulum in motion, providing finely controlled voluntary movement. It's not quite that clean a separation, but it's better than the shared roles required by most other putters. Does it always work? Nothing always works. But such golfers' tricks can often do more than sports psychology to overcome the yips.

So why does it happen under stress? Why are the yips more likely to break up an important shot than just any old putt in the backyard? Why does a Parkinson's tremor always get worse in public? Doesn't that make it psychological? Nope, it just proves that it is neurological. The brain must integrate everything. Those added inputs, the added activation and attention demanded by being in public, change the output. All Parkinson's patients get more tremors in such situations. One hundred percent. But their nerves aren't shot. Nor were Ben Hogan's. He didn't understand that, nor did very many neurologists in the 1950s.

Recognition that the yips are a neurological disorder is a recent development. Only in the last decade has this disorder received any attention in the medical literature. Most of this attention has gone to professional golfers. Who else would go to his doctor and complain about the yips? Who were these pros and of what did they complain? Their average age was about fifty, and they had been playing competitive golf since their teens. Typically, they first developed the problem during a tournament and it was described as a jerk, a spasm, or freezing while putting, or on rare occasions during chipping. The rest of their shots were rarely disturbed. The problems seemed to wax and wane. The yips were most likely to have waned in those who developed tricks. What sort of tricks had these pros used? Heavier putters. Pendulum putters. Changing the grip. Putting cross handed. Changing the stance to putt sidesaddle. Changing the line of vision. Changing the visual input. Shades of Parkinson's disease and those lines drawn out on the floor.

Some pros even tried hypnotherapy. As far as I know that has never been shown to work. But then again I know of no neurological problem for which hypnotherapy has ever been demonstrated to have any significant long-term efficacy. Why should yips be any different?

Professional golfers in general thought that, on the average, the yips accounted for about five extra strokes per round of golf. Five shots per round. In my circles, the estimate is much higher than that, and the disease far more common. How common? A recent survey suggests that about thirty percent of all male golfers have some degree of the yips. The incidence in females is not known. Yips are the same in professionals and in amateurs. Sunday morning golfers have the same jerks, the same spasms, the same freezing. The disorder afflicts still putting far more than any other stroke. In almost everybody the yips are worse in tournaments than during practice. I'm not sure we needed a scientific survey to learn that. Even for amateurs, tricks help, and there are almost as many tricks for golfers as there are gestures for patients with torticollis.

In my own less scientific survey there is one difference in the manner in which yips alter the games of professionals and those of amateurs. I have never talked to an amateur whose yips cost him only five shots per round. Perhaps they have an even more insidious form of the disease. A recreational dystonia. The worst type of dystonia of them all.

One medical question remains unanswered. Hogan was left-handed. He golfed right-handed. Those right-handed clubs were the only clubs the impoverished young man could afford. Was that the root of his problem? Is that why his nondominant extrapyramidal system finally gave out? Was it trying to do too much? More than it had been designed to do? I cannot tell you. As far as we know, there is no dominant extrapyramidal system. Handedness is a cortical issue. The extrapyramidal system has never been proved to be made up of distinguishable dominant and nondominant spheres. Most of what it does is bilaterally relevant. Postures are not one-sided affairs. In my thirty years as a movement disorder specialist, I have never seen a left-handed person who had been forced to write right-handed and then developed significant writer's cramp on the right that was eliminated by learning to write with his dominant hand. But I'm still looking.

How good was Ben Hogan? Despite missing two years because of World War II and another year because of injury, he won sixty-two professional tournaments. Only two men ever won more during their careers, Sam Snead and Jack Nicklaus. Arnold Palmer won sixty-one.

The Nineteenth Hole:
Wolfgang Amadeus Mozart

ACCORDING TO THE *ENCYCLOPAEDIA BRITANNICA*, golf is a cross-country game played by striking a small ball with various clubs. The striking starts on a series of teeing grounds and ends when the ball goes into a series of holes on a predetermined course. What could be easier to do than that? Almost anything people have ever tried.

The problem with this description is that it ignores the very nature of the game, which is a form of competing against yourself to reach your own level of perfection, and the fact that in that quest any failure is the responsibility of the player. It is like giving a solo performance. There is no one else to blame. The soloist picks the instrument, the program, the tempi, the dynamics. And this is as true of the youngster playing in his own living room as it is of any virtuoso playing in Carnegie Hall. That's how it is in golf. The golfer is his own virtuoso. He or she picks out the ball to be used—its make and compression ratio, the design of the clubs, their style. their weight, their length, the materials out of which they are made. Few of us end up playing as modern-day versions of left-handed Ben Hogan using borrowed right-handed clubs. The golfer chooses the specific club to be used on each and every shot and, on all but a few, picks the exact target for the swing. The golfer can even pick out the height of the tee. If Michael Jordan had been able to pick out the height of each incoming pitch, this book might have had to have a different title.

It is the golfer against himself, with the course supplying the battlefield, a battlefield, by the way, that in most instances has been chosen by the golfer. There is no one else to blame in golf for anything that goes wrong on any particular shot. And no one else can take any of the credit.

Music shares with golf much more than this ultimate acceptance of personal responsibility and the frequent occurrence of occupational dystonias in their devoted exponents at both professional and amateur levels. One other fact is apparent on even the most casual inspection. Both fields are dominated almost exclusively by early starters. The biographies of famous composers almost invariably make note of the subject's exceptional musical ability at a very young age. So, too, with golfers. Almost every player who goes on the tour began playing before the age of eight. Almost all composers began playing long before that age. By the age of eight most were already proficient at their instrument and had even begun to compose music.

In the old days the youngsters were prodigies on the organ. Today it is usually the piano that takes center stage. The story is often told that, in true Broadway tradition, little Leonard Bernstein's aunt moved out of town when the boy was only three or four years old and left her piano with his parents for safekeeping. Leonard took one look at the piano and it was love at first sight. By the time he was in his early twenties, he had written a hit Broadway musical comedy, *On the Town*, a Pulitzer Prize–winning symphony, a ballet that would enter the standard repertoire, *Fancy Free*, and had made a successful debut as conductor of the New York Philharmonic. A true prodigy in a field dominated by prodigies.

Or take a look at the life of Mozart. He was born into a musical family. His father, Leopold Mozart, was a distinguished and accomplished musician. Certainly if it had not been for his son, he, like Salieri, would be forgotten today. Leopold, however, was well able to make a comfortable living at his chosen craft, no mean feat in the eighteenth century. The elder Mozart decided to train his children to follow in his footsteps. It was the lessons that he gave to his daughter, Maria Anna, that first attracted the then quite young Wolfgang to music. Was it mere sibling rivalry or love at first sight for the instrument that got him started? When the young Mozart was three he was receiving lessons of his own, and by age four he reputedly sat on the lap of a dowager countess in Vienna in order to give a public performance. He did not pick out the particular harpsichord in this instance, nor the chair.

By the time he was eight, Mozart was a veteran performer who made concert tours around Europe. One of these brought him to London. While there he was "examined" by a certain Daines Barrington. Barrington had more than a passing interest in scientific inquiry and was a member of the Royal Society. This is where he eventually presented the results of his study of Mozart, in a paper entitled "An Account of a Very Remarkable Musician." Barrington was particularly intrigued by musical prodigies, and what better subject for study than young Mozart? In retrospect there was none. This was not, however, a retrospective study. Mozart was only eight years old. He had written nothing that without his later work would stand the test of time on its own merits. It was 1773; there was as yet no later Mozart. No one knew that he would become a musician of such lasting significance and greatness, much less that he would become Mozart.

So what did Barrington "test" in experimental subject Mozart? Barrington started with sight-reading, using the score of a symphony by an obscure English composer of the day—a redundancy, I admit. Barrington chose that particular work because he was confident that it was a piece the boy could not ever have heard. In Barrington's own words, "The score was no sooner upon his desk than he began to play the symphony in a most masterful manner as well as in the time and style which corresponded with the intention of the composer." Barrington concluded that the young Mozart was better at sight-reading than the senior Mozart. In the experiment, Leopold seems to have acted as what would today be called a "control." Wolfgang Mozart also excelled at extemporaneous composition, in which he demonstrated "most extraordinary readiness of invention." The young Mozart then played one of his own compositions. His playing was amazing considering that "his little fingers could scarcely reach a fifth on the harpsichord."

It was time to resume the tour, so the Mozart family moved on. The entire tour took eighteen months, including a break in the middle for a production of the eight-year-old composer's opera, *Bastien and Bastienne.*

The essence of what was learned by Barrington was that Wolfgang had started his training in music when he was quite young and that he came from a musical family. Is the inheritance of musical skills genetic, or is it environmental? Early exposure to music followed by early training? Obviously, young Mozart's skills were recognized at an early age and fostered by his father. Soon the life of the entire family centered around Wolfgang and his music. He was the paradigm of a prodigy, but he was far more than that. At around the age of eighteen many prodigies' talents wane. Not so young Mozart's. It was at that point that he burst forth as a brilliant and original composer whose creativity and productivity have rarely been approached, much less equaled.

Today in golf we are in the presence of an analogous prodigy, Tiger Woods. Like Mozart, he began playing his instrument in early childhood, almost as soon as he could walk. And now, as a junior in college, he has already won the U.S. Amateur championship title for the third straight year. Is Tiger Woods another Ben Hogan in the making? Another Jack Nicklaus? A Mozart of the links?

Not all prodigies become Mozarts. In fact, most don't. Barrington studied four other musical prodigies who were contemporaries of Wolfgang Amadeus Mozart. They included two brothers, Charles and Samuel Wesley, W. H. Crotch, and Lord Mornington. All had brilliant abilities. All had started young and performed amazingly well when tested by Barrington. All were still under the age of ten. All were extraordinary prodigies. But the testing could not predict future greatness. Only one of those tested became Mozart and that was Mozart himself.

What, then, is the success rate of such child prodigies? Many who have studied this question have been bothered by an apparent contradiction. It has been reported that only a mere ten percent of child prodigies go on to become virtuosi as adults, yet the vast majority of adult virtuosi started life as child prodigies. How could that be?

I am reminded of an introduction to the logic of neurology I once read. Most patients with brain tumors have headaches. Patients with headaches rarely have brain tumors. This is no contradiction, not even an oxymoron. In adults, the incidence of brain tumors may be no higher in those with headache than those without, if you can ever find enough of the latter to put together your study. The neurological solution to this logical dilemma rests on the fact that there are many common causes for headaches and that brain tumors are not a common disease.

In musicians the conundrum has a different solution. It is not merely early musical skill that produces continuing adult success. In prodigies it is a talent for physical skills that counts. True, the physical skills are often quite awesome, but they are skills that have been taught and learned. In adult musicians we expect far more. Not everyone has the innate abilities or the drive or ambition to develop them. It takes far more than skill to be the best of the best.

Hitting a drive three hundred yards is not the secret to becoming a great golfer. Like baseball, golf is ninety percent mental. It is only the remaining ten percent that depends on the physical skills that must be recognized and fostered at an early age.

The type of motor performance demanded of a virtuoso musical performer is not identical to the physical demands of putting and chipping. A late nineteenth-century English surgeon, Sir James Paget, once studied an expert English pianist as she played a presto from an octet by the renowned prodigy Felix Mendelssohn. The octet that Mendelssohn completed when he was only sixteen is generally regarded as the greatest single composition by any adolescent composer. Paget, by the way, was no minor character. This is the same Paget who described Paget's disease of the bones and the far rarer Paget's disease of the breast. Few physicians have ever won two eponyms. One is usually sufficient to ensure immortality.

The pianist played the Mendelssohn presto in four minutes and three seconds. In order to do that she had to play five thousand five hundred ninety-five notes, or an average of twenty-three notes per second. Even more significantly, this feat required approximately seventy-two manual finger movements per second. No wonder it is more common to get a par than to play a Chopin étude flawlessly. Considering the demands, the question may be why so few pianists develop occupational dystonias.

It was another nineteenth-century Englishman, the neurologist William R. Gowers, who first recognized that the occupational dystonias of musicians represented a form of neurological disease, not a variety of psychiatric disability. The "yips" did not achieve such recognition for almost another century.

Golf was also slow to make the jump from occasional brief appearances in weekly newsreels seen in neighborhood movie theaters to becoming a regular feature on the small screens in living rooms across the United States. That transition occurred in the mid-1950s, long after baseball, football, boxing, wrestling, and even Roller Derby had become regular TV features. It was still in glorious black and white, but it was available for people to watch regularly and watch it they did. In my own naive way, I attributed the success of televised golf to the inherent lure and fascination of the game itself, to say nothing of the charisma and skill of such big-name golfers as Bantam Ben Hogan, and of course to the drama of the competition that is golf. A golf tournament is never over in the first round. There is no such thing as a blowout in a golf tournament. If only Superbowls and World Series games were that way.

Other observers have been far more sanguine in evaluating this evolution. They have attributed the success of televised golf to the insatiable appetite of Americans to watch others perform well those very activities that they themselves do so poorly. A sort of watered-down masochism. What else could explain the continuing lure of televised golf or bowling, to say nothing of Julia Child and all those other cooking shows? How else could you account for the fact that there is an inverse relationship between the number of such cooking shows and the percentage of American meals actually cooked from scratch in American kitchens?

Perhaps they are right. If they are, it is natural to wonder whether this same rule of thumb applies to the fascination with watching pornography. It might not be a legacy of our reproductive past, but a form of recently acquired masochism that is the basis of watching sexual performance on the screen. It certainly is neither the charisma nor the skill of the stars that count here.

Whenever I play golf, I choose to play with Ben Hogan golf balls, even though I am well aware that he sold both the company and the right to use his name long ago. It is both the neurologist in me and the future patient as I wait for my writer's cramp to realize that it is time to branch out into the yips. Maybe I should order one of those long pendulum putters and start practicing now. Or change my hand grip. Or . . .

chapter 7

Muhammad Ali's Brain

HE WAS THE GREATEST OF CHAMPIONS in the worst of times. Hyperbole? Perhaps, but to many sports fans, Muhammad Ali will always be "The Champ." He is the one man who symbolizes what boxing, as a sport, should be all about but all too rarely is these days. Yet Ali was one of those many boxers who were all but destroyed by the game. Unlike so many of the others, from Joe Louis on down, Ali was neither cheated by crooked promoters nor swindled by his own managers. He was far too smart to let things like that happen to him. His life was destroyed by the boxing game itself, by the nature of his own work. As Ali himself once put it, "It's just a job. Grass grows. Birds fly. Waves beat the sand. I beat people up." The sad fact is that other boxers also beat him up. Year after year, especially late in his career. This continuous punishment, this continuous barrage of head trauma, repeated hundreds of times, eventually took its toll. It's like the toll that the waves exact upon the beach. Boxing's toll came as a relentlessly progressive disorder of the brain, a form of Parkinson's disease caused by repeated head injury. "The Champ" had become the proverbial stumblebum.

Ali became an international sports figure long before he took the name Muhammad Ali. He initially fought under the name he was given at birth, Cassius Marcellus Clay. As Cassius Clay, the son of a house painter, he first burst into prominence in 1960 when he won the Olympic Gold Medal in the light-heavyweight class. He was only eighteen at the time, and his young, handsome, smiling face was a welcome relief to most American sports fans. Clay's victory smile was one of the few pleasant moments in those Rome Olympics, disrupted as they were by angry Black Power salutes from winning American track stars.

Clay's boxing career had not started in Rome. His victory there was his one hundred and eighth as an amateur. The previous year, at the age of seventeen, he had won the Amateur Athletic Union light-heavyweight boxing championship, a feat he repeated in 1960 on the way to his Olympic medal. He had no more worlds to conquer as an amateur. It was time for him to move on to the promised land of professional boxing, a twilight world where potential glory often went hand in hand with dangers for the unsophisticated. Clay was anything but sophisticated.

Good fortune can do a great deal to compensate for lack of sophistication and Clay had more than his share of good luck. Soon after he returned to his hometown of Louisville, Kentucky, a local millionaire sportsman named Bill Faversham stepped into the picture. He put together a group of investors and took over Clay's career. The investors, known as the Louisville Sponsoring Group, worked out a contract with Cassius Clay, Sr., for the younger Clay's debut in professional boxing. That contract required the group to pay all expenses and give Clay a small monthly stipend plus fifty percent of all of his earnings. Faversham also created a trust fund for most of Clay's earnings. The monies in the fund could not be touched until Clay was thirty-five years old. Unlike Joe Louis, Cassius Clay would not be required to crown his career by greeting people in Las Vegas gambling halls. When the roar of the crowd quieted down, he would be provided for.

Muhammad Ali dealing out punishment to another opponent who, unlike Ali, never developed parkinsonism as a result of recurrent head trauma. Sometimes it is far better to be lucky than good. In this case the luck was in the genetically determined robustness of the substantia nigra.

The young boxer turned professional and went to work. His style as an amateur had been based entirely upon his amazing foot speed and his lightning-fast hands. To this was added some savvy of the game gained through both coaching and a carefully chosen series of opponents. After he had won nineteen consecutive professional fights, Clay was ready for the big one, a battle for the heavyweight championship of the world. There was only one heavyweight championship then and it was held by Sonny Liston, a big, tough fighter who had twice battered the previous champ, Floyd Patterson. In both matches, Liston had knocked Patterson senseless in the first round. Most sportswriters and fans did not give Clay much of a chance. Liston was thought to be unbeatable, if not untouchable—a towering machine of destruction, a street fighter who was at the top of his game. Cassius was an ex-Olympian pretty-boy, ready to be hammered.

Opinions did not change when Clay threw a highly theatrical, carefully planned outburst at the prefight weigh-in. Today we accept verbal banter between the fighters as part of the game. It was Clay who started it all.

He called Liston "the bear." Clay chanted that he would "float like a butterfly and sting like a bee." To Liston he cracked, "I got you now, Sonny; I got your championship now!" No one had ever spoken to Liston in that way. The champion was more than perplexed. He was psyched out. Clay stole the stage and the psychological advantage with his continued ranting and raving. He continued to chant his butterfly-bee mantra until Liston and the reporters were gone. It had been the first of many such performances that later won him the title of "the Mouth That Roared." Few of those who had been in attendance recognized what they had seen and heard. Even fewer seemed to notice that Clay was taller than "the bear" and had a longer reach (arm span). That meant that Clay could hit and not be hit in return. At the time, Clay was seen as a scared kid ranting out of fear. But as he put it, "Black guys scare white guys a lot more than black guys scare black guys."

Came the day of the fight and sting he did. Taller, faster, and quicker, he hit Liston early, often, and hard. For six rounds, the far more clever and faster Clay danced around "the bear" and stung him so hard and so frequently that Liston failed to come out for the seventh round. Clay had won by a TKO (technical knockout). He was the one and only world heavyweight champion.

But he was no longer Cassius Clay. On the eve of that 1964 title bout with Liston, he had converted to the Muslim faith and changed his name from a "slave name" to a Muslim name, to Muhammad Ali. It was a stance and a change that won him few friends and little popularity. Ali, formerly Clay, was not one to shy away from his beliefs. His next stand would be even less popular.

Ali reigned as champion for four years (1964 through 1967), beating everyone who dared to enter the ring against him. Liston got a rematch that lasted less than one minute and ended with a short, fast jab to the ex-champ's jaw, which sent him crumpling to the canvas for the count. The punch was so fast that many called it the "phantom punch."

Had Ali destroyed "the bear" physically with a single short jab? Or had he so psychologically mastered his opponent that the mere hint of a punch sent Liston to the canvas? Did it matter? Ali was "the greatest," a fact that he proclaimed at every opportunity, and those opportunities came very often.

In 1967, as President Lyndon Johnson continued to expand the unwinnable war in Vietnam, Ali, aka Selective Service Number 15-47-42-127, became reclassified by his draft board as 1-A. He was twenty-five years old and physically fit to go into the army, and was almost immediately sent his induction notice. He had been drafted to fight in a war that the country had not yet come to realize it neither wanted nor understood. Few young men had as yet burned draft cards or moved to Canada or Sweden. "Hell, no, we won't go" was not yet a battle cry.

Ali, however, refused to go. He believed that such a secular war was against his faith. Besides, as he told the press, "I ain't got no quarrel with the Viet Cong." Not exactly "Hell, no, we won't go," but nonetheless true. It was a stance that won him very few fans, even among those of his own faith. Ali was quickly indicted by the federal government and his passport was taken away. The boxing world stripped him of his heavyweight crown and turned its back on him. Elijah Muhammad denounced him and cast him out of the Black Muslim movement. Only one sports commentator, Howard Cosell, publicly took his side. And Howard did not represent a groundswell of opinion.

Ali was cast down and cast out. He was a pariah, an outcast, a leper. He went into a form of internal exile. Stripped of his passport, he could not leave the country. He could not fight, which was what he did for a living. He could make no public appearances because no one was willing to sponsor him. There was no product he could endorse since no manufacturer wanted to be associated with a "draft dodger." He had become an American version of a Soviet nonperson.

It didn't take forever for public opinion of the war and of Ali to change. By 1968, times and emotions were "a changing." LBJ withdrew from the presidential race. No American president who had wanted to run had ever been forced to withdraw because of public opinion, before or since. Richard Nixon was elected to bring the nation peace with honor. Ali was no longer the only American who had "no quarrel with the Viet Cong." The domino theory that suggested that if Vietnam fell to the forces of atheism, the rest of the world would quickly follow suit, had lost all credibility.

Ali had appealed his indictment as soon as it had been handed down. But the world has not changed that much in the last thirty years; the legal process even then was far slower than the change in public opinion. The Supreme Court finally ruled in Ali's favor. His exile was over. He was no longer a nonperson just a step removed from being a traitor. In a way he was a hero, a public figure who had risked everything to stand for what he believed and against the war. It was time for him to get back into the ring.

Three years is a long time to be away from any competitive sport, and boxing is no exception. Ali had trained and stayed in shape but that wasn't the same as boxing against actual opponents. Could he come back? Did he still have all of his gifts? Was he the same fighter he had been three years earlier? Would he still be "the greatest"?

Yes and no.

Ali had lost some of his skills. Most alarming was the fact that he had lost some of his edge in foot speed. His amazing quickness, his greatest asset, was not what it had once been. He could still sting like a bee, but he no longer flew like a butterfly. It had always been his creed not to take any punishment. Now he could be hit. Could he take it?

Ali's tune-up fights demonstrated that he could. The first of these took place in October 1970. The opponent was Jerry Quarry. Ali won by a technical knockout, but Quarry had been able to get in his licks. This was the good news: Ali could take hard punches and win. The bad news was that he would have to take such punishment in order to win. There would be no more psyched-out Sonny Listons waiting to fall without landing a punch. Ali could take a punch and come back punching. It was time to win back his championship.

The champion then was Smoking Joe Frazier, a strong, tough, hard-hitting fighter who had never been beaten. They fought in March 1971. The fight was dubbed "the Battle of the Century." That certainly must have been a surprise to anyone who remembered anything about Jack Dempsey and Gene Tunney, to say nothing of Joe Louis. The Ali-Frazier match went the limit, fifteen rounds. It was a fight between an undefeated champion and undefeated ex-champion. The two fighters punished each other through all fifteen rounds, and in the end Frazier retained his crown. This fight set a new economic standard for boxing. Each fighter received two and a half million dollars, while boxing fans paid an unprecedented twenty-five dollars each to watch the fight in movie theaters on closed-circuit TV. Ali later won a nontitle twelve-round rematch. He had broken even in two matches with Frazier, but Frazier was still the champion and he was in no mood to fight Ali a third time.

Ali got his second chance at the crown in 1974 against the new champ, George Foreman, who had taken the crown from Frazier. This was the same George Foreman who would return as champ twenty-one years later at age forty-five. By then, Ali had had the symptoms of Parkinson's disease for a decade. To the victors go the spoils? Not always.

The championship match between Ali and Foreman was fought in Zaire and was dubbed by Ali "the Rumble in the Jungle." Ali won. He was champ again. A second reign as world heavyweight boxing champion was not the only legacy of this fight. It also served to introduce an ex-convict named Don King into the role of the world's foremost boxing promoter, a role he retains to this day. "The Rumble in the Jungle" was followed by "the Thriller in Manila." "The Thriller" was a rubber match with Joe Frazier. Each fighter had won one of the two previous bouts. This one would tell the tale. It was Ali who got the last word. Ali won and retained his crown. "The Mouth" continued to win and roar.

Ali fought on and on, getting older and slower and taking more and more punishment. He fought every major contender. He avoided no one. In early 1978 he had what appeared to be a breather, a bout with a kid named Leon Spinks. This would be no contest. Spinks hadn't even fought ten professional fights in his entire career. He would be no match for "the greatest." Spinks won. Even though Ali regained his title in a rematch, he was no longer the boxer he had been. It was all downhill from there until he finally retired for good in 1981.

Within a few years it was not just his footwork that was slow. Everything was. While his opponents were still fighting each other, Ali was battling parkinsonism.

Ali had truly been a world champion. He had won the crown three different times. He had fought title bouts in North America, Europe, Africa, and Asia. Altogether, he fought twenty-five championship bouts, more than any heavyweight champ except for Joe Louis. Ali had won twenty-two of those twenty-five fights. Both the wins and the losses took their toll.

But what a career! Ali had fought a total of sixty-one professional bouts and won fifty-six of them. He had triumphed in thirty-seven of those fifty-six by knocking out his opponents. He lost only five fights, four by decisions of the judges and one—only one—by a knockout. One KO in sixty-one fights. Yet despite this apparent success, it was Muhammad Ali who developed parkinsonism from the repeated head trauma he received. It was not his opponents—not Sonny Liston—or Joe Frazier, not George Foreman, who at age forty-five regained the heavyweight crown and seemed destined to go on fighting forever. How could that be?

Many of Ali's opponents took as many hard blows as he did, and many had fought more fights. Most were knocked out more than just once in their careers. Almost all of them took more blows to the head over the years than Ali. But Ali was the one who developed Parkinson's disease from repeated head trauma.

Why? Why "The Champ"?

The answer to this question lies in the very nature of Parkinson's disease. The real question is why anyone even gets the disease. It is never just bad luck; there is always a reason.

Parkinson's disease is categorized in every neurology textbook as one of the degenerative diseases of the brain. Its cause in most patients is listed as unknown. Most texts, in fact, call it an "idiopathic" disorder—a disease that causes itself, a disease without a cause. But there is always a cause. The question is whether we, as neuroscientists, have been smart enough to discover that cause.

At one level, however, what is happening in the brains of these patients is well known. Selected groups of nerve cells in the brain stem, the nerve cells of the substantia nigra, are dying. These cells, sitting in the depths of the midbrain, send their axons deep into the hemispheres of the brain itself in order to reach large collections of nerve cells called the basal ganglia. These are the centers for hard-wired movement programs and for the learning of such basic movements as walking. Once there, the axons make contacts with millions of the basal ganglion cells and control the function of these cells by producing and releasing a specific neurotransmitter (chemical messenger) named dopamine.

In Parkinson's disease, the cells of the substantia nigra die off. As they die, there is less and less naturally occurring dopamine left to act in the basal ganglia. A fifty percent loss of dopamine shows no effect. An eighty percent loss means trouble: slowness of movement, tremor, stiffness, shuffling gait, imbalance. All of the signs and symptoms of Parkinson's disease.

A word about words. Medical scientists like to reserve the eponym *Parkinson's disease* for the specific disorder described by James Parkinson in 1817. The use of the word *disease* implies more than just a set of symptoms that go together. It implies that this symptom complex is a single disease entity and that everyone with this clinical picture has that same entity with the same cause or set of causes. If the symptoms in a patient occur from some other cause, we use a somewhat different term, parkinsonism, not Parkinson's disease. So, strictly speaking, Ali does not have Parkinson's disease but a form of posttraumatic parkinsonism—a Parkinson's disease–like state due not to whatever causes Parkinson's disease but to all of those punches that connected with Ali's head. This may be a distinction with far less difference than we used to believe, since the same factors may play a role in both processes.

But how did this happen to Muhammad Ali? How did the function of his brain become so deranged that his gait became a grotesque caricature of his "rope-a-dope" shuffle? And what did boxing have to do with it?

What are the clinical symptoms that James Parkinson brought together for the first time in his essay "The Shaking Palsy"? The first of these is obviously the tremor. A tremor is not just any form of abnormal movement. To be a tremor, a movement must be made up of successive alternating, rhythmic movements at any one specific joint or location. Rhythm is the key. Up, then down, over and over again in a rhythm. Back and forth. It has to be that way whether it is the fingers that look as if they are at work rolling a cigarette or a pill ("pill rolling" tremor), or toes that seem to be tapping out a melody (or an SOS).

But not all patients have the tremor. About one-third never do. Many patients with parkinsonism, not Parkinson's disease, have little or no tremor. Like Muhammad Ali, these patients have the palsy without the shaking, and it is the palsy that causes most of the problems.

The palsy is made up of several components. The first of these is rigidity or stiffness. If you try to move the patient's arm, it is stiff. It resists such movement even though the patient is not trying to resist. This rigidity makes it feel as if the arm is being pulled over a ratchet or cogwheel, hence the descriptive term "cogwheel rigidity."

The most important of these components goes by a number of names and covers a multitude of problems. The names include hypokinesia (decreased movement), bradykinesia (slow movement), and akinesia (without movement). Whatever term is used, and they are all interchangeable, the term includes most of the symptoms of Parkinson's disease.

The patient has difficulty initiating movement. At first he can't get out of a deep easy chair or out of a car. It becomes hard to initiate walking, as if the feet are glued in place, and the gait becomes slow and shuffling. The usual play of spontaneous movement is lost; no more spontaneous smiles. The face becomes more like a mask than a face. In our usually inventive way we call it "the masked face" of Parkinson's disease. The voice gets softer. It becomes harder and harder for others to hear and for the patient to initiate. The mouth seems at times to be glued shut. Handwriting gets smaller and smaller and tighter and tighter. Spontaneous movements are also lost. the patient becomes a statue. Even the movements we never think about, like swinging the arms as we walk, disappear.

Ali once had lightning speed. Quickness had been his hallmark. No more. His movements began to get slower, his stride shorter. His feet no longer floated over the ground but began to shuffle. He had been transformed from a butterfly into a caterpillar. For the man who had shuffled more for effect than anything else, shuffling became a way of life. Life itself seemed to leave his face. The famous smile was not there as often, and never spontaneously. His face resembled the Ali masks that kids once wore on Halloween, but he wore it all year long and not out of choice. The voice that had entertained us with sound bites before the term was invented was hard to hear and even harder to understand. The winner of "the Thriller in Manila" had become a slowed-down caricature of what he had once been.

This hypo-brady-akinesia combines with one other factor to eventually reduce many patients to dependency, and that is an inability to respond to postural threat. Suppose that you are standing at a street corner waiting for the light to change to green, and the person behind you gives you a slight nudge. Your body adjusts itself automatically to the shift in dynamics and you don't really move. Not so in Parkinson's disease. The Parkinson's patient cannot respond normally. He falls forward, taking step after step in a propulsive gait. Or, as the disease advances, he makes no response at all and crashes forward, with the potential for breaking a hip.

What makes the clinical picture that Parkinson described a disease and not a syndrome, or a group of symptoms that hang out together? The main fact is that the patients all have the same pathology. Examine the brains of deceased patients and you discover the same changes. The cells of the substantia nigra begin to die, and in dying have specific pathological changes visible under a microscope.

Like any other specific disease, Parkinson's ought to have a specific cause. But does it? Can an idiopathic disease be caused? Is that not an oxymoron?

The fact is that Parkinson's disease is not as idiopathic as it once seemed. Medicine has come to reject the concept that diseases are caused by themselves, that they have no true cause. Diseases don't just happen, any more than maggots appear by spontaneous generation.

This breakthrough in our thinking began in the early 1980s in California. There was an epidemic of young patients who developed severe Parkinson's disease quite rapidly. Most of the patients were in their early twenties. The average age of the onset of true Parkinson's disease is the early sixties. Occasionally patients do develop it in their twenties, but such patients are uncommon. And seven such patients were seen in San Jose in a matter of weeks. It was clearly an epidemic.

Was this an epidemic of early onset Parkinson's disease?

No. The patients did not have true Parkinson's disease. Parkinson's disease begins subtly and progresses slowly. Even parkinsonism due to repeated head trauma progresses slowly. Ali did not wake up one morning to find himself suddenly transformed from butterfly to caterpillar; he had undergone no sudden metamorphosis. His disease had progressed slowly, over months and years. There was nothing slow or subtle in whatever was happening to these patients. They became all but bedridden in a few days. That was not what happened to patients with Parkinson's disease. But these young people had all of the cardinal features of Parkinson's disease: rest tremor, cogwheel rigidity, bradykinesia, and impaired postural reflexes. It was an epidemic of some sort of parkinsonism, but of what sort?

Epidemics of parkinsonism are nothing new. The best known epidemic swept across the world from 1914 through the late 1920s. It was part of the worldwide pandemic of sleeping sickness, or encephalitis lethargica. Many of the victims of encephalitis lethargica, also known as Spanish flu, died during their sudden illness. Others survived but developed postencephalitis parkinsonism. (These were the patients studied and documented by Oliver Sacks, many years after the epidemic, in *Awakenings*.) Was this outbreak the beginning of another such epidemic? Would this become known as the San Jose flu?

This is where a neurologist named William Langston entered the story. Langston recognized that these California patients had a distinct and probably new form of parkinsonism. He soon learned that all of them were drug addicts and were all customers of the same drug distribution system. Hence, it was not merely an epidemic of a new disease, but an epidemic with a point source.

The point source was quickly located. He was a local chemist who manufactured and distributed his own drugs. Unfortunately, he was far better at distribution than he was at manufacturing. He had no quality control. What he thought was a Demerol-like narcotic had very little actual narcotic effect. Most of the drug was a chemical analogue of Demerol, known in the chemical world as MPTP.

When injected into monkeys, MPTP caused parkinsonism. It caused all of the classic signs of parkinsonism: rest tremor, cogwheel rigidity, akinesia, and impaired postural reflexes. MPTP did this in monkeys and dogs and every other species to which it was given. This is now called MPTP-induced parkinsonism. We knew the cause of the California epidemic.

Was MPTP-induced parkinsonism an entirely new disease, a separate form of parkinsonism, or did it have something to do with true Parkinson's disease? After all, the fact that an influenza virus caused the epidemic of postencephalitis parkinsonism never got us any closer to the cause of Parkinson's disease. We were still calling it idiopathic.

One of the first seven addicts died. His brain was studied. The changes that were found were the changes of Parkinson's disease. Loss of cells of the substantia nigra. The cells that die in Parkinson's disease were the cells that died in MPTP-induced parkinsonism.

The same was found to be true in other species. MPTP selectively destroyed the cells of the substantia nigra as it induced parkinsonism. Suddenly, Parkinson's disease no longer seemed so idiopathic. It could be caused by a toxin. Not MPTP, of course, but some sort of a toxin.

Since the discovery that a man-made toxin (MPTP) could produce a syndrome that clinically mimicked idiopathic Parkinson's disease, more and more research has been directed toward identifying the environmental toxins that might be the possible causes of Parkinson's disease. Unfortunately, this research has often ignored many of the known features of the disease. Any hypothesis that environmental toxins have significant roles in the occurrence of idiopathic Parkinson's must explain what we already know about the disease.

Whatever its structure, the toxin must have been present in the environment since sometime before 1817. That was the year in which the disease was first definitely described. That leaves out such man-made products as pesticides, herbicides, and MPTP.

The toxin must be widely distributed. Idiopathic Parkinson's disease occurs throughout the entire world, having been reported from every continent and from every region of every continent, and in all climatic zones. The toxin must also be ubiquitous. Parkinson's disease has been diagnosed in individuals residing in widely differing environments: city dwellers, farmers, hunters, hermits, even "primitive" hunters and gatherers. No one is immune. Exposure has to occur almost everywhere, for no large population of people has lived anywhere that we know of without some occurrence of Parkinson's disease sooner or later.

The toxin must not be increasing in concentration since there is no evidence that the prevalence of Parkinson's disease is increasing. As far as we know, it is no more common today than it was one hundred years ago.

The distribution of this toxin would have to be relatively uniform throughout the world, since the comparative prevalence of Parkinson's varies over a fairly narrow range and few, if any, pockets of the disease have ever been described. Unlike its MPTP-induced cousin, Parkinson's disease is never naturally epidemic.

No matter what the concentration of the phantom toxin is in any environment, only a very small minority of those exposed in that locale or any other locale ever develop idiopathic Parkinson's disease. In many ways this is key to understanding why particular persons develop Parkinson's disease and others living in the same environment do not. It may also be the key to understanding MPTP-induced parkinsonism. Our old friend, the chemist who sold the drugs laced with MPTP, had a distribution chain that reached far more than seven customers, and probably closer to seven hundred. Why were there only seven patients with MPTP-induced parkinsonism? Why not seven hundred? It wasn't that the afflicted seven injected more MPTP than anyone else; they didn't. There had to be another reason. And of course our initial nagging question still remains. Why Ali? Why not the losers? Why not George Foreman, or Sonny Liston, or the oft-battered Floyd Patterson?

Whatever the toxin, humans are uniquely susceptible to it. We are the only species to develop Parkinson's disease or anything resembling it. Almost every species when exposed to MPTP gets MPTP-induced parkinsonism, but only we get true Parkinson's disease. It has never been seen in domesticated species of dogs, for instance, although such species live long lives under conditions of close observation and develop parkinsonian features when given MPTP.

How can this be? If Parkinson's disease is caused by a toxin in the environment, why does this toxin only kill substantia nigral cells in humans? MPTP causes the same symptoms in virtually every species.

This list of requirements seems to be a strong argument against the role of any toxin whatsoever in the etiology of Parkinson's disease. But that argument would be false. In order to understand how this could be possible, you need only consider the implications of the evolution of human beings.

Unfortunately, most of us equate evolution with progress. This, in a Darwinian sense, is not necessarily true. Evolution involves change. It is a form of descent with modifications, but neither the descent nor the modification has any predetermined direction. As pointed out by Stephen Jay Gould, Darwinian paleontologist and baseball aficionado, the Darwinian model of evolution consists of "two undeniable facts and an inescapable conclusion."

Fact 1. Organisms within each and every species vary. These variations represent genetic variations, and such variations (perhaps with even further minor modifications) tend to be inherited by the offspring. Zebras vary in speed. Some are faster than average; some are slower. Most are pretty average in speed.

Fact 2. The organisms within each and every species produce more offspring than can survive. Each generation some new zebras don't survive into adulthood. It is a way of life for zebras. This results, of course, in a struggle for survival.

Conclusion. Those offspring that vary in a way that is for any reason more strongly favored by the environment will be more likely to survive. There are any number of environmental threats to survival that zebras must face, but one of the prominent, ever present threats, generation after generation, year in and year out, are carnivores such as lions. The fastest zebras are obviously less likely to be caught and eaten than their slower herd mates. In an evolutionary sense, it is not survival into old age that matters but survival to adulthood when reproduction becomes possible. This is referred to as reproductive fitness. As long as there are lions in the environment, faster zebras will be more likely to become reproductively fit than slower zebras.

The descent with modification envisioned by Darwin slowly results in increasing adaptation between organisms and their environment. The essence of this process is the hypothesis that natural selection ("survival of the fittest") is the creative force of evolution. Two other aspects of this process must be kept in mind. First and foremost, the variations are random. They are not in any predetermined direction. Changes are not designed so that each generation of zebras will be faster than the prior generation. Variations are a matter of chance. In each generation some zebras will be faster and some will be slower. But not by very much. That is the second condition; variations are each relatively small, not sudden, major leaps. And it goes without saying that this process, this interaction with genetic modification and the environment, goes on in each and every generation. It is a never-ending process.

People are different from all other species in the degree and manner in which they can change their environment. In Darwinian terms, what does this mean? It means that the inescapable conclusion no longer applies. Survival of the most fit is dependent on the role of the environment, an interaction between random variation and competition within the environment. But what happens if the species can change the environment? If the zebras could eliminate the lions? Speed becomes irrelevant and is no longer a virtue. Lack of speed is no longer a detriment. A slow zebra would be just as reproductively fit as a fast zebra.

A rather simple hypothesis based on the evolution of humans can explain how an environmental toxin or toxins could cause Parkinson's disease despite all of the inherent problems.

According to this view, the same prolonged, protected dependency of human offspring that allows for interaction between the developing brain and the environment—so key to the acquisition of language—is also responsible for other uniquely human susceptibilities to toxin-induced parkinsonism. How could that be? How could descent with modification lead to a disease?

The rearing practice of humans is geared to guarantee reproductive survival for as many offspring as possible. Human beings usually have only one offspring at a time. There is no excess of offspring. The battle is not one of survival among offspring but of the parents or clan to keep all of the offspring alive to assure reproductive fitness for all. This is not always the case, however. There are tribes in Brazil where weak or deformed children are allowed to die. We consider such peoples to be "primitive," but they represent an anomalous stage of civilization that is quite recent. There is no reason to believe that such practices occurred in earlier stages of human development. The child survival practices of many third world nations today are also irrelevant. They are by-products of a peculiar stage of economic development dating back a generation or two at most, and are tied to an industrial age economy. None of these would ever have had any long-term genetic consequences for the entire species.

The protective practices that have characterized human descent would have assured survival of those offspring that would be more susceptible to a toxin than any surviving individuals of any other species would be. It may be analogous to complete herd protection from lions. Welcome to a world of slow zebras.

How could this happen, and what would it have to do with Parkinson's disease?

It all has to do with the role of the substantia nigra in movement. Much of our knowledge of this body is based on clinical observations of patients with Parkinson's disease. It appears that the substantia nigra plays a determining role in most movements that are learned by the maturing nervous system early in life without the benefit of any instruction. These are the movements that are most affected in Parkinson's disease. These symptoms reflect damage to the substantia nigra, ergo the substantia nigra is responsible for these movements. Furthermore, these are movements that are acquired during that period of almost complete infantile dependency and parental protectiveness. These include such movement patterns as sitting up, obtaining an upright posture, walking, maintaining balance in the face of a postural threat, and associated swinging of the arms during walking. All of these are learned without being taught and even without being observed (they are all learned by blind individuals).

These movements are among the motor behaviors that are primarily lost in idiopathic Parkinson's disease. Every experienced clinician is well aware that loss of spontaneous swinging of the arms while walking occurs quite early in the disease. Often, family members notice this before any of them ever suspect anything is wrong with the patient. Patients and their families are also aware that patients often have less trouble dancing than walking. The ability to carry out these "primitive" motor skills seems to be dependent upon function of the substantia nigra.

This set of motor skills is so basic it is usually considered to be acquired equally well by all humans. That is merely an assumption. As every neurologist has been taught, normal babies learn to carry out these tasks over a wide range of time and with different rates of acquisition. Obviously, some babies acquire these skills more quickly than others and perform them better. This is true of humans and of all other species. It is the first of the simple observations that can be put together to explain why toxin-induced Parkinson's disease occurs only in humans and then only in a small percentage of exposed individuals. *Self-acquired motor skills depend on the function of the substantia nigra.* This is the first step in helping us understand why Muhammad Ali became one of the victims of posttraumatic parkinsonism.

Every ability of the nervous system is susceptible to genetic variation, from intelligence to running speed to the ability to hit a curveball. We are our genes. Some of us are faster and some are slower, both in the speed we can attain in running and the rate at which we acquire the ability to run.

This is the second self-evident observation: *There is a genetic variability in the aptitude of individuals to acquire these skills.* This variability applies to all species. Obviously, other factors could also alter these abilities, but those variations would have nothing to do with this process.

In a parallel to Darwin's own logic, there is one inescapable conclusion to be derived from these observations: *This variability must be a reflection of genetic variability in the robustness of function of the substantia nigra.* But couldn't other, nongenetic factors also play a role in this variability? The reason Parkinson's disease was called idiopathic in the first place was that there were no factors that could specifically alter the structure of the substantia nigra without also doing injury elsewhere in the brain at the same time. That is the key to this entire hypothesis. The rest of the brain is normal. The substantia nigra varies independently. The infants are normal. They are not deformed. They are not weakened. They would never have been selected for non-survival, even if that had been the normal practice of child rearing. It is just that over time the lower end of the normal range has been expanded.

The variability in the robustness of the substantia nigra could come about in any number of ways, including alterations in the total number of cells, alteration in the manner by which they branch to reach their target cells, differences in enzyme concentration or function. The mechanism can be almost anything, but it will be under genetic control. The exact process is unimportant.

For the sake of understanding the process, it can be assumed that robustness is directly related to the number of cells of the substantia nigra. The average number present on each side of the human brain is about one hundred thousand. Infants born with about this number learn to walk at an average age. Those born with significantly more would walk a little sooner. Those with fewer, a bit later, but they would all still learn to walk. There is a great redundancy in the nervous system. We have a lot more neurons than we need. This is especially true of the substantia nigra. So to be really slow in learning to walk or run, the infant must have a lot fewer cells. Perhaps only thirty or forty percent of normal.

This variability, whatever its anatomical or biochemical basis, must occur in all species. Despite this, Parkinson's disease remains a uniquely human condition. Why? This is where Darwin's specific logic comes into play. Those zebras with only half the normal number of substantia nigral cells become prey for predators. They never become reproductively fit. Not so in humans. Remember, *humans are unique in assuring the survival of all offspring over a wide range of such robustness.* In any species in which survival of the fittest operates, any deficiency in the system would be selected against generation after generation after generation. Slow-learning or slow-performing prey would be unlikely to survive. They would be weaned out in each generation. The same fate would befall slow predators, hence maintaining a balance. This, in general, has not been true for humans. This means that humans have randomized the variability of the robustness of the substantia nigra for hundreds of thousands, if not millions, of years. All Darwinian modifications (genetic changes) are both small in degree and random. Hence, if selection is eliminated for any selected genetic variable, there must be an increase in random distribution of that variable. In any generation, even in a dozen generations, this would be slight, but this process has been going on forever. This is essentially a process of deselection or randomization. It is not merely a shift of the normal distribution curve of the number of cells but a flattening and denormalization of the distribution, resulting in the birth and survival of humans whose systems are comparably far less robust than any member of any other species.

If zebras with less than half the normal number of cells are not reproductively fit (get eaten by lions), very few zebras will ever be born with less than half the normal number of cells.

Recall, modifications are small. But if those with fifty percent survive as well as those with one hundred percent, you get a different situation. If two fifty-percenters mate, why not get a forty-eight percent offspring who will survive and, in turn, mate? No reason at all.

This, over time, has a number of implications. It explains those kids who get picked last for each and every team throughout their lives despite hard work and coaching. More importantly, it explains the appearance of Parkinson's disease as a uniquely human disease.

As a result of this denormalization, individual humans with extremely nonrobust substantia nigral neuronal systems are born and survive. It is these nonrobust systems that then succumb to a ubiquitous toxin that is unable to produce disease in individuals with more robust systems.

An example of this mechanism would be the situation in which robustness is directly related to the number of nigral neurons. Eventually, some humans would be born with only thirty or forty percent of the usual number of nigral neurons. No other species would be expected to produce such offspring in any significant number since reproductive success depends upon nigral robustness. All individuals of all species are then exposed to this ubiquitous toxin. This toxin is relatively ineffective and can only kill the weakest surviving cells, and then only through a relatively slow process taking many years. What would happen?

The occurrence of Parkinson's disease depends upon there being only twenty percent of the normal number of nigral cells. Suppose that in a lifetime of exposure the toxin can only kill fifty percent of the usual number of cells. One hundred percent minus fifty percent is still fifty percent, and that is enough to function normally. No animals of any other species would develop parkinsonism. No zebra or lion would ever be born with so few cells that a fifty percent decline would result in parkinsonism. Only a small number of humans would develop Parkinson's disease. This would happen to those few humans with the least robust systems.

This proposal explains the uniquely human nature of Parkinson's disease. The inherent contradictions are no longer contradictions; they are the expected results. Parkinson's disease has to be unique to humans, and despite the widespread nature of the toxin and universal exposure, only a small percent of humans ever fall prey to it.

What does all of this have to do with "The Champ"? None of his opponents ever slipped him a mickey made up of poisons that would injure the cells of his substantia nigra. Not even Joe Frazier. They just hit him, over and over again.

That is precisely my point. Those punches injured the substantia nigra. Not intentionally, but unavoidably.

The axons of the substantia neuron have to travel a long way in order to get from deep in the brain stem to deep in the hemispheres. Along the way they pass from the immobile brain stem to the far more mobile brain. The brain itself is separated from the skull by the spinal fluid in which it floats. This watery fluid protects the brain. Any sudden, severe blow to the head displaces the brain, which then moves backward and forward within the protective fluid. But the brain stem is tied down. It cannot move. Each time the brain is suddenly displaced by a blow to the head, the axons that cross from the brain stem to the brain are stretched, bent, distorted. Think of a length of wire being bent back and forth. That is what a blow to the head does to the wires coming up from the brain stem.

Each hard blow to the head of a boxer causes a sudden movement of the brain, a displacement. Each time the head is snapped back, the brain is sent sailing back and forth within the spinal fluid. Acceleration and deceleration. Once. Twice. Hundreds of times. And in Ali thousands of times. Each displacement, each acceleration and deceleration, leaves its trace in the axons that cross from the brain stem to the brain. The process is much like breaking off a length of wire to hang a picture. A single bending of the wire, no matter how sudden or vigorous, leaves the wire still intact. Small, repetitive bends back and forth do the trick, but only if you bend it often enough. Some fibers break quickly, others far more slowly, but eventually they all become weakened and frayed and then snap.

This is what happened to Muhammad Ali. The axons of the substantia nigra travel as a single bundle of nerves, or axons, one pathway among the complex wiring of the brain. And once an axon of a brain cell is destroyed, the cell itself dies. The axons of Ali's substantia nigral neurons started to be destroyed long ago. As a result, the cells themselves died. Some of Ali's substantia nigral cells died long ago. Others, long ago injured and unable to repair themselves, died off slowly over the years until only a small minority were left, and shuffling became a way of life.

But is boxing designed to injure these axons? Make no mistake about it: the answer is yes. Grass grows, fish swim, and boxers attack each other's brains and especially the wires of the brain that travel from the brain stem to the brain proper. The damaged axons of the substantia nigra are not the prime target, they are a form of what we call collateral damage—quite a euphemism for death and destruction. It is a form of collateral injury that cannot be avoided. And it's all part of the game. Direct injury to cells that are neighbors of the substantia nigra is the goal of boxing. In professional boxing the goal is the KO, the knockout. What is a knockout? It is nothing other than a violent displacement of the brain. It sends the brain careening within the skull. The occipital lobes crash against the back of the skull. The brain then bounces forward until the tips of the frontal lobes smack against the front of the skull. But the brain stem never moves. All the fibers, the axons, that go from the brain stem into the brain itself are bent backward and then forward. With each and every blow.

The real targets are the axons of the reticular activating system coming up from their home deep in the brain stem. These are the cells that keep the brain awake. They maintain consciousness. Disrupt them and consciousness is lost. And that is what boxing is all about. A KO, a win, and a few more cells injured and dying; a bit more collateral damage to the substantia nigra. Another stumblebum in the making. The collateral damage is often worse than any permanent injury to the primary targets. Why? Because some boxers just can't afford to lose very many of these cells.

That is the point of the entire tale. That is why Ali developed parkinsonism while most of his opponents haven't yet and probably never will. The fact is that Ali wasn't dealt a full deck, in that he was more susceptible to injury. He probably had fewer substantia nigral cells and axons to start with, a less robust system.

True, Ali would never have been the last one chosen on any team. He was not the slowest zebra in the pack. Abnormal slowness requires the loss of eighty percent of the cells. Ali had far more than that to start with. But if injury can knock off sixty percent of a normal number, then Ali could have had eighty percent to start with and still end up with parkinsonism caused by trauma. Eighty percent is four times more than is needed to perform normally. Thank God for redundancy. But Ali was more than normal; he had speed, grace, quickness, rhythm, and athletic skills beyond average.

But he did not have these other skills because of his substantia nigra. The human brain has two other motor systems. The three systems play different but complementary roles. The substantia nigra has nothing to do with coordination; that depends upon the cerebellum. Nor rhythm; the patient with Parkinson's disease who cannot walk can often still dance. Nor quickness; rhythm and quickness depend upon the pyramidal system, which starts in the cortex and directs such learned (and taught) behaviors. Ali's skills in these areas were beyond compare. Just think how great he might have been if he had been dealt a full deck.

How can this concept of denormalization or randomization of nigral robustness, manifested by acquisitions of motor skills, be explained in terms of classic genetic theory? Mendel, Watson and Crick, DNA, and all that? Fortunately, genetics is not what it used to be.

Mendel's laws of segregation and their interpretations resulted in a system peopled by dominant and recessive genes. The dominant gene expressed itself whenever it was present;

that was why it was called dominant. If there were no dominant gene but just two recessives, then they would express themselves.

Research into two neurological disorders has robbed us of such elegant simplicity. The first of these is Huntington's disease. This disease was described by an American physician, George Huntington, some thirty years before Mendel's work was translated into English. Once Mendel was published, Huntington's chorea became the perfect example of a dominant disease.

Huntington's chorea is characterized by both abnormal involuntary movements and mental and psychiatric disorders. It usually starts in a patient's late thirties or early forties, and results in death in about fifteen years. It is what killed the great American composer of folk songs, Woody Guthrie. And his mother. The first signs of Huntington's usually start after the age by which most reproduction has taken place, so the gene does not limit reproductive fitness.

If either parent has (or later develops) the disease, each child born to that parent has an independent, fifty-fifty chance of receiving the gene and developing the disease. Ergo, it is a classic dominant gene. If a person has a parent with Huntington's disease but himself does not ever develop the disease (did not inherit the dominant gene), then his offspring cannot inherit the gene or the disease. Good old Gregor Mendel's theory at work.

Until recently this was all theoretical in a sense, because children were conceived before the disease developed. But now we can test for the gene, hidden away or not, on the fourth chromosome.

The structure of the gene for Huntington's has been analyzed, and guess what? It is not simply all or none, not just dominant or recessive. DNA, if you recall, consists of strings of two interlocking helixes made up of four different nucleotides. The gene for Huntington's is made up of repeats of three nucleotides in the same sequence, over and over again. Geneticists call these trinucleotide repeats. Sports fans would recognize them as a scientific variant of a "three-peat," so to speak. The "gene" for Huntington's chorea, hence, is nothing but a long series of such three-peats (even more than the Boston Celtics amassed in their best years), but so is the normal gene. Normal individuals can have anywhere from nine to thirty-four such repeats, although the number is usually between fifteen and twenty. Thirty-six or more repeats means Huntington's. The range here is quite wide. The average number of repeats in a patient is around forty-five, but there can be well over one hundred.

And this is where the new information may shed light on Parkinson's disease and Muhammad Ali. Huntington's can begin far earlier than the age of forty and can be far more rapidly progressive than usual, resulting in death in half a dozen years. This has been known since the days of George Huntington. Now we know that onset and severity have a relationship to the number of genetic three-peats. Those patients with the greatest number tend to develop their disease far earlier in life.

The more repeats the worse the condition. And those with early onset progress faster. That is only logical. The genetic defect is there from inception. The patient with one hundred and twenty repeats becomes symptomatic at age fifteen; the one with forty develops problems at age forty-five. But the fertilized eggs got the disease when the parents' egg and sperm combined. In the former, it took nearly sixteen years (fifteen years and nine months) for that disease to progress to cause clinical disorders. In the latter, the process took nearly forty-six years. So, of course, the disease in the former patient progresses more rapidly. It already had been doing that. That is why he was sick by the age of fifteen.

But of more interest to us is the phenomenon that geneticists call anticipation. In relation to a genetic disease such as Huntington's, anticipation means that the disease tends to start earlier in successive generations. And guess what? The number of the repeats also tends to increase slightly in succeeding generations. Scientifically, it is the other way around. Some members of each generation have a few more three-peats than their parents. More three-peats means more abnormality. More abnormality means a shorter time until the threshold for clinical disease is crossed. So the disease starts earlier in the offspring. It's a form of expectation which, in a way, is worse than the disease.

The way to eliminate Huntington's may be to reverse the anticipation by reducing the number of three-peats. Go down from forty to thirty-six, from disease after the age of forty to disease that might start at age ninety but, because of that, is hardly any disease at all.

What does this have to do with Ali and parkinsonism? Assume that running skill and robustness of the nigra depend on the number of three-peats. Not the same three-peats as Huntington's, of course. Not the same nucleotides, not even the same chromosome, but some gene somewhere else in the human genetic material. A gene that has to go with growth and development of the substantia nigra. Too many three-peats is bad news. The cells of the substantia nigra do not develop as they should from the time of inception. In zebras that's fatal news. Slow afoot and quickly eaten. It is the eventual fate of all of them. These zebras "anticipate" and suffer their fate far earlier in life. But not so in humans. A few too many three-peats means a little more work for the parents but not a failure of the offspring to survive. For survive they will and for them, like others, reproduction will go on. And in the next generation there may even be more three-peats in some of the offspring, resulting in the same outcome: more three-peats, less robustness, greater dependency for a bit longer—but survival and reproductive fitness. This is the process that assured survival of the whole species to become modern humans.

What happens, eventually? Some individuals survive with more three-peats than any single person was ever born with, and it's all part of the human condition.

But Ali was never slow. How many three-peats could he have been born with? Understanding the genetics of another disease may explain this. Dystonia musculorum deformans is another genetic neurological disease causing abnormal movements (dystonic movements). It is a dominant disease. If either parent has the gene, each offspring born to that parent has a fifty-fifty chance of inheriting that gene, but not a fifty-fifty chance of getting the disease. This is called incomplete penetrance. The gene is there in all its glory, but it may have little or no effect and certainly may not cause the full-blown disease.

So Ali had his excess of three-peats, but they didn't penetrate fully. Just enough to cause a mild reduction in nigral robustness, but not enough to limit his athletic prowess in any way. Just enough to set him up for traumatic parkinsonism. His wires were thinner than the average wire. Thick enough to do their job, but so thin that they were more easily frayed and fractured than those of some others. It took fewer bends and twists to break them. So Ali developed posttraumatic parkinsonism while Foreman was still winning championships and Leon Spinks was still contemplating yet another comeback.

What do we know about the toxin that causes Parkinson's disease in those parkinsonism patients who did not beat up people in order to make a living? Very little, but that is our own fault. Few perspectives of our world are more egocentric than our usual view of the toxins that threaten mankind. Any mention of the word *toxin* conjures up images of pesticides and herbicides and industrial waste. PCBs. Dioxin. Love Canal. A man-made wasteland yearning for its "organic" saviors. "Organic," even when misused in this sense, does not imply safe. Ask anyone who ever ate the wrong mushroom.

The organic world is made up of toxins. It is how the world survives. Plants survive because of toxins; animals that eat plants survive because of their ability to detoxify at least some toxins. The others they learn to recognize and avoid, or they are not even attracted to them. Which substances are toxic and which are not results, for the most part, from our old friend natural selection, acting on both the producers of toxins and the consumers. People eat almost everything. This implies that we must have the genetically determined ability to detoxify a wide range of naturally occurring organic toxins. The idea that everything that is natural is safe is merely a dream. There is no reason to believe that there is a perfectly natural, totally toxin-free diet.

Plants defend themselves against herbivores mainly by synthesizing toxic chemicals, which may comprise ten percent of the weight of some plants. Vegetables all contain at least trace amounts of such toxins. The complex chemicals that make coffee so appealing to most of us are toxins that protect coffee seeds from insects and small mammals. We can safely consume vegetables and coffee because we have evolved effective detoxification mechanisms. Also, like many other animals, we prefer diverse diets. This avoids overloading any one aspect of our detoxification mechanism and helps to provide all the needed trace nutrients. No diet is perfectly safe; all are compromises arising from the plant-herbivore arms race.

These facts have any number of obvious implications. In relation to Parkinson's disease, there is no reason for us to have developed any detoxifying mechanism at all. The disease starts after reproductive fitness has come and gone. Or perhaps that has been our defense, to slow the toxic process into one that, in relationship to reproduction, has no meaning. A tremor at age sixty has no effect on the number of offspring one has or their ability to survive and reproduce. So the toxin may well be there. We may eat it every week of our lives but so what? It's safe.

There are also implications for the current belief that we can develop strains of plants that require no protection from pesticides. They will be able to protect themselves. But how? Obviously, artificial selection for such disease-resistant plants should make it possible to reduce pesticide use, but we must expect such selection to increase the concentrations of natural plant toxins. Which toxins will be increased and whether they will affect humans is hard to predict. But they might. And perhaps only after a lifetime of consumption.

When Ali fought his last match, he was no longer the fighter he had once been. He no longer floated like a butterfly or stung like a bee. His face looked as young and handsome as ever, yet behind that face his brain was already beginning to show the effects of the wear and tear of all those hits that had sent the brain careening back and forth within the skull. He had become a tragic variation of Dorian Gray. *The Picture of Dorian Gray* is the only novel written by Oscar Wilde. In that Gothic tale, it is the painted portrait of Dorian Gray that undergoes alterations and shows the ravages of his dissolute life while the subject's own face remains unchanged, unweathered by time or sin. Like the face of Dorian Gray, the face of Muhammad Ali remained undamaged. It was his brain, not his face, that paid the price for the life he had lived and the genetic predisposition with which he had been endowed.

chapter 8

Between
Rounds

AS A NEUROLOGIST WHO HAS DEDICATED his professional life to helping patients with injured brains recover to a better level of function, I find it impossible to write about boxing and the brain damage boxing induces without confronting the question as to whether boxing as a sport is justified. It is a question I have thought about for thirty years. It arose the first time I treated a boxer for a neurological disease related to his career. Unlike Ali, this fighter had never been a world champion. He had been what was known as a club fighter. He fought in the various boxing clubs in Chicago, and not just a couple of times a year. Ali's entire professional career included only sixty-one matches. For Battling Bill Browne, that would have been a busy year's work.

When I first met Bill, I was just finishing my residency. In a couple of months I would start my career as a neurologist. I was twenty-nine years old. He was almost twice that age and his career had wound down about a decade earlier. We met in the hospital. He had been admitted to be evaluated for a progressive deterioration of his ability to walk.

We talked for over an hour. He had been born in Georgia. He never had much education and had been a boxer all his "adult" life.

How long had that been? About thirty-five years, starting at the age of fourteen.

How many fights had he fought? He had no idea.

How often had he fought? At least once or twice a month, and sometimes every week. In a good week, two or three fights. He had to fight that often.

Why? "To make a living, Doc." It seems he only got paid twenty to fifty bucks per fight.

"How good were you?" I asked.

"Good enough to win more than I lost."

But he had lost hundreds of fights over most of four decades. He had also been a sparring partner for real boxers, a punching bag for some of the best: Joe Louis, Joe Walcott, Ezzard Charles. Some of the greatest champs ever. Bill had been hit by them all, early and often. He had to be punch-drunk, I thought. Posttraumatic encephalopathy of boxers. Dementia pugilistica, as the English liked to call it. It was said to be related to the number of punches to the head a boxer took in his career—the number and their force. No one could have been hit more often or by harder punchers. Louis. Charles. Walcott. Charles had once even killed an opponent.

Yet Bill's memory was good and his speech was fine. He was certainly not demented. So much for classic dementia pugilistica. His problem was walking. It was, in fact, the only problem he had. If we could fix his walking, he could go back to making a living. I wasn't so certain we should try if that was our goal.

As he sat on the side of his bed, everything that I examined was normal, just like he said it would be. It was time to bite the bullet. I asked him to walk for me.

He quickly got up from his bed. That agility ruled out parkinsonism as a possible diagnosis. He had no evidence at all of bradykinesia. He stood erect. His balance was good. He tried to walk. He couldn't. It was as if his feet were nailed in place. He started to weave and jog but his feet never left the ground. Finally, his feet dragged along on the floor and he shuffled toward his left. He looked more like a boxer weaving and shuffling than a man trying to walk. It was hard to tell if he was dragging his feet or if his feet were dragging him, as if the floor had shifted and he had tried not to move at all. Then his feet suddenly locked in place again. The floor was no longer pulling him along. He tried valiantly to move again but couldn't. He started to shift his weight to force the issue, trying harder and harder, but his feet stayed frozen in place. He started to sway. Luckily, I caught him before he hit the floor. He was truly a stumblebum.

But was it due to his boxing? And if so, how and why?

It didn't take long to get the answer. An angiogram provided it. That was in the antediluvian age before CAT scans and MRI scans. Battling Bill had hydrocephalus. Hydrocephalus literally means water in the head, or to be more specific and accurate, too much cerebrospinal fluid (CSF) within the skull. Traditionally, there are two major types of hydrocephalus. The first has been labeled hydrocephalus ex vacuo. In this condition, the brain is shrunken by disease, and cerebrospinal fluid fills up the excess space available between the brain and the skull— hydrocephalus to fill up the vacuum.

The other variety is called obstructive hydrocephalus, indicating that spinal fluid collects because of obstruction of the usual pathways for the spinal fluid flow. The cerebrospinal fluid is formed in the cavities of the brain's two hemispheres, travels down through narrow channels in the brain stem, and then escapes to the space that surrounds the spinal cord. There it circulates down and then back up over the brain to be absorbed into the various spaces of the skull.

There are a number of places where this flow can become obstructed. One of the most common is the narrow channel, or aqueduct, in the midbrain. If this becomes blocked, the flow stops and CSF builds up inside the brain. The pressure mounts and the ventricles expand. Hydrocephalus. And in an infant whose skull can expand, the head then enlarges.

So what had happened to Battling Bill? An unusual form of obstruction brought on by dozens and dozens of head traumas. One of the common accompaniments of such trauma is a small amount of bleeding. And there shouldn't be blood in the spinal fluid space. It abhors blood more than it abhors a vacuum. The blood causes inflammation, which in turn causes scarring of the delicate structures that normally absorb spinal fluid. Absorption of the fluid is decreased but production continues. Fluid collects slowly but surely in the entire system. The condition is called normal pressure hydrocephalus because there is never the severe elevation of pressure that occurs in classic obstructive hydrocephalus. The symptoms are also different. There are no headaches or vomiting. Instead, the patient no longer knows how to walk. It's called apraxia of the gait—walking as if the feet were nailed to the floor. Bill went from boxer to stumblebum. Was there anything we could do to help him?

Fortunately, there was. We were able to put a shunt in his brain, which drained fluid from the swollen ventricles into his abdomen. The next day he was running down the hallway. The nails were gone. He could lift his feet off the ground. He felt so good he thought he might make a comeback.

Heaven forbid.

I saw Bill on and off for a couple of years. His apraxia never came back but he never went back to boxing. He worked in the gym cleaning up and helping other boxers. And he never developed posttraumatic encephalopathy. No dementia pugilistica. No posttraumatic parkinsonism. Why not? Because he was fortunate enough to have normal nigral cells from the start.

Brain injury is a goal of boxing, even of amateur boxing. Anyone who maintains otherwise is either naive or too close to the sport to be honest. If it wasn't a goal, hitting in the head would be illegal, just as hitting below the waist is illegal. Why we are more interested in protecting the testes than in protecting the brain is an interesting question that I can neither fathom nor answer. As an old friend of mine, and an ex-president of the American Academy of Neurology, Nelson Richards, once said, "In football if the referee sees a blow and believes that it was intended to injure, he usually throws that player out of the game. If that happens in boxing, the boxer wins the match." It didn't make much sense to him, nor does it to me. There is no way for us to screen for chronic progressive brain damage from blows to the head, and no way to prevent it from occurring after the blows have been struck. We try to teach teenagers not to smoke but instead to hit each other in the head under controlled conditions. That's called boxing. If anyone else treated an adolescent that way, it would be called abuse.

Ali is far from alone in suffering the long-term consequences of boxing. Jerry Quarry, whom Ali beat during his return from exile, has that form of progressive dementia caused by recurrent brain injury suffered during his boxing career. It's called dementia pugilistica. Quarry had once been fairly successful as a boxer. He had fought a total of sixty-six professional fights from 1965 through 1992 and lost only nine of them. When Ali had been stripped of his crown, Quarry was one of eight fighters selected to compete for the title. He never made it, losing to Jimmy Ellis in the semifinals of the tournament. A year later he fought Joe Frazier in a title match. Frazier battered him and won by a technical knockout in the seventh round.

In his career, Quarry won more than two million dollars in purses. Today he lives on social security and can't even remember his own phone number. But he's not alone. His younger brother, Michael, who once fought for the light-heavyweight crown, also has dementia pugilistica. Two members of the same family with the same predisposition and the same disastrous outcome. Most boxers have no pension, no disability plan, just their battered nervous systems. They can't even sue for workers' compensation.

But boxing is one of our eternal verities. There has always been boxing. Cockfighting has been made illegal—for the good of the cocks. So has bearbaiting. We no longer go to the Colosseum to watch gladiators gladiate each other into oblivion. We haven't since Constantine the Great made such contests illegal in A.D. 325. Boxing had already been outlawed in Rome for almost four hundred years by then.

To the best of my knowledge, boxing is not our oldest sport. The first historical reference to boxing is in the Twenty-third

Olympic Games, which took place in 688 B.C. The contestants were drawn by lot and were bare-fisted. The Greeks soon developed leather thongs to protect the knuckles. Later, a leather glove was introduced. The Romans modified this by reinforcing the gloves with lead and metal spikes, but this did not last for long. The Emperor Augustus put an end to boxing because the sport was ruining too many prospective soldiers. After that, there is no mention of boxing in any ancient sources. Civilization was making some headway.

In the late seventeenth century boxing made a comeback, especially in England, which became the cradle of pugilism. Modern boxing is usually dated to the revision of rules proposed by the Eighth Marquis of Queensberry in 1867, and to the reign of John L. Sullivan, who fought the last bare-knuckle bout in 1889. This was the same Marquis of Queensberry who denounced poet and playwright Oscar Wilde as a sodomist. Wilde sued him for slander. Wilde should have known better: he had been upstaged by boxing once before in his career. He arrived in Chicago on a speaking tour on the same day John L. Sullivan got into town. Needless to say, brawn took precedent over wit. Sullivan made the front pages. Wilde was lucky to make the newspapers at all.

The Marquis of Queensberry won in court. Even back in those days the truth was a defense against the charge of slander. The government had no choice but to arrest, try, and jail Wilde. Sodomy was a crime then. It was the beginning of the end for Wilde.

One of the subjects on which Ali is often quoted is the role of sex, or more correctly the role of abstinence from sex, in athletic performance. Ali claimed that he abstained for six weeks before each fight. That abstinence made him mean and frustrated and angry. Did it help? His record speaks for itself. Or does it? Was that part of his act, part of the Ali show? If he abstained because it helped him fight more ferociously, what should his opponent do? Wonder and worry? Was the advantage physiological or psychological?

The truth is that no one knows whether abstinence helps or hurts. The coaches of the Minnesota Vikings separated the players from their wives before each of the team's four Superbowl appearances. Their record in Superbowls is no wins and four losses.

Coitus itself is probably more helpful in building than depleting energy. The late-night socializing and drinking that often precedes such activity is another story. Legendary New York Yankees manager Casey Stengel, who managed a number of Hall of Fame–caliber carousers, put it this way, "It wasn't the catching that caused the problem for my guys. It was the chasing."

chapter 9

The Men with the Not-So-Golden Arms: J. R. Richard and Whitey Ford

"BASEBALL," AT LEAST ACCORDING TO YOGI BERRA, "is ninety percent mental and the other half is physical." Many other equally knowledgeable, if somewhat less succinct, observers have claimed that pitching is ninety percent of the game. If that is true, the 1980 Houston Astros should have walked off with everything. Their pitching was beyond compare. Their rotation of starting pitchers began with Nolan Ryan, who, before he retired, amassed more strikeouts and no-hitters than any other pitcher in the history of the game. Nolan was at his peak. While pitching for the California Angels the previous season, he had led the American League in strikeouts for the fourth straight season. Nolan continued to throw aspirins for the Astros. His fastball was almost unhittable.

Then Joe Niekro joined the team. Niekro threw nothing but junk, knuckleballs that fluttered and jumped unpredictably as they slowly approached the plate. If it hadn't been for brother

Phil and Hall of Famer Hoyt Wilhelm, Joe might have gone down as the best knuckleball pitcher in the history of the game. But his career was then peaking. In 1979, he tied for the lead in National League games won, with twenty-one. His brother also won twenty-one games that year pitching his knucklers for the Atlanta Braves, the only time in baseball history when two brothers, pitching for different teams, tied for the league lead in wins, no matter what type of pitch they threw.

Then there was the ace of the staff, the best of the best, a pitcher whose aspirins made Ryan's pitches look as big as houses—J. R. Richard. There was only one problem. Humans, as they descended into their present form, did not survive because of the ability to pitch a baseball. Or at least they were not designed for that specific task. Not as well and as hard and as often as J. R. Richard did.

J. R. Richard had made the big leagues to stay in 1975. He was twenty-five years old, six feet eight inches tall, and weighed about two hundred twenty pounds. He threw right-handed, and as the saying goes, he could throw a baseball through a brick wall.

In his first full year he won twelve and lost ten, striking out one hundred seventy-six batters in just over two hundred innings. A good year but not a great one. The next year he threw better. He won twenty games for the first and only time in his career, struck out two hundred fourteen batters, and lowered his earned run average (the number of earned, or deserved, runs the opposition scored against him each nine innings) by over a run and a half, from 4.39 to 2.75. He had become a very good pitcher. He also led the National League in an obscure and underrated statistic that season. The opposing players hit worse against him on the average than they did against any other pitcher, compiling a composite batting average of a measly .212. He had a very, very good year.

Over the next three years he moved beyond very, very good. He averaged only eighteen wins each year, but he twice led both leagues in strikeouts. In 1978 he amassed three hundred three strikeouts and in 1979 three hundred thirteen. Those same two

J. R. Richard rearing back to heave another aspirin. His right arm is cocked into a position where the blood flow to that arm is interrupted, the pitcher's version of the Adson maneuver. In 1996, Yankee pitcher David Cone underwent surgery for an aneurysm of the subclavian artery of his pitching arm. Cone's pitching motion, like Richard's and Ford's, had injured the artery of his arm. Cone's artery developed a blister (an aneurysmal dilatation), not a thrombosis. Hopefully the corrective surgery he underwent will save his career. Whether the surgical site of his arterial wall will withstand years of further abuse remains unknown.

years he also led the league in lowest batting average by opposing hitters (.196 in 1978 and .209 in 1979); and in 1979 he also led the league in lowest earned run average.

What a season that was for J. R. Richard. He was the league leader in three of the toughest categories: strikeouts, earned run average, and opponents' batting average. He did everything but collect the tickets. He had become a truly great pitcher.

J. R. was not yet thirty years old. If he was destined for continued greatness, this would be when that greatness would express itself by a string of continuous, consistently outstanding seasons. If not, this would be his pinnacle.

True greatness meant more such seasons. More strikeouts. More stifled hitters. More low earned run averages. Those were the statistics that he could control by his own abilities as a pitcher and if he could, the wins would come his way. And with those wins a pennant. An appearance in the World Series. Richard, Niekro, and Ryan. What more could a team want?

The problem for Richard started during spring training. J. R. never felt quite right. His arm felt tired. He would start the game and he would feel fine in the first few innings, but then his arm would feel tired. He had always felt a little tired after pitching a complete game, but this was different. His arm tired far more quickly than it ever had before. In 1979, he had started thirty-eight games and had completed eighteen. In those thirty-eight starts, he had averaged just short of eight innings per start. Here was a pitcher whose middle name was stamina.

But pitchers aren't supposed to have stamina when spring training starts. That's what spring training is all about for the J. R. Richards of this world. Start slowly, a few innings at a time, and then each time successively pitch a little longer. More innings. More pitches. More stamina. Until opening day and another complete game. It happened every spring, just that way.

But not the spring of 1980. Something had to be wrong. Richard's arm felt heavy. The more he pitched, the heavier it became. And once the season started it didn't get any better. In fact, it got worse. He felt fairly good when each game started but he felt worse and worse as the game progressed. The arm got heavier and heavier. It started to hurt. But J. R. was a trooper. He continued pitching.

How well he pitched is, in retrospect, all but miraculous. He started seventeen games but completed only four of them. That number is less than twenty-five percent of games completed, in contrast to the previous year's almost fifty percent. In 1979 he had pitched just short of eight innings per game. In 1980 this declined to an average of just over six innings per game, and after his early complete games his average fell even further. But the innings he could pitch, before pain and fatigue took their toll, were amazingly good. The opposition, which had hit .209 against him in 1979, was hitting only .166 against him in 1980. His earned run average was lower than it had ever been (1.90 per nine innings), and for the third time in his career he averaged more than one strikeout per inning. His record was ten wins against only four losses, a win-loss percentage of .714, by far the best of his career.

J. R. knew that something was wrong with his arm. But what? Neither the team physicians nor the team's orthopedic surgeon had any idea at all. His arm seemed to be fine to them. Fine as it may have seemed, it still hurt. It got tired too soon, far too tired and much too soon.

Then tragedy struck.

If from this point forward the saga of J. R. Richard seems to read like a neurological case history taken from some academic medical journal, I apologize. That, unfortunately, is precisely what it is: a case history that was published by a friend of mine, neurologist William S. Fields, and two of his associates.

The tragedy hit J. R. in the fourth inning of a game he was pitching in June 1980. He wound up to throw yet another fastball and suddenly his right arm went dead. It was no longer just tired or aching. He had numbness and tingling in the first three digits of his right hand. He could not hold the ball, much less pitch it.

That pitching appearance was over. It was time for a rest, and more than the usual four days between starts. There are, however, grave limitations as to the efficacy of rest, especially in pitchers with sore arms. A couple of weeks passed and J. R. felt no better. The one remaining alternative was to try to find out what was wrong, so he was admitted to a hospital in Houston. By this time, given his history, the diagnosis had to have been fairly certain. J. R. Richard's right subclavian artery, the artery that conveys blood from the aorta toward the right arm, must have become obstructed. The right subclavian becomes re-named the axillary artery as it moves toward the arm in order to supply the vast majority of blood to the shoulder and arm muscles, especially the arm muscles. A simple physical exami-nation confirmed that this was most likely the case. Richard's blood pressure in his left arm was normal. In his right arm it was almost nonexistent. A completely obstructed artery has no blood pressure.

What was needed was not clinical confirmation but defini-tive proof, which was quickly obtained. An angiogram of the aorta and its branches demonstrated that Richard's right sub-clavian artery was completely occluded. The obstruction was at the level of his first rib. His arm was still receiving some blood by way of collateral blood vessels that traveled around the shoulder. These small vessels usually do not have the burden of trying to supply all the blood needed, but under such circum-stances they can often become dilated and enlarged to carry more blood than usual. This dilation of collateral vessels had occurred in and around Richard's right shoulder, supplying the blood his arm needed to survive.

The doctors now knew exactly what had been happening to J. R. all year, as well as what had happened during that last pitch he had thrown in June. His right subclavian artery had become occluded. But that raised more questions than it had answered. Why had this happened to him, a pitcher with a golden arm, and how?

J. R. Richard was a young man, only thirty years old. He was an athlete who was in excellent physical condition, with none of the usual risk factors for such occlusive vascular disease. He did not smoke. His blood pressure was normal. Neither the good nor the bad serum cholesterol level was sky high. Yet he had a completely obstructed major blood vessel. Why?

We, I repeat, were not designed to throw baseballs. Certainly not at over ninety miles per hour, inning after inning, often totaling one hundred twenty or more pitches in a game, and not counting an almost equal number of warm-up throws. All of the pitches were thrown with an overhand motion in which the arm rotates high above the shoulder and the head. In the millennia of millennias before "Lucy" and her even relatively recent predecessors, those mammals who gave rise to the line of descent that was to be selected into Lucy did not throw anything. They did not stand upright. They walked on all fours. Their upper, or more correctly for them their front or fore, limbs were carried in a dependent position reaching down at a right angle from the plane of the trunk and shoulder girdle to the ground. They were all quadrupeds. They always had been and always would be. Their shoulders were designed to support weight, not to throw balls. They were quadrupeds that used their front extremities to support the weight of their bodies while walking and running. Just the way their descent and that of virtually all other land mammals had designed it.

Then along came the Lucys of this world—using the concept of Lucy as an early biped in a very broad and generic sense. In order to get to Lucy, all of that quadrupedal locomotion had to have changed. Lucy no longer had front legs sticking out at a ninety-degree angle from the plane of her trunk. She now had upper extremities as befits someone with an upright posture. She, just like her fellow "Lucys" with whom she mated, had arms, and these arms were parallel to the trunk and now resided within the same plane. There had been a remarkable change in the ground plan of the upper body and in its basic geometry. This variety of "genetic engineering," in the original sense, had to involve the entire shoulder girdle as well as the nerves, arteries, and veins that had to get back and forth from the trunk to the arms. These had to move laterally (meaning away from the center of the trunk) and blaze a new, previously uncharted pathway in order to maintain access to the arm. In so doing, they had to pass out of the chest cavity through a small outlet formed by three bones: the clavicle, that oft-fractured collarbone of fastball players; the scapula, better known as the shoulder blade; and the first rib. This three-cornered space is known in anatomy as the thoracic outlet. The subclavian artery, by the way, gets its name from the fact that it passes through this space below (sub) the clavicle. The bones that form the boundaries of the thoracic outlet are bound together by ligaments and muscles. These are muscles that, in specialized athletes, can and do get quite large and strong. No athlete is more specialized than a pitcher who throws fastballs one hundred or more times every fifth day of his professional life.

The smallness of this outlet, combined with the downward pull of the arm, might suggest that we should all get problems from this anatomical arrangement. Most of us, however, never have any problems because the support given by the various muscles of the shoulder girdle is sufficient to keep the thoracic outlet open. But sometimes the support isn't sufficient to do the job. It certainly wasn't in J. R. Richard's right thoracic outlet. Problems that arise from overdevelopment of the ligaments and muscles around the outlet are grouped together under the rubric thoracic outlet syndrome. This syndrome implies that one or more of the structures passing through the thoracic outlet is being compressed. These structures are the subclavian vein, which transports blood from the arm back toward the heart, the subclavian artery, and the parts of the brachial plexus, a group of nerves connecting the structures of the arm to the spinal cord and carrying messages back and forth.

In Richard, compression of the structure in the thoracic outlet had been occurring all year. All the thoracic outlet compression syndromes share the same anatomical basis, namely, that neurological and vascular structures get caught between the clavicle and the first rib. If the nerve gets squeezed, the patient feels pain, numbness, tingling. If it is the vein, the arm may get swollen. If it is the artery that receives the brunt of the pressure, the blood flow in the arm decreases. The muscles feel the initial effects of any loss of blood flow, and especially any muscles performing strenuous activity—like throwing a baseball at nearly one hundred miles an hour. Those muscles become fatigued.

They feel weak. They tire easily. The arm begins to weigh a ton. This is precisely what happened to J. R. Richard whenever he pitched in 1980.

In the first inning or two, he was great. No one could hit his aspirins. He was able to strike out hitter after hitter. Damn few hitters got any hits and fewer scored runs off him. His earned run average was a minuscule 1.90. A few innings later, his arm began to ache, then to hurt, then to feel heavy. He couldn't throw another pitch. J. R. Richard had a classic thoracic outlet syndrome. He was compressing his subclavian artery at the point where it changed names to become the axillary artery and entered the axilla, the space below the shoulder, in order to get out of the thorax and into the arm. All this is a part of the uniquely human design of the structures of the shoulder. By the time he took his shower, he felt like he could throw again. It was, in a way, Darwin at work.

Thoracic outlet syndrome is a peculiar variant of angina pectoris, the chest pain that comes with exertion and is so often the first evidence of partial obstruction of the coronary arteries. In angina, one or more of these coronary arteries are partially obstructed. As long as the heart is not working too hard the obstruction is usually asymptomatic and the patient feels fine. The heart is receiving sufficient blood to pump along. Sort of like J. R. playing a game of catch. But the patient runs to catch a train or a plane, the way O. J. Simpson used to run through airports in those immortal Hertz advertisements, and the patient's heart rate goes up. The amount of work his heart muscle is performing doubles. It needs more oxygen, more energy, more blood. But it can't get any more blood; the coronary artery is partially blocked. Suddenly, there is not enough fuel for that heart that's pounding away. The result is called ischemia—lack of blood and oxygen. Clinically, this means pain, excruciating chest pain, crushing chest pain.

The patient stops running and sits down. His heart slows down. The metabolic demands of the heart decrease. It is now getting just a barely sufficient supply of blood and oxygen. The pain becomes discomfort. The discomfort becomes a bad memory. Angina pectoris. It's time for coronary angiography and an angioplasty or two.

So, too, with J. R., but with some differences. He, too, had sufficient blood flow at rest and insufficient blood flow during exercise. His muscles also cried out in pain caused by the ischemia. His pain was just in different muscles. And his obstruction of blood flow arose from a far different series of events. It wasn't atherosclerotic plaque that was obstructing his blood vessel. There was no hardening of the subclavian axillary artery, no buildup of cholesterol and calcium. His own muscles had been causing the obstruction. When he had started the season, his arm felt fine for the first thirty or forty pitches of each game. But feeling can be so deceiving. Each time he elevated his strong right arm above his head to heave his fastball toward home plate, those powerful muscles pulled the bones to which they were attached closer together. What resulted was almost like the closing of a scissors, a scissors made up of his clavicle and his first rib. The paper within these scissors were those structures passing out of the thoracic outlet. Nerve, vein, and artery. Especially the artery.

Each time J. R. took that big windup of his and flung his strong right arm above his head, the scissors closed, and every time it closed the artery passing through the thoracic outlet was compressed, and while it was closed nothing went by. No blood at all, no oxygen, no glucose.

Then comes the big kick and the throw. Strike one.

The scissors opens up once again. Blood flow is restored. It's time to get ready to throw another pitch—just twenty seconds after the first one. Here we go again.

The muscles of the arm require oxygen to efficiently burn the glucose they store. They also need a continuous supply of new glucose since their store of glucose is quite limited. During the windup and pitch the blood flow is cut off. Not enough oxygen or glucose is supplied; the muscles are on the edge of deprivation.

J. R. looks in to get his signal. The muscles are relaxed. The obstruction is gone and the blood flow returns. It's time to burn another one by the batter, precisely what had been going on year after year after year. But not in 1980. Why? His pitching motion had not changed. There had been no buildup of atherosclerotic plaque. So why did his arm ache so damn much? All of those scissorlike cuts across his thoracic outlet had finally damaged the wall of his axillary artery. It had become beaten and battered. Small collections of platelets started to gather on the roughened wall. These small platelet aggregates became small clots of blood filling the lumen of the artery. Initially, all they did was cause partial obstruction to the flow of blood. But that obstruction caused the problem.

His windup and pitch, with their associated complete obstruction of the axillary artery, caused the same cessation of blood flow. The relaxation phase no longer did its job. There was still a recovery phase, but with only partial restoration of blood flow. The axillary artery was always partially obstructed. There was just not enough blood flow in those brief twenty-second respites to restore the missing glucose or the missing oxygen. And this went on pitch after pitch, inning after inning. J. R. was now like that man with angina running to catch a train. He could no more finish a game than that man could catch his train.

Then came his own private variant of a heart attack. The clots that had been forming in Richard's axillary artery, as a result of the recurrent battering it took every time he flung that baseball, suddenly expanded. Clots in the wrong place beget more clots. That's how normal coagulation works. When this happens, partial obstruction becomes complete obstruction. His arm was now dead. It had no blood pressure and very little blood flow. What to do?

He was developing collateral blood vessels that were supplying enough blood for most normal functions. He felt fine just as long as he did nothing strenuous with his right arm. Doing nothing much, however, was not his way of life. What would be considered "normal" function of his right arm was not what he did for a living.

The collateral flow was not good enough for him to pitch fastballs, but collaterals tend to increase with increased demand. Perhaps his would. At least enough to get him through the season, through the pennant race, and into the World Series. Richard, Niekro, and Ryan. Or the doctors could operate on him, although removing the clot was not an option since that rarely worked. The artery was too damaged for that. What was needed was an entirely new blood vessel, a bypass. That meant major vascular surgery.

The bypass graft might supply enough blood to his arm so that he could pitch again, and by the next year he would be back on the mound.

Think of the World Series! This was the Astros' year.

It was decided that they would watch and wait for a while. Perhaps nature would be kind to J. R. and the Astros. J. R. went back to the team and started working out again. It was like a second spring training designed to slowly increase those collaterals by slowly increasing the demand for blood. Pitch by pitch by pitch.

It was hard work. Torturous work. Slow work. But J. R. was a worker. He worked at it every day. It was harder than starting every fifth game, but he never once complained. He knew just what he wanted. Then tragedy turned into disaster.

On the morning of July 30, 1980, he went to see a chiropractor who manipulated his neck. That afternoon, while working out, J. R. became confused. He had a headache and felt weak. He couldn't see well. His left arm and leg didn't work the way they should. The left side of his face felt strange. Once again he was admitted to the hospital. Neurological examination confirmed that his left, nonpitching, arm was weak. It had lost sensation. He had trouble seeing to the left side, a left visual field defect. He still had no blood pressure in his right arm, but that was as expected.

The rest was not. Thirty-year-old, nonhypertensive, nonsmoking, nonobese J. R. Richard, the best pitcher in the National League, was having a stroke.

Another angiogram was performed. The clot had expanded. It had built up backward toward his heart and his aorta. More than that, parts of the thrombus had broken off and entered his right carotid artery. That artery supplies blood to the right side of the brain—or at least did before the clot screwed things up.

An operation was performed to remove as much of the offending clot as possible. This might not help make J. R. any better, but at least it would prevent any more clots from breaking off and causing more strokes. There was a lot of clot to remove, but in one sense the horse was already out of the barn. In fact, he was all the way off the farm. Richard had suffered a stroke. That wouldn't just go away, not overnight. It was time for rehabilitation. This is where William S. Fields, neurologist and recognized authority on strokes, became involved in his case.

Fields examined the pitcher neurologically. Richard's left side had improved slightly. J. R. could walk with only minimal difficulty, but he still had detectable weakness of both his left upper and lower extremities and the left side of his face. He had trouble seeing objects on the left side of his visual field. If there was only one object he was fine, but if there was one on the left and one on the right he only saw the one on the right. If there were both a batter and a catcher to see, he might only see one of them. Not a good thing for either the pitcher or the batter.

A CAT scan of Richard's brain showed that he had experienced three separate strokes from a shower of pieces broken off from that clot in his arterial system. And, of course, the arteries to his right arm remained obstructed, though the arm continued to be fed by collateral flow. But there was still not enough flow to pitch, much less recover between pitches.

It was decision time once again. J. R. needed and would get a bypass. The season was over. His Houston teammates had won their division championship. Niekro had again won twenty games, although Nolan Ryan had won only eleven. They played the Philadelphia Phillies in the five-game play-offs. Cy Young Award–winner Steven Carlton pitched the Phillies to victory in game one. All of the other games went into extra innings, and when Nolan Ryan could not hold a three-run lead in the eighth inning of the fifth game, the handwriting was on the wall. The Phillies won in the tenth. There would be no World Series for the Astros.

Surgery would not be easy. J. R. Richard was six feet eight inches tall. That meant that he needed a long bypass, much longer than usual. Segments of both of his external iliac arteries were taken out of his legs and replaced with synthetic grafts. These were then spliced into place as a single bypass. The procedure went well. J. R. now had normal blood pressure in his right arm, the same as in the left, and good blood flow.

On to rehabilitation. The outlook was good. The strength on his left side was almost back to normal. His vision came back more slowly. It was hard for him to see throws from his catcher to his left side. That made catching them all but impossible, but this, too, improved over time.

But he still wasn't ready to pitch in the major leagues. All of 1981 was spent in rehabilitation and so was 1982.

Things looked good for 1983. This was his year to make it back into the major leagues. Then came yet another setback. You were warned that this was more of a clinical case study than a sports biography. His left calf hurt whenever he walked or he ran or pitched. It felt cool. Even J. R. could tell that he had no pulse in his foot. That meant only one thing and it was not good. The synthetic graft in his left leg had closed off. That meant more vascular surgery.

Another bypass. In his left leg this time.

His career was over. His neurological exam by then had returned to normal. Strength, sensation, vision, depth perception, everything. All were normal. So much for the value of the neurological examination.

In writing up this clinical report, Fields discounted the possibility that the chiropractic manipulation had played any role in J. R.'s disability. There is no question that such manipulations of the neck can cause strokes. But those strokes do not take place in parts of the brain supplied by the carotid arteries. They occur in the back of the brain, in those regions supplied by the vertebral arteries. These arteries wind in and out of the vertebrae of the neck, hence their name. As they do that, they become susceptible to the sudden shearing action of a chiropractic manipulation. The carotids have a simpler course. Chiropractic manipulation does not injure them.

What happened to J. R. Richard was quite different. He had a fresh clot growing inside his right subclavian artery, a clot that was expanding back toward his heart. It had begun in his axillary artery and moved backward, or retrograde, into his subclavian artery. The right subclavian begins in the chest as a large trunk called the innominate artery, or the artery with no name. This comes directly off the aorta and divides into the right carotid artery and the right subclavian artery. In J. R., the clot had continued its retrograde expansion. It was advancing to the rear with a fresh, easily broken up clot attached to the better organized one further downstream. The clot now reached back into the innominate and then up the carotid, where pieces just happened to break off a couple of hours after manipulation of his neck and got sent crashing up into his brain.

Bill Fields was probably right. It was just a coincidence that it happened after the chiropractic manipulation. Perhaps I am just too damn skeptical of chiropractics at times.

Not all stories of pitchers with occlusions of their arteries end this tragically. Left-handed pitchers have a natural advantage here. There is no left innominate artery. The left common carotid artery comes directly off the aorta. Clots coming back retrograde from the left subclavian cannot break off and get into the left carotid. There is no risk of stroke. The medical literature contains a well-hidden but far happier tale with a far happier ending for a left-handed pitcher. This pitcher was none other than Edward Charles "Whitey" Ford, the man who broke Babe Ruth's record for most consecutive shutout innings pitched in the World Series. Ford's career began in 1950 when he was just twenty-one. He came up in midseason, started twelve games for the New York Yankees, and ended up with a record of nine wins and only one loss, helping the Yankees to win both the pennant and the World Series. Following two years in the service during the Korean War, Ford returned to the Yankees for good in 1953.

In his first thirteen seasons the Yankees made it into the World Series eleven times, interrupted only by the Cleveland Indians in 1954 and the Chicago White Sox in 1959. The Yankees won the World Series six times. For most of these seasons Ford was a major factor in winning the pennants as the pillar of the Yankee staff. Three times he led the American League in wins: 1955 with eighteen, 1961 with twenty-five, and 1963 with twenty-four. Three times he led in win-loss percentage (1956, 1961, and 1963), and twice in earned run average (1956 and 1958). He was a great pitcher. His lifetime win-loss percentage of .690 is the highest of any pitcher in the history of baseball. He never led the league in either strikeouts or lowest opponent batting average, but why quibble?

Quibble we did, though, we Chicago White Sox fans. To us Ford was little better than a glorified pansy. Between the years 1953 and 1960, he averaged a mere twenty-nine starts per season. In his youth, fellow Hall of Famer Bob Feller had averaged well over forty. In many of those years Ford completed ten games or fewer. Over that same time span, White Sox left-handed pitcher Billy Pierce completed an average of sixteen games per season, including at least one 1 to 0 loss to Ford almost every year. Sometimes two or three.

To us, Ford's arm was suspect. What else could we do but make such snide attacks? We could not win the pennant. Not when the opposition had Mantle and Berra and Ford and all the rest, but why go on?

In 1964 the Yankees won the pennant yet again. And the World Series. Ford won seventeen and lost six. Even Sox fans had to admit his greatness. In the previous four years he had improved to average thirty-seven starts and had even led the league in most innings pitched twice. The pansy had become a workhorse. And Bill Pierce had gone on to win a pennant for the San Francisco Giants.

Those last two years as the workhorse of the Yankee pitching staff had not been very much fun for Ford, nor had all that work been so easy for him. His arm started to feel fatigued in the late innings. Game after game he made a good showing, but he still only completed about a third of his starts. By those late innings, his arm ached. He could hardly toss those last pitches of the game. In the World Series it was even worse.

Ford went to Houston to be evaluated by a team of physicians, including noted cardiac and cardiovascular surgeon Denton Cooley. When first tested, Ford's blood pressure in the right arm was normal but in his left arm it was unobtainable. Shades of J. R. Richard fifteen years later. Only in Richard's case it was the other way around—Richard was a right-hander, not a lefty—déjà vu in reverse.

That, of course, is what the arteriogram revealed: a complete occlusion of the left axillary artery. Denton Cooley came to the rescue. But what should he do? Was it time for a bypass? Ford wanted to pitch the next season and so decided against it.

Cooley had an alternative plan: a sympathectomy. That would destroy control of the sympathetic nerves over the collateral vessels in Ford's left arm. It was a far simpler procedure and it might increase blood flow enough for him to pitch again. For a while at least.

Ford opted for a sympathectomy and it worked. In 1965 Ford never missed a start. He pitched two hundred forty-four innings. He won sixteen and lost thirteen, the most he ever lost in a season. And the Yankees did not win the pennant. They were not the team they had been. But Ford's arm felt stronger. It did not ache as much nor did it tire out as easily.

Wait 'til next year, everyone thought. The Yankees would be back. So would Whitey Ford. Except neither happened. Ford's arm got worse and he finally needed his bypass. The obstruction had progressed. He tossed in a few more games but he never really pitched again. The sympathectomy had bought him a year.

Thoracic outlet syndromes are not restricted to great pitchers. In fact, the reverse is more likely true. Great pitchers become great in part because they are less prone to this problem. The dimensions of the outlet vary from person to person, too. Those in whom there is the least amount of space never get to be even average pitchers, much less major leaguers. They give up pitching very early during their baseball experience. Significant thoracic outlet syndromes have been reported more often in teenagers pitching baseball than in major league pitching stars. Such teenage players usually become outfielders.

J. R. Richard did not undergo a sympathectomy after his right subclavian artery initially became blocked. He was not, as best as I can tell, ever offered this option, despite the fact that fifteen years earlier it had allowed Whitey Ford to once again become the workhorse of the Yankee staff. By 1980 it was generally known that sympathectomy was rarely, if ever, therapeutic in such cases. Fortunately, neither Denton Cooley nor Whitey Ford knew that in 1964.

Compression of structures within the thoracic outlet has long been a controversial subject in medicine. In patients such as J. R. Richard there can be very little doubt as to what happened or why it happened. Most patients don't throw fastballs for a living and most don't have overdeveloped shoulder muscles pulling their outlets shut with such enormous force. Some do have anatomical abnormalities that could push against the contents of the outlet. One of these could be a cervical rib. Normally, only the thoracic vertebrae have ribs; occasionally an individual has a rib on one of the cervical vertebrae, a cervical rib. If that patient has pain and numbness in the arm suggestive of compression of one of the nerves that traverses the thoracic outlet, perhaps that rib is compromising the thoracic outlet. Surgical removal of the offending rib, which is serving no other particular purpose, ought to be curative.

How can that conjecture be proved?

Enter Dr. Adson and his maneuver, designed to diagnose thoracic outlet syndromes. The way I learned the Adson maneuver, the seated patient elevates his arm laterally, palm up, until it is parallel to the ground but still in the plane of the body. At a ninety-degree angle to the floor. He then bends the elbow ninety degrees so that the forearm is now parallel to the spine and the hand is above the head. Next, he moves the shoulder back as far as he can until he looks just like a pitcher throwing a fastball almost fully overhand. The physician then feels for a pulse in the wrist. Is it still there or has it disappeared? Disappearance means that flow has been cut off in the subclavian artery. The more sophisticated variant involves listening to the subclavian artery in the neck and hearing a bruit, or murmur, as its blood flow is strangled. Off to the operating room and out with that cervical rib?

But that strangulation happens to patients without cervical ribs. It also happens to people without any symptoms at all. To pitchers who throw thousands of fastballs each season and never feel anything beyond the usual fatigue that comes with overuse of a muscle. To most of us, occasional numbness in a limb is a fact. Who among us hasn't awakened at night with one arm all but dead, stretched into an odd position and compressed by our own weight. Compression like that is normal. It's the price we pay for having freed our hands from carrying us around. It is only rarely an anatomical variant like the cervical rib that causes symptoms and needs to be treated. Unless you pitch for a living.

chapter 10

The Tenth Inning: Bruce Sutter

BLOOD VESSELS ARE NOT THE ONLY anatomical structures that can become entrapped as a result of trying to throw a baseball. Self-entrapment is a fairly common neurological problem. It has become part of our lives, even us nonpitchers of the modern world, as we engage in activities for which our bodies were not really selected. What usually gets entrapped are the peripheral nerves. After all, pitching is not the only recently invented human behavior that our bodies were not selected to perform. If only Darwin had been a bit more imaginative.

The increasingly ubiquitous carpal tunnel syndrome—that foe of workers, employers, and the workplace—is nothing more than an entrapment syndrome with its own name. It indicates compression of the median nerve as it passes through the carpal tunnel, leading from the forearm across the wrist into the palm of the hand. The carpal tunnel is a tight space without much room to spare. Anything that makes the space tighter or stretches the nerve more tautly against the tunnel's edges can cause trouble. The most common factors are simple trauma or injury to the wrist, and contorted, repetitive, or sustained postures that stretch the median nerve against the tunnel. What we now observe in keyboard operators was originally seen and described in cleaning ladies who scrubbed floors by hand. For some, this change in population at risk is what is meant by progress.

Why is carpal tunnel syndrome seen more commonly in women? Is it because of the nature of the jobs they are forced to perform, or could it be the nature of their bodies? There are differences between men and women. Women's wrists are smaller, hence so are their carpal tunnels, but their nerves are no thinner. As a result they have less room inside their smaller canals, less margin for error, less tolerance for stress. It is more anatomy than any other factor that seems to be the culprit.

Major league pitchers are all males and they neither scrub floors nor operate keyboards. They throw baseballs. Few pitchers ever threw better than star relief pitcher Bruce Sutter. Pitching for the Chicago Cubs and later for the St. Louis Cardinals, Sutter led all National League pitchers in games saved five times in the six years from 1979 through 1984. A relief pitcher is credited with a save if he enters the game with his team already in the lead and preserves that lead until the game is over. Sutter saved so well that he made the All-Star team four times. Pitching for the Cubs precluded any appearances in a World Series, but this was rectified almost immediately after he switched allegiance to St. Louis, a franchise that has never been allergic to postseason play.

Sutter was not a candidate for a thoracic outlet syndrome. He rarely pitched in a game long enough to compress his thoracic outlet so much that it made his arm ache or feel fatigued. In his over six hundred appearances as a major league pitcher, he pitched less than two innings per game. And in many of his best years, his typical appearance lasted just one inning. He never once was a starting pitcher. Yet he still fell victim to his own anatomy. Man was just not meant to pitch, and not only because of the dimensions of his thoracic outlet.

The thoracic outlet was not the only part of the upper body that was altered by the selection of bipedalism. That switch changed the forelimb into the upper limb. This could only be accomplished by changing both the structure and the function of the entire shoulder girdle. In its own simpler way, the shoulder girdle in humans is as unique as is humans' ability to speak. The ability of the shoulder joint to bear weight, along with its basic stability, has been sacrificed for increased mobility and versatility in movement. In humans, there are four pairs of muscles that have come to maintain the stability of the shoulder and to permit it to perform selective degrees of rotation. These are the muscles that make up the rotator cuff.

Injuries to these muscles are common in pitchers. The cuff wasn't built to do what pitchers do to it and with it. The rotator cuff muscles try to perform their selected degree of rotation and then stabilize the shoulder in that posture. It is the larger, stronger, external muscles of the shoulder that whip the arm around through this angle of rotation, producing the speed of the arm and then of the baseball on its lonesome way toward home plate and the enemy batter. The shear forces that these external muscles exert on the muscles of the rotator cuff are enormous, and they are exerted each and every time the pitcher throws a fastball. Bruce Sutter rarely threw anything other than fastballs. His specialty, the pitch that made him the outstanding relief pitcher of his day, was a variant of the standard fastball known as the split-fingered fastball. Most of his pitches were split-fingered fastballs. That made him a perfect candidate for a rotator cuff tear, a shearing lesion of one of his rotator cuff muscles.

It never happened to him.

Instead, Sutter's arm began to hurt every time he tried to pitch, every time he cocked his arm back in order to throw his fastball. Every time. Even the first pitch as he warmed up. And it was no simple ache. It was a sharp, shooting pain in his shoulder bone. To Sutter that pain meant no more pitching. No more appearances even as short as one inning and certainly no more saves.

To neurologists, that sort of pain means one thing and one thing only. That pain comes from direct involvement of a nerve. Direct compression. But which nerve and why?

It was not a simple question; a number of nerves innervate the various muscles of the shoulder. Examination of Sutter's shoulder girdle and the muscles that control its movements showed that one of the shoulder muscles of his rotator cuff was weak and atrophied. This was the infraspinatus muscle, located below the spine of the shoulder bone. It is innervated by the suprascapular nerve, located above the shoulder blade. Stretching or compressing that nerve would cause shooting, electric-like pain, just like the pain that had sidelined Bruce Sutter.

Bingo. But where was the nerve being compressed, and why had it happened?

The why was the easy part. As the scapula rotated into its present position as part of the transition to bipedalism, it took its nerves along with it. As a result, some of these nerves follow twisted, tortuous courses that bring them dangerously close to various bones and notches in these bones, so close that extreme stretching could rub a nerve against one of these bones. The suprascapular nerve has just such a complex course that makes it susceptible to stretching. And there is no extreme stretching of the upper extremity quite like that of cocking an arm to hurl a fastball. Unless it is reaching back to serve a volleyball. Injury to this same nerve was reported in a volleyball player before it happened to Bruce Sutter.

The only question left was where along its tortuous course the suprascapular nerve was being compressed. The first surgeon looked in the commonest site for such injury. The surgery was a complete success, but the pain was still there. Sutter still could not pitch.

About six months later, Sutter was evaluated at the University of Colorado by neurologist Steven P. Ringel. Sutter's infraspinatus muscle was still weak and shrunken. The pain had not gone away. Steve, who was one of my first residents, was certain that the first surgery had been the right operation but in the wrong place, and after careful study a second freeing up of the suprascapular nerve was carried out.

It worked. Although the nerve injury was permanent and the infraspinatus remained weak and shrunken, the pain disappeared. Bruce Sutter, after over a year and a half of being totally incapacitated, was once again able to pitch.

He pitched for one more season and rang up another fourteen saves. He had only managed three in the season that had been ended by the pain. All in all, it was not a bad year for a thirty-five-year-old relief pitcher who was thought to have been washed up two years earlier.

Flying Like a Butterfly: Wilma Rudolph

HOLLYWOOD MADE A MOVIE of the life of Wilma Rudolph, one of the greatest female track stars America has ever produced; and well they should have, for hers was a life made for the movies. Her story tops that of Cinderella or Snow White or Pocahontas. None of them had anything on her. In many ways her life story was far better and far more dramatic. Wilma Rudolph rose up from the poverty of the rural South to become an Olympic Gold Medal winner. While myriads of athletes have overcome poverty, Wilma triumphed over poverty complicated by an attack of polio that left her with a weakened and twisted right leg. Despite this handicap, she became the fastest woman in the world and the first American woman to win three Olympic Gold Medals in track. Her life story was certainly the stuff of fairy tales and Hollywood movies.

Wilma Rudolph, an African-American, was born in 1940 in St. Bethlehem, a small town in rural Tennessee. That was supposed to have been an Olympic year, the games having been scheduled to be held in Tokyo. In retrospect, that makes for interesting speculation as to the politics of Olympic scheduling, with Berlin in 1936 followed by Tokyo in 1940. Another example of freedom, democracy, and the moral authority of pure amateurism at work for the benefit of all. But the Olympics were not what they had once been. In ancient Greece, wars were suspended so that the games could be held. In our modern world it is the games that are suspended. In 1940 this was because of the war raging in Europe and Asia. Needless to say there were also no Olympic Games in 1944. The next Olympics were held in London in 1948, three years after V-J Day.

Wilma was the twentieth of twenty-two children in her family. When she was still an infant, the family moved to Clarksville, Tennessee, where Wilma grew up. Her father did odd jobs and worked as a railroad porter. Her mother, aside from raising her children, also cleaned "white people's houses." Wilma estimated that her parents never made more than $2,500 in a single year, but the family was entirely self-sufficient. There was no welfare for them; they were far too proud for that. The Rudolphs were a family that took care of their own.

When Wilma was still a very young girl she developed a number of serious illnesses. Neither the number nor the sequence of illnesses is entirely clear, nor the true nature of the diagnoses. The unsophisticated medical care available to her as a poor black child living on the impoverished side of Clarksville, Tennessee, during World War II may well mean that no one ever really knew for certain. Wilma herself was probably too young at the time to be a reliable witness. In her autobiography, *The Story of Wilma Rudolph*, the evidence is far from clear-cut. She tells of a series of childhood maladies including scarlet fever, whooping cough, double pneumonia (which she was said to have had twice), chicken pox, measles, and acute infantile paralysis.

Polio! That was undoubtedly the most dreaded infectious disease in America during the forties and fifties. Anyone who was alive during the era of the annual polio epidemics recalls the vivid, chilling image of the ravages wrought by this unseen enemy. Franklin Delano Roosevelt had been transformed from a vigorous, athletic man into one who was all but bound to a wheelchair. Even so, the true extent of FDR's disability was not fully appreciated by most Americans. Though he had only minimal use of his legs, and could not stand or walk without support, FDR never permitted photographs of himself in his wheelchair. He was only photographed sitting or standing, with the discreet support of others.

Other images from the age of polio were far more frightening. There were children and teenagers being transported to hospitals by ambulances when general use of ambulance trips was few and far between. Some children died. Others became confined to iron lungs because they could no longer breathe for themselves. Their confinement often lasted for years, only to end all too often with a fatal attack of double pneumonia. Those who were lucky recovered to the point where they could breathe without the help of an iron lung, yet were still disabled by varying degrees of weakness and paralysis. All too often they had shriveled arms or legs.

When I was growing up it seemed as if one day you could be playing baseball with your friends and the next day you could be paralyzed for life. In Chicago, every summer, you had to stay away from crowds, especially the crowds at the beach. Otherwise polio might get you. Clarksville was no safer, no more protected from the onslaught of polio in 1944 than any other town in the country.

Wilma was never taken to a hospital. Ambulances rarely came to that part of town. Fortunately, she never needed an iron lung. She did, however, develop paralysis of her right leg and her right foot turned in. The exact age at which Wilma became stricken is also hard to confirm. Her polio must have occurred during early childhood, for in none of her interviews and reminiscences does she ever relate not remembering that crooked leg. It was certainly there long before she entered school. In order to walk, she had to wear a brace. This was not a very promising beginning for a future Olympic champion.

Our knowledge of polio as an epidemic disease, as a recurrent plague, is restricted to less than two centuries. In this sense, polio is thought of as a modern disease. In reality, polio isn't a new disease and almost undoubtedly has been occurring since at least ancient times. Ruma, an Egyptian priest of the eighteenth dynasty, is portrayed on a stele with a withered and crooked leg, the typical residuals of polio. That dynasty ruled Egypt at the time of the incursions of the Hyksos, during the fourteenth and fifteenth centuries B.C., some thirty-five hundred years ago. But the ancients who chronicled all sorts of human disasters recorded no epidemics that resembled polio. In fact, no epidemics were ever recognized until the second half of the nineteenth century.

By the late eighteenth century, occasional cases of infantile paralysis were a part of life. One eighteen-month-old child, who was to grow up and become the great writer Sir Walter Scott, had an attack of polio. He became affected with a fever that was thought to be due to teething, but on the fourth day of his febrile illness he lost the use of his right leg. He was left with permanent weakness of that leg. Later in life, he described his "rehabilitation": "The impatience of a child soon inclined me to struggle with my infirmity, and I began by degrees to stand, to walk, to run. Although the limb affected was much shrunk and contracted [shades of both Ruma and Wilma] my general health which was of more importance, was much strengthened by being frequently in the open air, and, in a word, I, who in the city had probably been condemned to hopeless decrepitude was now healthy, high-spirited and my lameness apart, a sturdy child." It is a perfect sketch of a young child left with a paralysis of one leg from an attack of polio.

Sporadic incidences of this disease had become well recognized by the early nineteenth century. The first recorded epidemic, however, was reported in Norway in 1868. Others quickly followed throughout Western Europe, and this phase in the natural history of the disease finally crossed the Atlantic and caused the first American epidemic in the 1890s, just in time for the four hundredth anniversary of the arrival of Columbus in the New World and the transportation of syphilis back to the old one. A fair trade of sorts.

As soon as these epidemics appeared, infantile paralysis was recognized as an infectious disease, a form of contagion, spreading from the sick to the well or from some infected source to the well. The last third of the nineteenth century was the heyday for the study of infectious or contagious diseases. In part, this was one of the benefits of applied technology. The microscope had come into its own and through the use of this instrument those two fields of medicine most dependent on its practical application, pathology and bacteriology, exploded into prominence. Pathology used microscopy to examine tissues and explain what was happening in the body, while bacteriology searched for the causes of the changes that were observed by the pathologists. These twin approaches resulted in a revolution in our understanding of most human diseases. Microscopic examination could even show exactly what changed in the nervous system in patients with neurological maladies.

What, then, is polio? *Polio* is short for poliomyelitis, or to be more scientifically complete, anterior polioencephalomyelitis, which is clearly a mouthful. The *itis* is a term that comes directly from pathology, meaning inflammation. Under the microscope, the involved tissue is flooded by white blood cells, which are there to fight off infection.

But what tissue? Since paralysis is a hallmark of this form of "itis," then the nervous system must be the site or sites of the inflammation or infection. The question then reduces itself to where in the nervous system the infection occurs to cause paralysis.

Encephalo is the root term for brain, hence encephalitis means inflammation of the brain. In polio, this inflammation is usually most prominent in the brain stem, that part of the hind brain that connects the cerebral hemispheres with the spinal cord. The lower two-thirds of the brain stem is shaped much like the bulb of a tulip in bloom, and thus is frequently referred to as the bulb. Polio can be restricted to just this part of the brain, a condition called bulbar polio. This is the most dreaded of all forms of polio. The bulb is not a trivial relay station. Those groups of neurons that direct and control the muscles of respiration are found here. It is the bulbar form of polio that causes failure of the muscles of respiration and with that an inability to breathe, resulting in life in an iron lung.

Iron lungs are now a thing of the past, but in their day they were a great advance. It was an advance that we have fortunately progressed well beyond, much as we have gone beyond artificial respiration based on compressing the wall of the chest. Today we know that mouth-to-mouth resuscitation is far more efficient, but we didn't know that then. Why, I have no idea. The scenario is all too familiar from old movies and TV shows. Someone nearly drowns, most often the staple Hollywood heroine or some other buxom young lady. Her heart is still beating but she's not breathing. No air containing oxygen is entering her body, no air filled with carbon dioxide is being removed. What to do? Move the chest wall; reproduce the movements of respiration. Artificial respiration does not do that, of course, since most of the expansion and contraction of the lungs during normal breathing is due to movement of the diaphragm. But moving the chest wall was all we could think to do (even though the prophet Isaiah had breathed life into the son of the Shulamite woman by mouth-to-mouth respiration, not by pushing on his chest). So, like the hero of those Hollywood B movies, we pushed on the wall of the chest and moved the bad air out. Then we relaxed our pressure, allowing the wall of the chest to expand and pull in the good air.

It had an element of logic to it, but the process was not very efficient, since very little air was being moved. That, however, was the model, so iron lungs were designed to do the same. Large tubelike structures fit around the patient from the neck down. They were airtight and attached to a pump that would increase the pressure around the body to compress the chest wall and the lungs and expel the bad air. Then it would pump air out of the iron lung, creating a vacuum that would expand and pull good air into the lungs.

That was the process. Over and over and over again. Ten times a minute. Sixty minutes each hour. Twenty-four hours a day. That was life in an iron lung.

Wilma Rudolph flying like a butterfly. Her legs show no evidence of her battle with polio.

Fortunately for most patients, the situation was not a permanent one. Some of the cells that controlled automatic respiration eventually recovered. Often, enough of them recovered so the patient could breathe on his own outside the iron lung.

What is *myelitis*? Myelitis is inflammation of the spinal cord. It, too, can contribute to respiratory failure because the nerve cells that control the diaphragm start in the spinal cord.

That leaves only the most recognized and fearful of all the terms. What does *polio* actually mean? *Polio* is the Greek word for "gray" and is a term that comes from anatomy, especially microscopic anatomy. The brain and the spinal cord are composed of two types of tissues. The first is called the gray matter and consists of collections of nerve cells such as the layers of cortex covering the cerebral hemispheres and the cerebellum, as well as the large groups of nerve cells deep within the brain. The other part of the central nervous system is the white matter, which consists of tracts that connect the gray areas with one another and with the world outside the brain and spinal cord. Any infection of the white matter of the brain is called a leukoencephalitis, for *leuko* is derived from the Greek word for "white." Infections of the nuclear structure deep inside the brain in the gray matter are called polioencephalitis.

Now we have pretty much put it together. Wilma had poliomyelitis. The name describes precisely what has taken place. It was her spinal cord that was the site of her infection, more specifically, the gray cells of her spinal cord. But not all of the gray cells are equally involved in polio; it is only the motor cells that become infected. If polio occurs in the upper part of the spinal cord, it causes paralysis in the hands or arms. Polio in the cervical, or neck, portion of the cord can also cause respiratory failure, since the diaphragm and other respiratory muscles are directly innervated by the cells that live here and receive their orders from the brain stem respiratory centers. Polio of the lower part of the cord causes weakness in the legs.

Within the spinal cord, all the gray matter is found in the center, and the white matter surrounds it. This is just the opposite of the hemispheres of the brain where gray matter covers the surface. The spinal gray matter forms an H-shaped structure and the limbs of this H are called horns. The motor cells are all located in the front or anterior horns, while the sensory cells are in the posterior horns. So the polio attack that paralyzed Wilma Rudolph has an even more complete name, anterior poliomyelitis, occurring in her lower spinal cord.

Inexplicably, polio attacks only the motor cells and never the sensory cells of the spine. The two anterior horns, one on each side of the spinal cord, supply the two legs. The one on the left goes to the left. The one on the right, the site of Wilma's polio, goes to the muscles of the right leg. As separate as they are functionally, these two horns are less than a centimeter apart. In Wilma's case the polio was so specific that it weakened only one of her legs.

That is the nature of the beast that causes polio. Viruses often attack very specific cells. Look at the AIDS virus. It does not attack all white cells, not even all lymphocytes or all immune cells, but specific subsets of T cells, the AIDS-specific subsets of T cells. In much the same manner, the polio virus attacks only motor neurons, and in the spinal cord this attack is almost always far more marked on one side of the cord than the other. This asymmetry has long been known and was, before the development of virology, one of the keys to making a correct diagnosis.

There is little question as to the correctness of the diagnosis in Wilma Rudolph's case. What had transpired was an attack of classic asymmetric anterior poliomyelitis. What it left behind was a little girl with a weakened, deformed right leg. For years it was never a question of Wilma learning to run; the problem was walking. Ruma had recovered from polio to become a priest and Scott had survived to become a writer. But neither of those occupations required much running.

Today we automatically connect the word *polio* with its cause, the polio virus. That was true when Wilma fell ill and had even been true some twenty years earlier when Franklin Roosevelt fell victim to the same disease. The discovery that polio is caused by a virus did not come easily or quickly. Today, with our impatience at the seemingly slow progress of medical research, it is important to recall the timetable of one of the greatest success stories in the history of modern medicine, namely, the elimination of epidemic polio. It took about one hundred years from the first epidemic to the last one. Scientific progress in this endeavor was closely tied to both technical advances and intellectual leadership. The technical advances started with the application of the microscope and the various techniques of bacteriology. The intellectual impetus was supplied by Louis Pasteur in France and Robert Koch in Germany. Pasteur's accomplishments were legion: the rabies vaccine, the proof that anthrax bacillus caused anthrax, the demonstration that spontaneous generation did not occur. Koch made a simpler and, in many ways, more profound contribution.

One of the problems that faced early bacteriologists was that bacteria were everywhere. They were in the throats of patients with scarlet fever. They abounded in the throats of patients with diphtheria. And they thrived in the throats of patients with no diseases whatsoever. The mere presence of bacteria did not mean disease. Nor did their presence in a diseased patient mean that they were causing that particular disease.

This is where Robert Koch stepped in and proposed a logical process designed to prove that a particular bacteria caused a particular disease.

Step 1.   The bacteria had to be isolated and identified in patients with one specific disease.

Step 2.   A pure culture of that bacteria had to be harvested.

Step 3.   That pure culture of bacteria, when given to a recipient (usually an appropriate experimental animal), had to cause the same disease.

Step 4.   The same bacteria then had to be isolated from this diseased subject.

This train of reasoning became known and revered as Koch's postulates. Using this approach, the causes of contagious diseases such as anthrax, brucellosis, cholera, and diphtheria were quickly identified. Tuberculosis was identified by Koch himself. Most of the important diseases of the day were traced: plague, typhoid fever, and even syphilis and leprosy. But not polio. A great deal was learned about the disease but not its cause. No matter how hard the bacteriologists tried, no bacteria could be found. By 1905, it was suggested that the primary infection did not take place in the brain, but in the gastrointestinal tract, and that in most people that's all that ever happened. In other words, most people infected with whatever it was that caused polio only developed a mild infection of the gut, a gastroenteritis, a summer flu, nothing more. These not very sick patients could spread the disease even if they never got classic polio. The next person in the chain, however, might.

Where to go from there? No bacteria could be identified or isolated. What to do? The answer was to short-circuit Koch. Sidestep the postulates. Polio was contagious. To prove it, all that had to be done was to go from step 1 to step 3 without ever going through step 2. This was accomplished by Landsteiner and Popper in 1909. They took brain tissue from fatal human cases of polio and injected that tissue into the brains of monkeys. The monkeys came down with polio, proving the disease could be transferred. It was contagious. Polio was not, however, caused by a bacteria but by a "filterable" particle, or virus, that was too small to be seen under a microscope. It was this virus that went from person to person, causing few if any clinical symptoms in most, and devastating disease in a very few.

Wilma Rudolph was one of the unlucky few. Wilma's recovery from her paralysis started slowly. She missed all of kindergarten and first grade. She needed a heavy steel brace in order to stand and walk and to keep her leg and foot as straight as possible. She would put it on as soon as she got up in the morning and she wasn't supposed to take it off until she went to bed at night. It was far better than an iron lung, but to Wilma it was just as disabling. She hated it. It made her stand out as a freak. She wanted nothing in life more than to get rid of that steel brace and those ugly brown oxfords, the only shoes she could wear with it. No girl wanted to wear such ugly shoes all the time.

There was only one way that this was ever going to happen: work, work, work. Today we call it rehabilitation, but the essence is still the same. Wilma was a worker with a goal. Her initial goal was to live her life as a normal kid without a brace and wear gym shoes not brown oxfords. It was a work ethic that would serve her well later in life in her athletic pursuits. She came to believe that goals could be set, and if she worked hard enough and long enough they could be reached. Not all at once, but eventually. Hard work did pay off even if you couldn't see any rewards for a long time.

Recovery from polio is a very complex process and occurs in two very different phases. The first is the acute recovery phase. The virus has attacked the motor neurons and overwhelmed them, resulting in acute paralysis. Most often there is complete paralysis of the muscles involved. Perhaps one leg. Perhaps an arm. Perhaps breathing. Bring on that iron lung.

The body begins to respond. It counterattacks with white blood cells and then specific antibodies, which immobilize and defeat those filterable viruses. The infection is over. The inflammatory response cools off. The motor cells begin to function once again. If they were merely overwhelmed but not seriously injured, recovery can come about surprisingly quickly. In two or three weeks, those stunned cells often recover much of their function, if not all of it.

The patient whose life was saved by that iron lung starts to breathe on his own. His own muscles can once again be directed to move the chest wall in and out. The patient can be taken off that iron lung. A life saved.

The second phase of recovery is far slower and involves motor cells that have been more seriously injured. These motor neurons are not just in a state of shock; their metabolism has all but come to a standstill, taken over by the foreign invader. For that's what viruses do, take over the cell's metabolism and use it to make more viruses. It's a form of survival of the smallest. Nerve cells that are injured in this way respond in a peculiar way. The motor cells that have been invaded by the polio viruses each have a long process that extends from the cell body all the way to the muscle it innervates. A motor cell of the spinal cord that innervates a muscle of the foot has an axon that is three feet long or longer. The axons carry the message from the cell bodies to the muscle and do very little else. They contain no proteins and no enzymes. Their metabolic needs must be supplied by the metabolism of the cell body of the motor neuron.

When the metabolism of the neuron fails, it is the axon that is most susceptible. It has the longest and most vulnerable line of supply. Soon the axon is not getting the energy and nutrients it needs and it starts to die, not all at once but from the far end back toward the cell body. This process is called dying back. By the time the cell body begins to recover from polio, the axon may have died back all the way to the cell body. Regrowth and regeneration can occur, but this is a slow process. The cell membrane, the membrane of the axon, can only be built in the cell body. It is estimated that a totally normal neuron, one not recovering from an invasion of polio virus but responding to a physical injury to its axon, can only regenerate the axon at a rate of one millimeter a day. A neuron that has been invaded by viral particles and has just regained control of its own injured metabolic processes—and may well recover to less than its normal robust condition—may support new axonal regrowth at an even slower rate.

If the axon is two feet long, that is well over five hundred millimeters. It could easily take a year or two for regrowth.

What happens to the muscles in the meantime? A muscle without its nerve withers and dies. This is true no matter what causes the muscle to lose its neuronal input. Death of the nerve from whatever cause results in a shrunken, atrophied muscle. The nerve, it seems, has two separate functions. It causes the muscle to contract and thereby produces movement, and it keeps the muscle alive, a trophic or nutritive function. Deprived of this function, the muscle cannot survive. In Wilma Rudolph's right leg, the muscles didn't survive. The result was the weak, crooked leg and turned-in foot. A leg that required a brace to keep it straight.

That is not the worst part. Some motor nerve cells can never recover and so die. And in the brain and spinal cord death is forever. If some liver cells die, others will reproduce and replace them. Not the motor cells. There is no recovery. No regeneration.

What to do? Work. Rehabilitation. And since you can't tell whether the cells will recover or not, you work that much harder. For a goal that cannot be guaranteed.

The recovery process begins almost as soon as the disease does. Here is where the brace comes in; it does more than just support a weakened joint. It prevents deformity. The brace keeps the joint in a normal position so that the shrunken muscle cells cannot turn into a fibrous band of connective tissue that would freeze the limb into an abnormal position. But it takes more than a brace to do that. Here's where Wilma's family stepped in. Her mother and an older sister would apply heat to her leg, and then they would move and massage the leg. By doing this, unknowingly perhaps, they helped her maintain a full range of motion in her joints by keeping those muscle fibers fully stretched.

When Wilma was six and still not walking any better, it was time to try to do more. She started a four-year series of treatments at Meharry Medical School in Nashville. Meharry was one of only two black medical schools in the entire country. These two schools supplied the bulk of America's black doctors. In Tennessee, Meharry also took a lead in tending to the needs of the state's poor black population. The school offered services that were hard, if not impossible, for blacks to find elsewhere. One of these was rehabilitation from polio.

Wilma's mother took her to Meharry. For the first two years, Wilma traveled to Meharry twice a week. It was a fifty-mile bus ride each way, in the back of the bus. This was the late 1940s; the buses in Tennessee were segregated. Wilma never went alone; her mother or an aunt always went with her. It was a full day's excursion, including four hours of work for Wilma and her therapist. What Wilma remembered about those sessions was the constant turning and twisting and pulling of her right leg, the hot whirlpools, and the traction. All of these were designed to do one thing and one thing only—stretch those muscle cells so that when the nerves finally grew back the muscles could respond and restore her strength.

The use of heat and rehabilitation in polio dated back to the 1920s when an Australian nurse, Sister Kenny, observed that hot packs helped to relieve muscle spasms caused by polio and to prevent permanent fibrous contractions. This became the basis of the "Sister Kenny method" and became widely adopted. The method not only helped the patients but it also revolutionized attitudes toward the entire concept of rehabilitation. Sister Kenny herself became very controversial. She refused to believe that polio was a disease of the nervous system or that there was any permanent paralysis. She felt that the muscles were "alienated" by the disease and that her treatment of the muscles always cured the disease. That's right, *always*, as in one hundred percent of the time. Such unscientific and insupportable claims hurt her cause, but the stimulation she gave to the role of rehabilitation was a major step in the right direction.

The unanswered question was whether rehabilitation would change Wilma's disability. It didn't change everyone's life, despite Sister Kenny's claims. Would Wilma's nerve cells grow back?

Recovery wasn't to happen overnight. Or even over a month of nights. Wilma never gave up, nor did her family. Progress or not, the trips continued. Weeks became months and months turned into years. But over the years, the first signs of progress occurred. They were the beginning of her personal miracle. All that hard work was finally paying a dividend just as Wilma began to grow. When you grow your nerves also grow—they have to. They still have to get from the spinal cord to the foot, and that distance becomes greater. How does that growth happen? The body produces factors that produce this growth. These are called nerve growth factors (NGFs). As Wilma began to grow, her body began to produce NGFs and these NGFs did their job. Not only did the nerves of her healthy left leg grow so that they accommodated her increasing height—which came to be six feet—but the nerves in her abnormal right leg grew as well. The bones there were growing and so were the nerves.

Did all her neurons recover? That's hard to tell. NGFs do two things. They cause growth of the axons and they also cause sprouting of those axons. It may be that virtually all of Wilma's nerves recovered and grew to innervate her muscles once again. More likely, some of her nerves had died but the others that recovered produced new sprouts and these new sprouts reached those muscle cells that were waiting to be reinnervated. Once there, these new sprouts from old neurons took over the role of the dead cells. All of Wilma's muscles now had nerves and were ready to go to work.

At nine and a half, Wilma walked into church for the first time without her brace. It was a personal triumph. She still needed the brace at times, but less and less often. She still wore those ugly brown oxfords, but they too would soon be discarded. It was a great step in her progress and every night her work continued: stretching, massages, hot baths, more stretching.

At ten she was discharged from the clinic at Meharry. She was on her own. There were no more long rides in the back of the buses. By the time she was twelve, she gave up the brace altogether. She was now entering seventh grade. It would be a new year in a new school, the first year of a new life, a life as a normal kid who wanted to try one thing she had never done. She wanted to play basketball. It looked like fun to her.

That was 1952, another Olympic year. The games were held in Helsinki, Finland. The U.S. track and field team performed brilliantly, led by future senator Bob Mathias. For the second consecutive time, Mathias won the decathlon. Wilma was not thinking about those games or the 1956 games scheduled to be held in Melbourne, Australia. She was only twelve. Her family had no TV set. She had no idea that the Olympic Games had ever been held.

From here the story moves into high gear. It's almost as if a Hollywood director, or at least a Hollywood writer, had stepped in. Wilma did more than play basketball in junior high school and high school. She became the star of the team, and when the school took up track so did she. She never lost a race in high school. In ninth grade she regularly ran in five events, ranging from fifty to two hundred meters, and won them all. She soon gained the attention of Ed Temple, the women's track coach at Tennessee State University. With his coaching advice and encouragement, she tried out for the U.S. Olympic team. She was still only fifteen; she would not turn sixteen until the time of the games themselves.

The tryouts were held in Seattle, Washington. The women athletes from Tennessee would travel there by car. That was better than a segregated bus ride. Coach Temple drove Wilma along with members of the Tennessee State University team, including senior Mae Faggs, who had won medals in those 1952 games that Wilma had not seen. Faggs took young Wilma under her wing. Wilma qualified in the two hundred meter dash and as a member of the relay team. She was fifteen and had overcome polio to become a member of the U.S. Olympic team.

So Wilma was off to Melbourne to compete for the gold, but she didn't win any gold. She did win a medal, though, a bronze, as a member of the four hundred meter relay team. She was disappointed, but she now had a new goal to aim for. She was very good at setting and reaching goals. The star of those games, among the women, was an Australian named Betty Cuthbert. Betty had won three track events: one hundred meter, two hundred meter, and four hundred meter. If Betty Cuthbert could win three gold medals there was no reason at all why, she, Wilma, couldn't. And she was willing and ready to work for four years to accomplish that goal.

The next games were to be held in 1960 in Rome. She would be nineteen, not a scared teenager but a seasoned veteran. She vowed to herself that she would be back in Rome, and she was.

The 1960 Olympics were not a happy one for the U.S. track and field teams. The men's team was in disarray. Everything seemed to be going wrong. There was bickering between athletes, friction between athletes and officials, low morale, bad luck, missed buses from the Olympic village to the stadium resulting in missed competition and medals, and poor performances. The heavily favored American team, which had won fifteen gold medals in track and field just four years earlier, won only three of the first eleven events.

Then it was Wilma's turn to run and she was set on reversing the trend. She had never run better or more consistently. On her way to the Olympics, she had set a world record of 22.9

seconds in the two hundred meter dash. It was a record that would hold for eight years. Wilma reversed the trend her team had set. She did it so well that she became the star of the games, hailed by the French as "La Chattanooga Choo-Choo."

She won her three gold medals. That had been her goal and she had accomplished it, becoming the first American woman to win three golds in track and field in the same Olympics. She won all three medals with real style. In the one hundred meter dash, she tied the world record of 11.3 seconds while winning her preliminary heat. In the two hundred meter, she won by tying the Olympic record. In the four hundred meter relay, she and her Tennessee State University teammates set a world record in their semifinal heat, and in the finals Wilma came from behind to grab the gold medal.

Honor after honor came to her, topped by the Sullivan Award as the nation's outstanding amateur athlete—male or female.

Wilma's accomplishments did not end there. When her running days were over she taught school for a while, but her interest in athletics persisted. She became assistant director of athletes for the Mayor's Youth Foundation in Chicago. She was very active in the Women's Sports Foundation and lobbied hard for the passage of Title IX, the law requiring equal treatment for women in college sports. She helped establish the Track and Field Hall of Fame in Charleston, South Carolina.

She even found time to set the record straight. In 1969, a communist newspaper in Rome wrote that, because of the way blacks were treated in the United States, Wilma was living in poverty and had to pawn her Olympic Gold Medals in order to buy food for her four starving children. Wilma was incensed. She flew to Rome to set the record straight. She told reporters there that she was not in poverty. She was not wealthy but she was rich in both freedom and opportunities.

Later, she settled in Indianapolis and started her own not-for-profit organization, the Wilma Rudolph Foundation, to promote amateur sports. After all, she knew what good foundations could do. There was no more polio in the United States and very little left anywhere in the world. In no small part, this was due to the efforts of the National Foundation for Infantile Paralysis (the March of Dimes), which had done so much to develop an organized program of research to eradicate the disease.

The elimination of polio, the end to those annual epidemics with their legacy of iron lungs and withered limbs, didn't happen overnight. Landsteiner and Popper had shown in 1909 that the disease could be transmitted. It wasn't until forty years later that it was known that polio was not caused by a single virus but by three separate strains of virus, and that all three could be isolated and grown in tissue culture. This was going back to Koch's work, but it was a miraculous advance that won the Nobel Prize in Physiology or Medicine for a doctor named Enders. Once you could grow the three strains in a pure culture, you could grow enough virus to make a vaccine. That could be done in one of two ways. The easiest and quickest would be to grow the viruses and kill them, and then inject the killed virus into the patient, hoping that the antigens would still be potent enough to provoke the production of antibodies to the virus itself. The production of antibodies would then produce immunity. That is what the team led by Jonas Salk did; and by 1954 and 1955 this killed virus vaccine was being used throughout the United States. The epidemics of polio became part of our past.

The other, slower, approach to eliminating polio was to produce an attenuated virus. This would be a live polio virus, which by passage through other hosts became attenuated or weakened so that it could no longer cause paralytic disease. The live but attenuated virus would enter the body and stimulate an immune response just like the natural, nonattenuated virus did. That would bring about lifelong immunity. No one had ever been infected by the polio virus twice. This research was done by Sabin and Koprowski and others. Such live vaccines were introduced in 1960 and over time replaced the Salk vaccine. Wherever these vaccines are appropriately used, polio has disappeared; no more epidemics and no more occasional cases.

Polio had never been just an epidemic disease that suddenly burst out and just as suddenly disappeared, like bubonic plague. Unlike the Black Death, it was also endemic, a disease that was always there. It had withered the leg of Ruma, the ancient Egyptian priest. Why in the nineteenth century had it changed and become an epidemic disease? It was a change in social conditions that changed polio from an endemic disorder to an epidemic disorder. The endemic disorder existed where people had not assured the cleanliness of their water supply. Under such conditions polio would spread rapidly and everyone would get the virus early in life. Such early infection has two advantages: the battle with the disease is usually trivial (only a small percentage of infants ever became paralyzed), and it is followed by lifelong immunity. Contact later in life is far more malignant and far more likely to cause paralysis. In regions of the world with poor standards of sanitation, most five-year-olds already have antibodies to all three strains of polio virus, clear evidence of already having the three viruses in their bodies.

Changes in living conditions and improved sanitation, ironically, caused the shift from mild endemic to terrifying epidemic polio as we knew it during the first half of this century. This may well explain why polio epidemics appeared as a new disease in the 1860s. Obviously, this should not be taken as a condemnation of sanitation. While our greatest medical advance remains separation of feces (especially, but not exclusively, our own) from the water supply, doing so left us prey to diseases to which we had previously built immunities through constant exposure.

Wilma Rudolph died in 1994, when only fifty-four years old, of a brain tumor. She is still remembered as a graceful runner and inspiring woman, one of the relatively few recent American athletes who gave back far more than they received. "When I ran," she said, "I felt like a butterfly." Unfortunately, butterflies are never with us as long as we want them to be.

The Four-Minute Neurologist: Roger Bannister

THERE ARE TWO SPORTS TRIVIA questions I ask to spark up what otherwise promise to be rather uninteresting lectures. The first is the identity of the only baseball player who played five years in the major leagues, enough time to qualify for the major league pension plan, and has both a Ph.D. (in neuroscience, no less) and an M.D. The second is the identity of the only neurologist alive and practicing today who will still be remembered one hundred years from now.

The second question often falls on deaf ears, although nowhere near as frequently as the first. Any failure of response all but contradicts any notion of validity. The answer to the second question, of course, is Sir Roger Bannister. He will not be remembered for his contributions to neurology, although they have not been insignificant. Bannister will be remembered because he was the first man to run a mile in under four minutes—the first four-minute miler. That had been one of the most illusive goals in all of sports for the first half of the twentieth century, and this medical student from England was the one who reached it. In light of what has happened in track and most other "amateur" athletic fields, the most fascinating aspect of his accomplishment is that he could have done it while he was still a full-time medical student. That could not happen today.

By now, well over four hundred men have run a mile in less than four minutes, and it is sometimes hard to recall or understand why this barrier seemed to be so absolutely insurmountable. In the 1950s, however, the perspective was quite different. The assault on the four-minute barrier had been going on for well over three decades, and while progress had been made, the goal had yet to be attained. The following is a summary of the world record times prior to Roger Bannister's historic run, beginning with Paavo Nurmi's record-setting run thirty years earlier.

1922	Nurmi (Finland)	4:10.4
1931	Ladoumegue (France)	4:09.2
1933	Lovelock (New Zealand)	4:07.6
1934	Cunningham (United States)	4:06.8
1937	Wooderson (Great Britain)	4:06.4
1942	Hägg (Sweden)	4:06.2
1942	Andersson (Sweden)	4:06.2
1942	Hägg (Sweden)	4:04.6
1943	Andersson (Sweden)	4:02.6
1944	Andersson (Sweden)	4:01.6
1945	Hägg (Sweden)	4:01.4

Progress had been slow but steady; nine seconds had been whittled away in just over twenty years. But it seemed to stop there. Hägg's mark stood unsurpassed. No one matched it for the next eight years. Just one and a half seconds were left to be chipped off for someone to become the first four-minute miler.

Yet why have so many men now done what was then deemed impossible? Why is the record time now closer to Roger Bannister's prediction of a three-and-a-half-minute mile than the old four-minute barrier? There are at least three factors that contribute to this phenomenon. The first is the construction of the tracks on which the races are run. Runners from well before the era of Paavo Nurmi until after Bannister ran on tracks made up entirely of cinders, the ash from coal-burning power stations. There are few such power stations left today, and this form of recycling has been replaced. Now tracks are made of synthetic materials created to assure speed. These materials do not become sticky and do not cling to the spikes of the runners the way cinders do. The adherence of cinders to spikes decreases the bite of the spikes on the track. The longer the race, the more this matters. How much difference does the track surface make? Observers of both tracks and middle distance runners agree that the tracks make a difference of at least a second per quarter mile. That means that both Hägg and Andersson would have broken the four-minute barrier during World War II.

The second factor is that the spikes of the track shoes changed; the long steel spikes worn by runners of that era have been replaced by shorter studs, which results in less resistance, or drag, when lifting the foot up from the track. This is thought to contribute another couple of seconds to a runner's time. Could Glenn Cunningham have done it? I like to think so, since his story, like Wilma Rudolph's, involves overcoming a significant medical handicap. In his case the handicap was a severe burn involving both legs, which resulted in scarring of the skin and connective tissue, as well as some impairment of the circulation.

The third factor is the way in which runners train. In the 1950s, runners were not full-time athletes in the way they are today. Training was not a one hundred percent effort that involved most if not all of the runner's life. Bannister was a full-time medical student in addition to being a successful runner. This was not an anomaly. Take Horace Ashenfelter, a contemporary of Bannister's and the best American middle distance runner of the 1950s. He won seventeen national championships and a gold medal for the three thousand meter steeplechase in the 1952 Olympics. Ashenfelter was an FBI agent by day. He trained as a runner by night, running through city parks and using the benches for hurdles. Big-city parks were safer in the 1950s.

So why was Bannister the man who succeeded where so many had failed? A look at his prior career would not show him to be the most likely candidate. His personal best times make an interesting comparison to the overall quest for the four-minute mile:

1950	Centennial Games	4:09.9

This was only half a second better than what Nurmi had run in 1922. Bannister was some thirty years behind the field.

1951	Benjamin Franklin Mile	4:08.3
	AAA Championships	4:07.8

He had now passed Lovelock's 1933 time, gaining a decade in one year.

In 1952, he raced only one mile run, finishing with a time of 4:10.6. Back to Paavo Nurmi. Bannister did, however, finish fourth in the fifteen hundred meter run in the Olympics (the "metric mile").

1953	AAA vs. Oxford	4:03.6
	Motspur Park	4:02.0

By now, Bannister was getting close. This was the third-fastest mile ever run. But others were getting close, too, especially the Australian runner John Landy, who had become the odds-on favorite to crack the barrier first.

Bannister, as a result of his medical training, understood that the barrier was both psychological and physiological. He was convinced that the physiological part could be overcome if approached correctly. He was certain the psychological constraint would then crumble, since he believed that the human spirit is indomitable.

But what was the correct approach? To Bannister, that flowed logically from an understanding of the energy needs of muscle. Muscles burn glucose to produce energy. If oxygen is available, the glucose burning is done quite efficiently. If no oxygen is available, the process is only ten to fifteen percent as efficient, and soon outstrips the supply of energy resources. The key then is to increase the efficiency of the cardiorespiratory system to supply as much oxygen and glucose to the muscles as possible for as long as possible. This was the goal of his training program, which he monitored in a physiology lab.

But a mile run is a peculiar task. It is far too long to continuously drive the muscles anaerobically as they are driven in dashes, and it is run far too fast with far too much energy consumption to rely entirely on aerobic metabolism. The solution was to try to decrease excessive demands on the muscles as they became depleted of their reserves. Many runners approached the four-minute goal by depending on their fourth-quarter "kick" to get them into the finish line on schedule. True, a great kick, or finish, is often the key to winning a race, as the runner with the best kick can storm past his opponents and get to the ribbon first. But there are limits to what legs that have already run three-quarters of a mile can do. Their energy reserves are depleted.

The goal Bannister had set for himself was not to win a particular race against the best runners in the world. He'd lost that race in the 1952 Olympics. The objective was not to be relatively faster than every other runner in the race that day. The goal here was an absolute one, and that required a different strategy. The way to run a four-minute mile was to run four sixty-second quarters one right after the other. That decreased the dependence on the fourth-quarter kick and required less from muscles already depleted by running three-quarters of a mile. The race at Motspur Park on June 27, 1953, came close to reaching this ideal. Bannister's times for the four quarters were 59.6 seconds, 60.1 seconds, 62.1 seconds, and 60.2 seconds. It was that third quarter that cost him a four-minute mile. Still, it was the third-fastest mile ever run.

How was that program of running four consecutive sixty-second quarters of a mile accomplished?

Bannister trained by running intervals, successive quarter-miles in sixty seconds with some two-minute half-miles thrown in for variety. He would run one-quarter of a mile then jog for another quarter of a mile. The jogged quarter took him two minutes and was followed by another sixty-second quarter. Most of the time, his entire workout consisted of ten sprinted quarters and ten jogged quarters. That meant that he only trained for about half an hour a day. All of this took place during his lunch breaks from his duties at the hospital. Looking back, Sir Roger remembers it this way, "No warm up or warm down. One quarter in sixty seconds plus one quarter in two minutes times ten. Twenty laps. This equaled five miles. A shower and back to work as a medical student. Five days training per week."

Bannister did not train alone; he ran with a number of other middle distance runners, all of whom followed the same system and two of whom agreed to help him with his goal. That goal was to break the four-minute barrier, not to win an Olympic Gold Medal. It was not one race that was the object. The effort would not be made in a major race. Bannister would attack the goal in a minor race, and two other runners would help by setting the pace so that the four minutes would be four one-minute quarters, or as close as they could be.

The site Bannister chose was an informal track and field meet at the Iffley Sports Grounds just outside Oxford. The date was May 6, 1954. This was not a major track meeting by anyone's criteria, but it was an official event. British track authorities were there, and all times would be official. Any record would stand just as official as if it had been set in a major meet, and there was no pressure to win the race. There were close to a thousand spectators at the field that day. According to Bannister, a much smaller crowd had been anticipated to watch the race, but apparently the word had got around.

Bannister and his friends ran according to Bannister's plan. Chris Brasher and Chris Chataway acted as pacers. The announcers cooperated by announcing the interval times. Brasher

Roger Bannister breaks the four-minute mile before a scant crowd. He maximized his efforts through an understanding of his normal physiology. He now spends much of his life studying the abnormal physiology of patients with Parkinson's disease and related disorders, hoping to find ways to help these patients to accomplish the same end, maximal performance in the activities of daily life.

set the pace at the beginning. He ran the first quarter in 57.4 seconds and the first half mile in 1:58.0. That was almost a perfect sixty-second quarter-mile. At the half-mile mark, Bannister was only two-tenths of a second back, at 1:58.2. If he could do the third quarter of a mile in not much over a minute, then the fourth quarter would only have to be run in approximately sixty seconds. This is where the run at Motspur had fallen short. In that race, the third quarter of a mile had been too slow. Brasher dropped out at the half-mile mark; he had done his job. Chataway took the lead. His job was to get them to three-quarters of a mile fast enough so that a sixty-second fourth quarter would do the trick. Chataway followed the plan to the letter. At the three-quarter mark Chataway, who had set the pace for most of the third quarter, was timed at 3:00.4. Bannister was timed at three minutes flat.

3:00.0 for three quarters!

He was on schedule. This was not Motspur all over again. All Bannister had to do was run the fourth quarter of a mile in a tenth of a second under sixty seconds; 59.9 and he'd have done it. That was one hell of a big "all." Most commentators who reflect on this race marvel at Bannister's big kick, his dramatic finish, but it wasn't his big kick that did it. It was the other three quarters. They had been planned perfectly, and the plan had been perfectly executed. Bannister ran the fourth quarter in 59.4 seconds. Moments after he crossed the finish line the announcement came: "The winner of the one mile event was R. G. Bannister of Exeter College running for the Amateur Athletic Union in a time which, subject to verification, is a new track record, English, British, European, and world record. The time was three minutes. . . ." No one heard the rest of the announcement above the cheering of the crowd. The official time was 3:59.4. Bannister had run that last quarter in 59.4 seconds.

The four-minute barrier had been broken by a full-time medical student and part-time runner.

Seven weeks later, Bannister's time was bettered by John Landy, who ran a 3:58 mile in Turku, Finland. This feat set up the race of the century, the first between the only two men who had ever run a mile in less than four minutes. The race took place in Vancouver, British Columbia, in the British Empire Games on August 7, 1954. Unlike breaking the barrier, there was a sellout crowd and the games were televised across the United States.

It was a race for all time, but this time the goal was to win the race. And this time it was Bannister's great kick that did it. I watched the race in a store window in downtown Chicago. Landy took the lead early and held it. Bannister fell off the pace. Landy's times were too fast for him; he needed to pace himself, and he had the discipline to do just that. At three-quarters of a mile Landy held the lead. He continued to hold it, and on the last turn he looked back over his inside shoulder to see where Bannister was. Bannister was coming up on the outside, kicking past him to win in 3:58.8.

That race had been the mile of the century and then some. Bannister never ran another mile race. He ran and won the European fifteen hundred meter. His time was 3:43.8. It was a new world's record and was the equivalent of a four-minute mile. Bannister finished medical school and then trained for another seven years to become a consulting neurologist. He has had a successful career in neurology with a major interest in the autonomic nervous system. That is the part of the nervous system that controls such automatic (nonconscious) functions as blood pressure, heart rate, sweating, bladder and bowel function. He also took over as author of a standard British textbook on neurology, *Brain's Clinical Neurology*.

Recently, Roger Bannister's name has once again been in the news. At first it was for the fiftieth anniversary of the accomplishment for which I am certain he will be remembered. Then it was for a far more controversial subject. He had the audacity to suggest that all men are not created equal, that they are not endowed by their creator with equal athletic ability, and that some of this lack of equality is actually inherited. It is genetic. Horrors!

I don't think that there is a single individual who could dispassionately look at all the evidence and come to any other conclusion. Suppose we stage a basketball game between a team of the best four-foot Bushmen we can find and a team of the best seven-foot Tutsi tribesmen.* Winner take all. It would be no contest and everyone knows it. Is that a racist statement? A claim with some hidden prejudice or agenda? Would it set back racial understanding two decades? No. The two-foot or more average height difference between the players on the two teams would put Bushmen at a distinct disadvantage. They would be disadvantaged in the matter of height. That difference is genetic, and it does determine an athletic disadvantage.

Reductio ad absurdum! I have reduced it to absurdity, right? I don't think so. The differences are genetic. The results would have been the same had I staged a weight-lifting contest between the best of the Tutsi and the best of the Russians. But both teams would not have been black.

What has Bannister said? Not much more than I have already written here. Athletes are not created equal. Some of those inequalities are genetic. Some of those genetic differences cluster among different races. That clustering creates different sets of athletic abilities.

Wherever studied, blacks have relatively longer legs (increased ratio of the lower half of the body to the upper half) than their white counterparts raised in the same environment. Are we to believe that such differences make no difference, that despite longer legs and longer strides blacks cannot run dashes any faster when given the training and opportunity, nor jump any higher? To suggest the latter would be racist in that it would directly imply some built-in inability to capitalize on "natural" abilities. Such inferences are by their very nature racist.

In his brilliant and entertaining set of essays *The Flamingo's Smile*, Stephen Jay Gould said, "Human equality is a contingent

*Bushmen are one of a number of closely related, small-statured peoples of southern Africa who were once called Pygmies. Bushmen, when first encountered by European whites, were hunters and gatherers. The closely related Hottentots were herders who raised cattle. These groups together are now known as Khoisan peoples, a word derived from each group's own name for itself.

fact of history." I in no way dispute that motto, and the inequalities discussed here are not inconsistent with it. For what is meant by equality? It is certainly not identity. Nor exact sameness. All evolutionary theory is based on the random inequality of individual members of a species. Without that there is no descent. Equality has to do with access to the same overall gene pool, with similar ranges of expression in all groups, not sameness or identity between individuals or groups. There are genetic differences between groups; skin color varies, as do hair color, and incidence of baldness, and height. Even genetic diseases such as dystonia and sickle cell anemia and many others are more prevalent in some groups than in others. This may not be politically correct; it is, however, an indisputable fact.

To answer my first sports trivia question, the baseball player who played for five years in the majors and has both a Ph.D. and an M.D. is none other than Gail Hopkins. He played first base for the White Sox, the Kansas City Athletics, and the Los Angeles Dodgers, from 1968 through 1974, hitting .266 overall. He received his Ph.D. from the Illinois Institute of Technology and his M.D. from Rush Medical College, where I teach. He worked his way through medical school, in part by playing first base in Japan.

As a neurologist who has become a writer, I hope that fellow writer and neurologist Oliver Sacks, author of *Awakenings*, *The Man Who Mistook His Wife for a Hat*, and *An Anthropologist on Mars*, will also be remembered in one hundred years. There is a possibility, of course; Michael Nyman composed an opera based on *The Man Who Mistook His Wife for a Hat*, and a movie was made of *Awakenings*. The smart money, however, is still on Bannister.*

---

*The author thanks Sir Roger Bannister for taking the time to read and comment on this chapter. I have attempted to integrate all of his corrections and reminiscences. If any errors have crept in, the fault is mine, not his.

A Break in the Action: Willie Mays, Vic Wertz, and Eddie Gaedel

ROGER BANNISTER GAINED SPORTS IMMORTALITY by doing the right thing, in the right place, at the right time. Had he run half a second slower on that famous day, he would have set a world's record that would have lasted less than two months. Had he run his first four-minute mile seven weeks later, he would have been the second four-minute man and still a second and a half slower than John Landy's record pace. He still might have beaten Landy in the British Empire Games, but that would have netted him little more than his allotted fifteen minutes of fame.

Bannister was in the right place at the right time. Other athletes have not been so fortunate. No one has had more of a penchant for being in the wrong place at the wrong time than Vic Wertz. Despite a major league baseball career that stretched out over seventeen seasons and included four appearances in All-Star games and one in the World Series, this left-handed-hitting outfielder and first baseman is remembered, if he is remembered at all, for hitting an out in that one World Series. Really, he is remembered as a trivia question about that out, for it has become legendary as "the catch." That miraculous catch was the one made by Willie Mays in the 1954 World Series.

That World Series was between the Cleveland Indians, who were led by a pitching staff that included three future Hall of Famers, Bob Feller, Bob Lemon, and Early Wynn, and the New York Giants, who had no future Hall of Famers on their pitching staff. And pitching is what the game is all about. All the Giants had on their side was Willie Mays, back after a two-year tour of duty in the army, a pinch hitter named Dusty Rhodes, and a peculiarly shaped ballpark called the Polo Grounds (having been designed for polo, not baseball).

It was game one, the eighth inning. The score was tied 2–2. There were two men on base when Vic Wertz came up to the plate. The Giants brought in left-handed pitcher Don Liddle to face the left-handed-slugging first baseman. Wertz had hit a triple off starting pitcher Sal Maglie in the first inning to give the Indians their two runs.

Vic Wertz hit that ball just about as far as a baseball can be hit. This is where fate, the Polo Grounds, and Willie Mays came together. Wertz hit it straight out into the long canyon that was center field in the Polo Grounds. This park had the longest center field and the shortest foul lines in the majors. In any other ballpark that blast would have been a home run, and with any other center fielder it would have been at least a triple. But that was Willie Mays playing center field for the Giants. He turned at the crack of the bat, raced back, and outran the ball, making an over the shoulder catch about four hundred and seventy feet from home plate. Wertz was out. The game was won when Dusty Rhodes came up as a pinch hitter in the tenth inning and hit a short fly ball down the right field line. It traveled no more than two hundred and eighty feet. It would have been an easy out in every other ballpark in America. In the Polo Grounds, it was a three-run home run that won the game. The rest of the series was all anticlimax. The Giants won it in four straight games.

The next season, Wertz was once again in the wrong place at the wrong time. This time he did more than hit "the catch." This time he developed polio. The Salk vaccine had just been introduced. Polio had not yet been eradicated. In midseason, Wertz became stricken and was soon near death. But he wasn't up against Willie Mays this time. He pulled through and after hard work was left with very little residual paralysis. Wertz worked at rehabilitation as hard as he could. He was never as fast as he had been before he got polio, but speed had never been his strong suit. He never played in the outfield again. He could not move quickly enough. He did not have the speed or stamina to chase fly balls across the outfield. He stayed on first base, and in 1956 he hit a career high thirty-two home runs. The next year he hit twenty-eight and made the All-Star team for the American League. All things considered, he made one of the most dramatic comebacks in the history of baseball, a return from paralytic polio in less than a year. Wertz finally retired in 1963. After all this he is remembered as a trivia question: Who hit the ball that Willie Mays turned into "the catch"?

It's like asking who was the second man to run a four-minute mile. Or the third? Or better yet, who was the pitcher who walked that midget who pinch-hit for the St. Louis Browns?

That feat was accomplished by Bob "Sugar" Cain of the Detroit Tigers. The midget was named Eddie Gaedel. He was an achondroplastic dwarf. Achondroplasia is a hereditary disorder of the cartilage, bones, and joints. Hereditary achondroplasia is not limited to humans. Dachshunds are all achondroplastic. They were originally bred to have that disease because it endowed them with short legs and a long, squat body so that they could burrow after their prey. They are one of the early examples of man manipulating genetics, long before Darwin or Mendel or Watson and Crick. Genetic engineering is not so new.

After Eddie Gaedel's one appearance, the forces who controlled major league baseball forbade Bill Veeck, the owner of the Browns, to play him in another major league game. Veeck and that midget were making a mockery of the game, the forces said. Today, it might be very different. Gaedel was being discriminated against because of a medical condition. Today that would be illegal. It is the owners and the other players who have now made a true mockery of the game, without any help from Eddie Gaedal. Or Bill Veeck.

After "the catch," Giant manager Leo Durocher again changed pitchers, bringing in right-hander Marv Grissom to face the right-handed power in the Indians' lineup. As Grissom approached the mound, Liddle turned to him and said, "I got my man."

Just Right: Mahmoud Abdul-Rauf

IT'S A SCENE THAT HAS BEEN PLAYED out thousands of times in high school gymnasiums and basketball courts across the United States for at least the last fifty or sixty years, if not longer. Ever since Dr. Naismith's invention became more than just a way for young men to get some exercise on free Saturday afternoons. It's a scene we can all image, one that we have come to honor and respect, even to expect from the most dedicated young players. It's late on a Thursday evening; the basketball court is all but empty. One lone young man is there; everyone else has finished practice and gone home. He alone has stayed behind to work on some aspect of his game, to perfect his skill. Hard work in order to succeed; the American work ethic. Perfection never comes easily.

But somehow this rendition of the scene isn't quite right.

The six-foot-tall young black male stands at the free throw line in the half-illuminated gym. He makes six quick, short dribbles with his hand down around his ankle. He brings the ball up to shooting position far faster than any coach has ever taught him to. He jerks his head slightly to the left. Suddenly the ball is in the air, arcing toward the basket.

Swish. Nothing but net. A perfect free throw.

The boy, for he looks no older than sixteen, sniffs once, lets out a brief grunt, and trots over to pick up the basketball. "Eight," he says under his breath. "Eight, just right." That should be enough to evoke a smile or at least a grin in him, but neither is evident.

He is almost immediately back on the line, ready to start his next free throw. Once again he goes through the same routine. He begins with his six quick, low dribbles, his hand very close to his ankle. He again brings up the ball with great speed and then jerks his head slightly to the left. Without any hesitation the ball is in the air following the same perfect arc toward the waiting net.

Swish. Nothing but net. Another perfect free throw.

He sniffs again once, lets out a repetition of the grunt he made less than thirty seconds earlier, and trots over to pick up the basketball. "Nine," he says under his breath. "Nine, just right. Please, God, this time let the next one be perfect." Perfection is his goal. Nothing else will do. He is still not smiling.

He is back on the line for his try at number ten. He is ready to start again, and once again he goes through the very same ritual. In a flash the ball is in the air.

Clang! The basketball hits the back rim of the basket, rolls around once, twice, and then slips through the rim and into the net. Ten in a row. A pretty good feat for anyone.

"Shit!" he shouts; then he clears his throat loudly four times in succession. "It wasn't right. It wasn't right. It has to be just right. It has to be. Why does it have to be?" He is almost crying as he takes his place at the free throw line.

He starts again and goes through the very same ritual. The jerk of his head to the left, however, is a little more forceful than before. In a flash the ball is projected toward the basket.

Swish. Nothing but net. Another perfect free throw. The first in a new sequence. The boy lets out a brief grunt and trots over

Mahmoud Abdul-Rauf looking just right while driving down
the court. During moments like this, his complete concentration
aborts the tics of his Tourette's syndrome.

to pick up the basketball. "One," he says under his breath. "One,
just right. Only nine more."

He never looks at the clock. Time does not matter. It is almost
ten; he has been at it for over two hours. He has made well over
ninety percent of his free throws. Merely making them doesn't
count, though. He has to shoot ten in a row that sound just

right—that *are* just right. And that he has not yet done. Until he does, he cannot quit. Only then can he go home and go to sleep, after he counts all of the books in his bookcase from right to left and then from left to right. Three times. That's a snap. That can always be done perfectly.

Swish. "Two."

Eight to go.

The American dream of sports perfection has somehow turned into a nightmare for this one lonely adolescent.

Scenes much like this were the life of a high school basketball player from Gulfport, Mississippi, named Chris Jackson. Most people kindly considered him to be "peculiar" at best. Others were less generous and considered him to be crazy. Neither opinion boded well for his prospects as a future basketball star.

Today he has a new name, Mahmoud Abdul-Rauf, a new religion, a new outlook on life, and a career as one of the best guards in the NBA; he is also one of the most accurate free throw shooters in the history of professional basketball. Most of all, he has a diagnosis, one that explains most, if not all, of his peculiarities and may even contribute to some of his successes.

Abdul-Rauf, the name he assumed in 1991 when he converted to Islam, has Gilles de la Tourette's syndrome.* Tourette's syndrome is a neurological disorder that produces pure neurological symptoms, such as abnormal movements, as well as other symptoms that in the past would have been categorized as belonging to psychiatric or behavioral disorders. The former symptoms cause public embarrassment and are never beneficial; the latter symptoms can produce a search for perfection that can lead to extraordinary accomplishments—like Abdul-Rauf's hitting over ninety-five percent of his free throws in a single season and threatening to break the all-time record of 95.8 percent held by Calvin Murphy.

---

*American patients and their physicians now refer to this as Tourette's syndrome, a usage that is a pure Americanism. The doctor whose name has become the eponym for this disease was a French physician named Georges Gilles de la Tourette. Everything but Georges was part of his last name. For the sake of familiarity, to say nothing of brevity, I, too, will use the short form of the eponym.

In most medical circles, Tourette's syndrome is classified as a movement disorder, in essence a type of neurological disease that is defined by the occurrence of abnormal, involuntary movements. The movements seen in Tourette's syndrome are characterized as tics. Tics are brief movements that could be purposeful in the right place at the right time, but are performed at times and frequencies that no longer serve any meaningful purpose.

How can tics constitute a disease? We all have had a tic or two at some time or other. What's the big deal? A tic or two, off and on, is no big deal. Consider blinking. Blinking is part of our normal, spontaneous range of activities. A failure to blink is one of the manifestations of the loss of spontaneous movement that characterizes Parkinson's disease. Everyone blinks, but not ten to fifteen times a minute for hours on end; and those normal blinks do not cause forceful eye closure. Nor are normal blinks accompanied by an uncontrollable urge to make such forceful blinks, an urge that can only be relieved by forcing the eyes to close. Ah, that feels better.

The tics of Tourette's can also be made up of more complicated patterns of movement. A single complex tic can consist of a shoulder shrug combined with a toss of the head and a loud sniff, always occurring together, in the same stereotyped sequence. The tic is often allowed to occur just to relieve the need for that specific movement. In a patient with Tourette's, the individual tics wax and wane. Any one tic or combination of tics starts up, intensifies, becomes more frequent and often more forceful, and then disappears, only to be replaced by other varieties of tics. A young boy starts to blink. Soon he is blinking away uncontrollably. Just as soon as his parents make an appointment with an ophthalmologist the blinks stop, and a few days later the boy is shrugging his shoulder. That lasts for a few weeks or months and then is gone. Good, all the shrugs were tiresome. Soon he starts clearing his throat and spitting. Time after time after time. Bring back the shrugging.

Individuals with full-blown Tourette's syndrome (I hesitate to label them as patients, since the majority of their problems are often more social than medical) invariably have uncontrolled noises, varying from grunts to vocalizations. These are merely another form of tic, but vocal tics have become a diagnostic necessity. Without them, we do not label a person as having true Tourette's. Occasionally, sudden, uncontrolled obscenities break through as one of the vocalizations—a condition known as coprolalia. Historically, this peculiar symptom was one of the major factors that led patients to be evaluated and diagnosed by physicians. It quickly became the most notorious aspect of the disease. A well-bred Victorian-era lady of social rank swearing like a drunken sailor was obviously noteworthy, but coprolalia is overall quite uncommon even when the disorder is otherwise full-blown.

Other rare and peculiar symptoms include echolalia, the compulsive repetition of someone else's words and phrases; echopraxia, compulsive repetition of someone else's movements; and at times even copropraxia, repetitive obscene gestures. In contrast to these rarities, compulsive movements, such as the need to touch other people or specific objects, and compulsive rituals that must precede a voluntary act, are not uncommon in individuals with Tourette's. Like Abdul-Rauf's six quick dribbles of a basketball. A ritual that had to be performed prior to a free throw.

Georges Gilles de la Tourette studied with and then worked under the great French neurologist Jean Martin Charcot, and has often been described as Charcot's most dedicated and enthusiastic disciple. Charcot held the first chair in neurology in the world. He achieved that position by recognizing the pivotal importance of careful clinical observation and description of the signs and symptoms of individual patients. This knowledge was then paired with meticulous postmortem examinations of the brain and spinal cord in order to correlate the clinical observations with the physical changes that were found within the nervous system. As a result of applying this approach, Charcot and his disciples were able to delineate myriad "new" diseases. Charcot became the most famous neurologist, and perhaps the most famous physician, of his time. People from all over the world, including the emperor of Brazil, came to Paris to be seen and evaluated by him. Not bad for a man who had once set up shop in an asylum for destitute prostitutes.

It was Charcot, accompanied by his entourage, who saw these patients, and it was Charcot who then assigned his disciples to study certain patients and write them up for publication. So, too, with Gilles de la Tourette. His thesis was the paper in which he described the disease that now bears his name.

In this paper, Gilles de la Tourette included nine patients, most of whom had been seen at one time or another by Charcot. The first of these was Madame de Dampiere. Her case had already been written up once before. She had started making involuntary jerking movements early in life, and these were soon complicated by occasional sudden shouts of obscene words and phrases (coprolalia). Because of this coprolalia, she was seen and evaluated by Jean Itard, the same physician who had tried to instill language into the Wild Boy of Aveyron without any success. He likewise had no success in treating Madame de Dampiere; but he had published his observations on her in 1825. The woman continued to be plagued by her disorder and became a social outcast, a recluse. Late in her life she traveled to Paris to be evaluated by the famous Charcot. She died at age eighty, still manifesting both uncontrolled tics and disruptive coprolalia.

Madame de Dampiere became case one in Gilles de la Tourette's study:

Soon it became clear that the movements were indeed involuntary and convulsive in nature. The movements involved the shoulders, the neck, and the face and resulted in contortions and extraordinary grimaces. . . . Her examination showed spasmodic contractions that were continual or were separated only by momentary intervals of time. . . . In the midst of an interesting conversation, all of a sudden without being able to prevent it, she interrupts what she is saying or what she is listening to with horrible screams and with words that are more extraordinary than her screams. All of this contrasts deplorably with her distinguished manners and background. These words are for the most part offensive curse words and obscene sayings. These are no less embarrassing for her than for those who have to listen, the expressions being so crude that an unfavorable opinion of the woman is almost inevitable.

She had been forced into a life filled with uncontrolled tics, vocalizations, and coprolalia, which caused social, not medical, disability. No wonder she became a recluse.

There was nothing that any of her physicians could do to help her. As Gilles de la Tourette remarked, "The treatment for this singular condition is still to be discovered. . . . The only treatment that has seemed to help the symptoms and has been associated with periods of remission has been isolation." On reading her entire, detailed case history, it seems far more likely that her remissions were more a part of the natural history of her disorder than anything any of her physicians did for her.

Itard's initial description of Madame de Dampiere had been published in 1825, just eight short years after James Parkinson's landmark essay "The Shaking Palsy." The timing of these two contributions to the history of clinical medicine is no coincidence. It has been suggested that James Parkinson was able to identify Parkinson's disease, when physicians before him had not, because there were more old people around to be seen and observed than ever before. After all, the disease is one that afflicts an aging population. Parkinson just happened to be in the right place (suburban London) at the right time. But several of the patients he described were only in their forties and fifties, not exactly aged. And Madame de Dampiere was a relatively young woman when her disease started and still young when she came under medical attention and written about for the first time.

The average age of the population was not really what had undergone the most important change. In fact, it had probably not changed much at all. Most people, even most physicians, confuse life expectancy with the average age of the population and the number of older people alive at any one time. These are not the same thing and should not be confused. Life expectancy is the average projected duration of life for a newborn child. The major factors in determining life expectancy are infant and childhood mortality rates for the given group. Declines in infant mortality have a profound effect on average life expectancy and on population growth and density, but little effect on the age distribution of the population after the period of infant and child mortality has passed. That distribution depends upon those factors which control life expectancy of the population that has already reached the age of twenty or twenty-five. This determines the relative number of aging people within the population at any one time, that is, the number at risk for those diseases that are related to aging.

There is, for instance, no evidence that the average age of a Roman senator was any less than the average age of an American congressman. Both positions have the same minimal age requirements. A U.S. congressman must be at least twenty-one; a Roman senator had to be at least twenty-five. Everyone in both groups already had to have survived infant and childhood mortality. Cicero, the most famous senator of his age, was an old man when he was murdered by agents of young Octavius, the future Augustus. Cicero was eliminated because of his political views and because no one expected him to die soon of natural causes. In the minds of his contemporaries, that particular old man still had a significant life expectancy. Octavius went on to become Augustus and died at age seventy-seven. His successor, Tiberius, died at age seventy-eight. No contemporary historian thought that their longevities had been that extraordinary. The essay of Cicero's that is most widely read and quoted today is entitled "On Old Age." In it he made numerous observations on old age that remain cogent, but not once did he remark that old age was a rarity. Washington, Adams, Jefferson, Madison, and Monroe all lived long enough to be at risk for Parkinson's disease. Hamilton didn't, but only because he was killed in a duel.

If it was not a simple matter of the changes in the age distribution of the adult population that led to the description of Parkinson's disease, then what was it? The answer is that we see what we as doctors are trained to see. If each disease is thought to be an imbalance in the body's natural "humors," or life fluids, to be treated by bloodletting and purges, then detailed clinical observations of the specific clinical aspects of a patient's disease—whether those include disorders of gait or the characteristics of the patient's abnormal involuntary movements—are meaningless and never even sought after. Tics do not matter except as a sign of imbalance of the system. It is their occurrence, not their characteristics, that count. Tics need not be differentiated from tremors.

Benjamin Rush, the physician who gave his name to the medical school at which I teach, and who was the most famous American physician of his era, believed in those time-honored methods of his predecessors. He was one of the leading figures of his day, a signer of the Declaration of Independence, and one of the first Americans whose medical writings were read in Europe. Rush believed that all fever was an imbalance in the body's humors, and he treated all fevers in the same way. Something was amiss with the precious bodily fluids that had to be corrected. He treated yellow fever with bloodletting and purges. That's the same way he treated George Washington during Washington's terminal illness, when he certainly did not have yellow fever. The clinical details of any particular fever were not that important to Rush or his contemporaries. It was the fever that signaled the imbalance and that had to be treated. We now know that the survival rate of those yellow fever victims who were treated by Rush was less than that of patients who underwent no medical treatment at all. This was first demonstrated during Rush's lifetime, and was one of the factors that led physicians to question traditional wisdom. Most modern authorities also believe that Rush's overly zealous bloodletting contributed to the death of our first president. And I teach at Rush Medical College.*

Revolution was in the air in Rush's day, and not just of the political variety. Medicine underwent its own revolution in the ensuing years, in part because of the obvious failures of men like Benjamin Rush, but more because of an evolution in how

*George Bernard Shaw was probably on the right track when he claimed that the reputation of a physician depended on the number of famous people who had died under that physician's care.

physicians thought about disease. All fevers were not the same. Smallpox was not just a fever. Jennerian vaccination prevented smallpox but nothing else. Different people died of different diseases. Those different diseases could be identified at autopsy by specific pathological alterations in different organs and tissues. It wasn't just an imbalance of the humors. Those ancient authorities had it all wrong. Just like Benjamin Rush.

It was this evolved scientific logic that Charcot pursued within the realm of neurological disorders, and that had finally come to dominate medical thinking in the early decades of the nineteenth century. Pathology mattered. That meant that clinical-pathological correlations mattered. And that meant that the clinical observation of details was paramount in understanding individual diseases. The leadership in this transition was taken by Karl Rokitansky, a pathologist from Vienna who insisted that physicians attend autopsies and see what had really been happening to the patients they had been treating. What an idea!*

Medicine had entered an age of clinical observation and Gilles de la Tourette became one of those observers. But he did more than just observe. Under Charcot's leadership, he reasoned from his observations. The disease he described was a single disease entity. The patients in his group weren't nine people with nine different disorders who happened to share a few clinical signs and symptoms; theirs was a specific disease entity. A breakthrough of a sort had been made. Men who could do what Gilles de la Tourette had done were few and far between. Such men, Charcot believed, deserved to be honored—especially if they were his disciples. That was why Charcot always felt it was appropriate to use eponyms.

More important than suggesting that it was a single disease with a wide range of manifestations beginning in childhood and extending throughout life was Gilles de la Tourette's insistence that the disease was a neurological disorder. Something was amiss in the brain, not in the psyche.

*Rokitansky collected data on all of his autopsies, which were numbered consecutively. Rokitansky's first was the autopsy he performed on a Viennese composer and piano player with alcoholic cirrhosis of the liver, who became delirious and then died of liver failure. The composer is somewhat better remembered today as Ludwig van Beethoven.

So it was not demons that drove Abdul-Rauf to make all those noises and jerks; it was a neurological problem. But what about those free throws that had to sound and feel just right, that quest for perfection that was beyond perfection? Madame de Dampiere had no such quest for perfection. She just wanted to stop swearing and jerking and be able to have coffee with her friends in peace. That need for perfection couldn't be neurological, or could it?

Gilles de la Tourette's paper was not a best-seller. In fact it wasn't translated into English until one hundred years later, on the occasion of its centenary. The disease also did not "sell" well. Between 1884 and 1965, only fifty cases of this strange and apparently rare disorder were published in the world's medical literature. Most of those were published by psychiatrists, and often by psychiatrists with an analytic prejudice. Reading those papers today is enough to reinforce the antianalytic judgments of any rational scientist. All those obscene words and gestures were too latent with symbolic meaning of an anal nature not to be misinterpreted. And those tics. They were something else. The thought seemed to be that all that eye closure must come from observing the primal scene, a phenomenon that must seem less repulsive among the impoverished who have forever lived in cramped quarters. And the switching from one tic to another. Symptom substitution in an attempt to . . . and on and on in the same vein. But if psychiatrists were treating these types of patients, then Tourette's had to be a psychiatric disease. A self-fulfilling proposition if there ever was one.

Gilles de la Tourette also fell out of favor. By 1960 he was no longer listed in *Grand Larousse Encyclopédique*.* That was the unkindest cut of all.

Then another evolution in thinking occurred and the theories all changed. Many psychiatric diseases were shown to have biological roots and could be treated with drugs. And, unlike psychoanalysis, the drugs could be proved to make a difference.

---

*This publication all but codifies who was who in French history and culture, as well as who wasn't. There is no equally important arbiter of significance in the English language.

Why not Tourette's? Why couldn't it, too, have biological, neurological roots? That was what Gilles de la Tourette had said in the first place. Why couldn't the syndrome be treated with medications? Some Tourette's patients were treated with antipsychotic medications and their tics got better. They improved with the very same drugs used to treat schizophrenics. That must mean that the psychiatrists were right all along. Or must it?

To get a feel for interpreting the results of these trials, it is important to understand how these antipsychotic drugs were developed in the first place. Developing antibiotics is easy, once the concept is understood. Bread mold kills bacteria on moldy bread. It does this by producing a chemical, and that chemical is what kills the bacteria. That chemical, it turns out, doesn't kill rats or mice. It became the first antibiotic, penicillin, and it won the Nobel Prize for Fleming, Florey, and Chain. To develop new antibiotics, modern pharmaceutical companies still follow the very same process. They discover which chemical kills a given bacterium in culture in a petri dish and yet is safe when administered to experimental animals. The concept is simple, straightforward, and easy to understand and apply. That's why so many drug companies have been able to do it. But you can't put schizophrenia in a petri dish.

The first antischizophrenic drug, chlorpromazine (marketed as Thorazine), was discovered by accident in the 1950s. It was serendipity twice over. The group of medications of which chlorpromazine is a member are called phenothiazines. They had been developed to deworm cattle. The cattle dewormed with some of these drugs became quite tranquil. They still went about their business of being cattle, but they were less easily startled. The first human application of this observation was the use of chlorpromazine as a preanesthetic medication to make the process of general anesthesia less startling and traumatic to the patient. It worked. It even made anxious schizophrenics who were awaiting surgery far more tranquil. Perhaps it would help them even if they were not going to undergo anesthesia. It did and it still does. Thorazine became the first truly successful treatment for schizophrenia. Today the use of such medications is

under attack. Before their use, the average length of hospitaliza-
tion for a newly diagnosed patient with acute schizophrenia was
more than two years. Within a decade of the widespread use of
these medications, hospital stays had fallen dangerously to less
than a month. It is now known that the drugs' effects are far more
complicated than simply providing a chemical straightjacket.

Drug companies found that there was a lot of money to be
made with such medications. These drugs were much more
profitable than antibiotics. Patients often only need to take
antibiotics for a week or two and are cured. Schizophrenics are
never cured; they remain on their neuroleptics forever. For these
drugs not only help patients recover from a first episode of
schizophrenia, they prevent recurrences of psychotic behavior.
The problem of how to create new neuroleptics was initially
solved by merely making minor adjustments to the pheno-
thiazine nucleus. Manufacturers made adjustments galore. The
resulting drugs became better known as Mellaril, Stelazine,
Prolixin, and a host of others.

Then came Paul Janssen, a Belgian pharmacologist and my
perennial candidate as the best medical scientist who has never
won a Nobel Prize. Janssen figured out how to make the first
neuroleptic that was chemically unrelated to the phenothiazines. He realized that the single characteristic that all successful neuroleptics shared, and that correlated best with their
antischizophrenic potential, was a propensity, when tested on
lab animals, to block abnormal movements induced by amphetamines and related drugs. All he had to do was test other chemicals for this exact property. It was not as simple a procedure as
killing bacteria in petri dishes, but almost as straightforward.
The result was haloperidol, better known as Haldol. Haldol
blocked the amphetamine-induced movements without doing
any harm to the animals. That suggested that it would be both
effective and relatively safe. Haldol became one of the most
widely used antipsychotic agents throughout the world.

Haldol was also the most effective drug for the management
of tics in Tourette's syndrome. Did that mean that all of those
psychiatrists had to have been barking up the right tree? After

all, Haldol was an antipsychotic drug, and now it could be used to control both the psychosis of schizophrenia and the tics of Tourette's. But haloperidol was developed because of its potency in blocking amphetamine-induced stereotyped chewing behavior in rats. Those rats were not schizophrenic. They had abnormal movements. Those abnormal movements were due to the activity of dopamine released by the amphetamines and then acting upon certain dopamine receptors within the brain—more specifically, the dopamine receptors of the striatum. What all of this meant was that a drug that blocked dopamine-related movements in animals blocked certain abnormal movements in humans. This suggests that in patients with Tourette's syndrome these tics were due to the activity of dopamine within the brain. Schizophrenia was irrelevant to the issue. Now that is progress.

Dopamine is the same chemical that is found to decrease in the brain in patients with Parkinson's disease. If the neuroleptics block dopamine receptors, then that should mimic the loss of dopamine that causes Parkinson's disease, and schizophrenics who are given these agents ought to look just like they have Parkinson's. They do, or at least many of them do. The condition is called drug-induced parkinsonism, and a majority of patients on neuroleptics develop at least some of the signs and symptoms. These are often mild, but they are there.

The tics of Tourette's syndrome are not the only movements that improve when a patient with abnormal movements is put on haloperidol. Choreatic movements in Huntington's disease also improve on haloperidol. No one believes that Huntington's is a psychiatric disease. It is a neurological disease in which the activity of dopamine at dopamine receptors, probably in the striatum, produces the abnormal movements. The same appears to be the case in Tourette's.

Huntington's chorea is a hereditary disease of the brain caused by a dominantly inherited gene. Scientists have even located the gene. Tourette's is also a dominantly inherited neurological disease. The specific gene, however, has not yet been identified. When I first started evaluating and treating patients with Tourette's syndrome, the available literature stated that it was not a hereditary disorder. I could not understand how that could be true. I would sit in the office with an adolescent boy with multiple tics and ask him and his parents if there was anyone else in the family who had tics. The father would sit there shrugging his right shoulder and sniffing away compulsively while the mother told me that no one in the family had ever had any tics. No one at all. The research that claimed that Tourette's was not hereditary was dependent on such anecdotal family histories, not on direct examinations of all family members. Psychoanalysts are not the only ones who make fundamental errors in scientific logic.

I have not stopped inquiring about any family history of tics or other abnormal movements each time I see a new patient with Tourette's syndrome. I no longer consider a negative family history to be meaningful. I once asked a potential patient about his family history and he said he didn't know most of his family but that he had an uncle who was the family's resident genealogist. His uncle knew everything about everyone for as far back as anyone could remember and even longer. He'd ask his uncle. On the next visit, he told me that he had asked good old Uncle Blinkie, and Uncle Blinkie had assured him that no one in the family had ever had any abnormal movements of any type. A negative family history direct from the horse's mouth, only this time the horse was named Uncle Blinkie, like someone right out of Damon Runyon. Uncle Blinkie, it seems, blinked from morning to night as if he had something in his eyes.

The heart of the problem is that the Tourette's gene is dominant, but with incomplete and variable penetrance. Not everyone who has the gene has the same symptoms. Some have the full-blown disease as described by Jean Itard and Gilles de la Tourette, a disease with severe tics and vocalizations beginning in childhood and lasting throughout life. Many more have tics that are less pronounced during childhood and by adult life have settled entirely into the background. Others have only minor tics that are never more than a part of who they are and are certainly never thought to be a neurological abnormality. Still others have no tics at all. These patients often have other problems; the most common of these are obsessive-compulsive personality traits.

Chris Jackson's mother had these kinds of habits. They were a part of who she was and had been all of her life. That was her personality. She would turn off the stove—once, twice, three times. Then she'd check again to be certain that it was off—once, twice, three times. This routine was not that much different from the rapid dribbles preceding her son's free throws. When it was time to go she locked the door—once, twice, three times. She'd check the lock. Another thrice-repeated task. Into the car and on her way, only to turn back after driving a couple of miles to make certain that the door was really locked. The psychological or mental components of these behaviors are called obsessions. The movements that are made in response to such obsessive thoughts are called compulsions.

The line between these two supposedly different forms of behavior is far more distinct in the mind of the observer than it is within the brain of the individual patient. The underlying mechanisms are tightly linked. The patient is forced to repeat the same behavior over and over again. If that behavior is a simple jerk, it's classified as a tic. If it's a complex motor behavior that is repeated again and again, it's called a compulsive movement, a complex stereotypy. These are much like the complex stereotyped behaviors caused by amphetamines in rats or guinea pigs and blocked so very successfully by haloperidol. Is it so strange, then, that obsessive thoughts and compulsive actions are part and parcel of the overall clinical picture of Tourette's syndrome? How could they not be?

Abdul-Rauf, when he was Chris Jackson, had inherited the gene for obsessive thoughts and compulsive behaviors at the same time he inherited the gene for compulsive tics. They may well be one and the same gene, or at least a single gene that is responsible for the altered function of the brain that sets the stage for both.

But aren't all successful athletes compulsive? Aren't biographies of great athletes replete with tales of compulsive dedication to their sport? The examples are legion. Pitching at targets for hours on end. Throwing footballs through suspended tires. Similar as these tales are, there is a difference. Abdul-Rauf didn't go home at night until the free throws were "just right." Not just ten out of ten, but ten out of ten that were *just right*— that *sounded* right. The sound of a free throw does not change the score of a game. Ten out of ten is good enough for everyone else, but it wasn't, and still isn't, for Abdul-Rauf.

Abdul-Rauf is not alone in this (although he may be among NBA players in this regard). It is a characteristic he shares with most other individuals who have Tourette's syndrome. The compulsive need to perform physical acts until they are just right is common in Tourette's. And the compulsions are no more fun for other patients than they are for Abdul-Rauf. Like Abdul-Rauf, they have a need to do what they have to do in a way that is just right. This is not some order that they are receiving from outside themselves. Their urges have no such schizophrenic connotations. These urges arise within them and cannot be ignored. They must perform the required task until it has been done "just right," or the urge will not go away. It will become an itch that has not yet been scratched. One of my patients told me that he would much rather have his teeth drilled without anesthesia than to have his urges to do things "just right." He had no choice; he went through every day with these feelings.

In some patients the required act must feel right. A patient may put on ten shirts until one feels right around the neck. Or tie a dozen ties, tying each three or four times until it feels right. Or maybe it has to look right. I once treated a young girl who would tie and retie the ribbons in her hair each morning until they looked just right. At times this took only a few minutes. At times it took far longer. She gave new meaning to the concept of "bad hair days."

In others, the act must sound just right. No matter that the act is one in which sound is considered irrelevant. Like shooting free throws. To the person who is performing the act the sound is what counts. If the sound doesn't sound "just right," the itch has not been scratched. Without the right sound, it is as if the free throw has not been made. Swish. Nothing else comes even close to doing the trick. No other sound is acceptable. This is Tourette's; not horseshoes or hand grenades. Close does not count. Just right or nothing at all.

So what do these people do? They learn to develop a level of concentration on the task at hand that allows them to perform that particular activity in just the right way. They become better and better at doing it until it is "just right" as quickly and as often as possible. They must keep that stay in the dentist's chair as brief as possible, just like the rest of us.

Swish. Ten out of ten. The best free throw shot in the world. Ain't disease a wonderful thing sometimes?*

Most Touretters also have premonitory urges before their tics. The tics relieve these urges. In a sense they are the right motor behavior needed to relieve that particular urge. But the two sensations, the compulsive need to perform a task in a specific manner and the urge to tic, are not identical; the patients themselves can usually tell the difference. One insightful patient of mine put it this way. "I have to tic to release a buildup of physical energy. But I can delay that tic for a long time. Once I let the tic happen, I'm relieved. The buildup is gone. It'll come back, but

---

*Abdul-Rauf was not the first person with Tourette's to succeed in a public way of life. Far from it. Nor was he the first in whom the disease may have been of some benefit. The first may have been Dr. Samuel Johnson, born in 1709. During his lifetime, he was acknowledged to be the greatest man of the era, an acknowledgment that continues to this day. A respected poet, playwright, biographer, and essayist, Johnson edited the greatest folio of the works of Shakespeare. But his most noteworthy and lasting accomplishment was his monumental dictionary of the English language.

Throughout his entire life, Johnson manifested the full gamut of behaviors Gilles de la Tourette would later describe. To Johnson's contemporaries, these were all considered to be the peculiarities of a man of genius. A friend of his, the noted eighteenth-century diarist Fanny Burney, described him in this way: "His mouth is almost constantly opening and shutting as if he were chewing. He has a strange method of frequently twirling his fingers and twisting his hands. His body is in a continual agitation seesawing up and down; his feet are never a moment quiet; and in short his whole person is in perpetual motion." Johnson also had some behaviors that had to be done just right. In one of these, he developed a ritual of stepping back and forth before crossing the threshold of a doorway into a house.

How did his disease help him? Samuel Johnson compiled the first comprehensive dictionary of the English language—all by himself, starting from scratch. What task could be more obsessive than collecting each and every word in an entire language? And each and every meaning and usage of that word? With appropriate examples from the literature for each usage? Not to be published until it was absolutely complete? I personally cannot think of one.

Johnson died in 1784 without the benefit of a diagnosis.

for that moment, it's gone. My compulsions are different. The urge is emotional, not physical. I can't do anything but satisfy it. It takes over. I'm not done until I do it in just the right way."

Tics, compulsions, and obsessions may all arise from the same genetic cause, but how do they arise? Some aspects of the way by which the still undetected gene for Tourette's syndrome produces the symptoms of the disorder are almost obvious. The brain itself in Tourette's has to be normal in the sense of an absence of any significant, permanent pathology. There can be no fixed structural abnormality. Nothing that Charcot or Gilles de la Tourette could have seen with their microscopes. Why not? Remember the natural history of the disorder; the tics come and go. The patient blinks. The pathologist would look in those parts of the motor system that control blinking. Something must be amiss there. The patient stops blinking. Now it is his right shoulder that is jerking. Look at the right shoulder motor control area on the left side of the brain. What about the area that controls blinking? It should be normal. Why? Because the patient stopped blinking and began another tic.

And so it goes. There can be no single fixed lesion of the brain. This disease has a wandering abnormality, an abnormality of process not structure, of neurophysiology not neuroanatomy. The answer to disease is not always to be found in pathology. It is an interesting irony that this disease, defined by the champions of the direct relationship between pathology and neurological symptoms, is the one that best illuminates the limitations of that approach. It is not that we have gone back to humors. It is that we must look beyond microscopic pathology.

Tourette's as a disease evolves more than it progresses. Tics come and go. Gestures come and go. The process continues as the tics wax and wane. The patient has good weeks and bad weeks, good months and bad months. Madame de Dampiere also had good months, unrelated to anything her doctors prescribed for her. Can there be good years and good decades? A good year is a wonderful respite, but a good decade or two means a change in diagnosis. The patient no longer has any disease. There is a critical period here, a classic window of opportunity. The tics almost always begin in childhood and early adolescence. They evolve; they come and go. And sometimes they go to a point where they become nothing more than background noise.

In most patients there is an evolution into extinction as the tics fade away into nondisease. This happens so often that it rivals Abdul-Rauf's free throw percentage. When do the tics fade? Usually during adolescence and early adulthood, right up to the early twenties, but never much later than that. If the tics are still a problem in the patient's late twenties, they will always be a problem. The patient now has as a lifelong disorder the syndrome described by Gilles de la Tourette. If a doctor only sees adults, he or she always sees these kinds of cases. In research that is called selection bias. Gilles de la Tourette saw no children and no adolescents. He had absolutely no idea what happened to his disease starting from the vantage of a youngster with multifocal tics and vocalizations. In most, the tics eventually become suppressed as the youngster grows.

The ability of the brain to suppress the tics has a window of opportunity, a critical period. It is Michael Jordan and the ability to learn how to hit a baseball revisited—only in reverse. If the neurophysiological mechanism needed for hitting a baseball is not selected by age twenty-five or thereabouts, it is too late. So, too, with Tourette's. If the mechanism to prevent or control the tics is not selected by about that same age, it never can be.

I once observed a monkey, alone in a cage, in a laboratory that studied monkeys as models of human movement disorders. This particular monkey had numerous facial tics. I watched the monkey for a full twenty minutes. He made movements continuously, three or four each minute. But the variety of movements that this monkey made was quite limited. He made only four different movements, performed in a random order. The lab had produced the perfect animal model of Tourette's syndrome. I asked about the monkey. What medicine was he receiving? None.

I was flabbergasted. A monkey with multifocal tics that was on no medications. Could this be a monkey with spontaneous Tourette's syndrome?

Not quite. When the monkey was very young, he had been given a large dose of apomorphine. Apomorphine acts like dopamine at certain receptors in the brain, and when given in large doses can produce ticlike movements in monkeys. That was nothing new. But apomorphine doesn't last very long. It's all gone from the animal's system in a couple of hours.

What made this monkey different from all other monkeys that had been given apomorphine?

He had been very young when the apomorphine had been injected and a large mirror had been next to his cage. He had watched himself tic and had been ticcing away ever since. That mirror had somehow made all the difference. But how?

We all tic from time to time, especially as children. We all have compulsions. We all have obsessive thoughts from time to time. These tend to start later in life than the tics. We learn to select against all of these behaviors, the tics, the compulsions, and the obsessions. Or at least those of us without the gene for Tourette's do. Those with the gene do not. Why not?

The selection against tics and compulsions and obsessions is all but automatic for the rest of us. In childhood we are like normal monkeys given apomorphine. A few tics and there's no reason to select to continue them. For once, then nothing. Having the gene for Tourette's makes that process more difficult. It's as if there is a positive feedback. Some sort of trick within the brain makes that pathway for a tic or a compulsion or an obsession, once innervated, continue to fire, to reverberate on its own. Is that what the visual feedback did to that monkey? Feedback is important here. Interaction with the environment guides neuronal development in the brain. It is the basis of language. It is the basis of hitting a baseball successfully. It is the basis of seeing with both eyes. It may also be the basis of the recurrence of tics, compulsions, and obsessions, of both their reinforcement and their resolution. If that shot through the hoop sounds right, the obsession ends. Once the movement is made, the urge is relieved. Feedback works to suppress the urge, to relieve the obsession.

Can a person with Tourette's learn to select against these reverberating cycles? That is what most such individuals eventually do, although the precise mechanism is unclear. It is partially conscious. Every kid with tics suppresses the movements to some extent. This suppression is as much a part of the disorder as the tics themselves. Shouting out in class causes a problem, so the kid suppresses that tic. Once school is out, he lets go and out comes a series of whoops and shouts. But he can't suppress all of his tics and certainly not forever, at least not at first.

But the brain learns, it selects the most successful strategies. The adolescent first learns willed suppression of the tic and then suppression of the urge as well as the tic that follows the urge. In part this process is not conscious. Where one stage ends and the other begins is often hard for the patient to describe and impossible for the outside observer to distinguish. The conscious-unconscious dichotomy itself may be more apparent than real in the context of motor control. How much of hitting a golf ball is conscious? How much is unconscious? How is that unconscious aspect learned via conscious effort? And which is which?

Our old friend conscious absorbedness also contributes to the control of tics. Concentrated mental effort, total absorption in a complex task, aborts most tics. Abdul-Rauf never tics while he is actually shooting the basketball. He goes through his compulsive ritual and tics, and then releases the tic-free shot. His head never jerks at the precise moment he takes his shot. Such absorbedness, to the exclusion of all other inputs and outputs, works. The tics go away to allow for the performance of the absorbing physical act. For the duration of that act, there are no other urges and no other distractions. This is an example of true complete absorbedness. It may occupy only the few hundred milliseconds it takes Abdul-Rauf to get off a jump shot, or it may last a surgeon all the way through a complex surgical procedure.

This raises a question for which I have no answer. Should the symptoms of Tourette's be treated during childhood and adolescence? If the natural history of improved suppression of tics depends on the brain receiving feedback of some sort that allows it to select against tics, then might not treating the tics hinder this process? Theoretically, it certainly could. But those tics may well reinforce themselves with reverberations that beget more reverberations. Again a theoretical possibility.

Fortunately, I do not treat theoretical possibilities. I don't even treat the signs and symptoms of Tourette's syndrome. I treat patients, and the decision to treat them is usually not a medical one. Treatment will not change the natural history of the patient's disease, as far as I know. It will not change his or her life expectancy. That's already normal. The decision is more a social one. Are the tics interfering with socialization? Schooling? Making friends? Is the person disrupting classes? Are the tics interfering with learning, or causing the child to get into disciplinary difficulties? These factors are what usually lead to medical intervention.

Abdul-Rauf was the number three pick in the NBA draft in 1990. He had been a consensus All-American at Louisiana State University. The Denver Nuggets traded their first round draft pick and an All-Star guard, Fat Lever, to get the rights to Abdul-Rauf. His performance during his first year was hampered by a congenital abnormality in the bones of his feet. He played twenty-two minutes per game and averaged just over three points per game. After that first year, he underwent foot surgery and tried to beef himself up. He may have tried too hard because he reported in overweight. The Haldol he was on to control his tics may have played a role in this. Haldol blocks amphetamine and even has the reverse effect of increasing appetite. In most patients an increased appetite results in weight gain.

During his third season in the league, Abdul-Rauf came into his own when he averaged over nineteen points a game and was voted the league's most improved player. He also hit almost all of his free throws. Better than that, they almost all sounded just right. Abdul-Rauf was off all treatment by then. He had lost weight, and he was faster. He practiced compulsively from morning until night. His obsessive advantage was back. He was also quicker. Haldol never makes a patient faster or quicker. Speed had always been a major part of Abdul-Rauf's game. During his two years at LSU he led the Southeastern Conference in scoring, both seasons. Attempts have been made to attribute his quickness to his Tourette's, as if the same neurophysiological process that had led his brain to select lightning-fast tics gave him the ability to select far faster moves than any other guard in the NBA. While this is an interesting conjecture, it is one without much scientific support. If it were true, the NBA should be filled with lightning-quick guards grunting and hissing their way up and down the court. It isn't.

Abdul-Rauf may simply have a far more robust nigrostriatal system than most people. That would make him two standard deviations faster than the average zebra. This would be independent of his Tourette's syndrome. It would just be part of that genetic drift that makes some players less robust and some players more robust than other NBA guards of the same age. Or he may just be faster for some other genetic reason.

One other professional athlete I know of playing today has Tourette's: outfielder James Eisenreich. Eisenreich has good speed but is not exceptionally fast. As expected, his tics are suppressed by the absolute concentration of hitting a baseball. When Eisenreich was playing in the 1993 World Series, my good friend Bill Brashler, author of *The Bingo Long Traveling All-Stars & Motor Kings*, among other books, asked how, considering all the scratching of private parts (copropraxia), swearing (coprolalia), spitting (complex tics), et cetera, I could tell which of the players had Tourette's. I told him it was easy: the player who wasn't swearing, scratching, jerking, or spitting was the one.

Why was that? He was the one on Haldol. It usually worked. That's how we learned that Tourette's syndrome is really a neurological disease.

chapter 15
One Fine Morning: Lou Gehrig

PROFESSOR SIGVALD REFSUM OF THE UNIVERSITY OF OSLO had become an eponym a couple of decades before I first met him. He was Refsum of Refsum's disease. Neither his name nor his disease are exactly household words, but what could a neurologist expect? All the good diseases had been taken up by the eighteenth- and nineteenth-century clinicians who got there first. There weren't many opportunities left for mid-twentieth-century neurologists to attach their names to diseases, and those diseases that were left were rare and hard to come by.

This habit of identifying a disease by the name of the person who first described it dates back to the era before the rise of pathology, bacteriology, chemistry, and other scientific disciplines within medicine. Once these disciplines became established, diseases came to be named for one of several different factors, whether it be the nature of the pathological change (as in myotrophic lateral sclerosis) or the causative agent (herpes encephalitis) or the name of the chemical that builds up to abnormal levels (phytanic acid in Refsum's disease) or the specific biochemical defect (omega oxidation deficiency, again in Refsum's disease). But eponyms antedated modern science. Most of them date to the nineteenth century, an era in which diagnosis was based almost entirely on clinical observation, and medical progress consisted of the ability to group together clinical observations into a single entity. One of the best ways to signal acceptance of the validity of such observations was to use the name of the observer as an eponym. This practice was not just done to honor the dead, it was useful. It organized knowledge and assisted in its dissemination.

The rise of technical expertise and scientific knowledge in medicine has given us far better ways to organize our knowledge and to classify disease, but they have yet to displace the need for clinical insight. It was Charcot who best acknowledged the primary importance of such clinical acumen. In one of his clinical lessons, published in 1872, he wrote: "How is it that one fine morning Duchenne discovered a disease that probably existed in the time of Hippocrates? . . . Why do we perceive things so late, so poorly, with such difficulty? Why do we have to go over the same set of symptoms twenty times before we understand it? Why does the first statement of what seems a new fact always leave us cold? Because our minds have to take in something that deranges our original set of ideas, but we are all of us like that in this miserable world." The disease was Duchenne's muscular dystrophy. Before Guillaume Duchenne's work in the 1850s, the condition was just an unidentified part of the morass of disabling diseases of childhood. It soon became recognized as the commonest type of muscular dystrophy. Charcot believed that anyone who was able to overcome the limitations of the human condition and discover a disease deserved to be honored. Much of the world of medicine, especially neurology, continues to agree with him.

The "one fine morning" came for Refsum during World War II while the Germans were occupying Norway. He observed a small group of patients with a disease he had never seen before. He had never even read a description of a constellation of neurological problems quite like it. The patients had pigmentary degeneration of their retinas leading to a severe loss of vision (retinitis pigmentosa). This condition was accompanied by a peripheral neuropathy (degeneration of the nerves throughout the body resulting in weakness and an inability to transmit sensation), ataxia (lack of balance due to altered function of the cerebellum), and a disorder in which the skin became thickened, scaly, and fishlike (ichthyosis). This collection of abnormalities traveled together within members of two different families. The togetherness of the clinical manifestations suggested that the abnormalities constituted a single disease entity. The familial distribution showed that this entity was hereditary. Refsum devised the perfect Latin name for his disease and published his observations. The name was *heredopathia atactica polyneuriti-formis*. Quite a mouthful, but accurate. The disorder he was describing for the first time was a hereditary disease with ataxia (atactica) in which there was major hereditarily determined pathology (heredopathia) in the nerves (polyneuritiformis). All of the other hereditary ataxias, from Friedreich's to Marie's to Sanger-Brown's and others, were diseases of the brain and spinal cord. This new disease was primarily an ataxia of the peripheral nerves. Refsum had isolated a new disorder from that jumble of things that could go wrong within the nervous system. He was deserving of the honor of becoming an eponym. Besides, his personal name was certainly easier to remember than the Latin name he had devised. And easier to spell.

The approach to naming diseases has become far more egal-itarian during this century. We have honored women by attach-ing their names to diseases. We have even begun to name diseases after the patients. Hartnup's disease was named after the Hartnup family in whom this hereditary disorder was first discovered. So, too, with Machado's disease, Joseph's disease, and many others. The first physician to start this practice was that trendsetter of trendsetters, Sigmund Freud. Freud forced medicine as a field and physicians as individuals to rethink many aspects of medicine and of life. Most of his pivotal contri-butions remain accepted, although often not clearly recognized as stemming from Freud. Before Freud, psychiatry textbooks were filled with pictures of the insane, as if visual recognition was the key to diagnosis. Today, it is hard to find a picture in a psych text, unless it a picture of some doctor who is being honored. It was Freud who proclaimed, in his subtext that it was what a patient said, not how he looked, that mattered. While we may debate how the unconscious works and what it does, we don't doubt its existence. Freud named the Oedipus complex after the character in *Oedipus Rex*, King Oedipus. The story that Freud used was handed down to us by the Athenian playwright Sophocles. It was the universal mythical nature of the character and his situation that led to Freud's use of his name. The complex's validity remains accepted, but its interpretation, like most literary interpretations, remains a matter of intellectual debate. It did set the stage for the patient as eponym, a democratic change in an increasingly democratic world.

Lou Gehrig was not the first patient to have amyotrophic lateral sclerosis. He was, however, at least in America, the most famous patient who ever developed ALS. Gehrig was a man whose acceptance of his fate has long been an inspiration to others facing incurable diseases. He achieved mythical stature, within the mythic nature of baseball. Such people can and should be honored. Besides, his name is far easier to remember and to spell, and it certainly helps in raising funds to support research.

Lou Gehrig was the greatest first baseman in the history of major league baseball. His career accomplishments are legion. The most famous was his feat of having played in two thousand one hundred thirty consecutive games, a record finally broken in 1995 by Baltimore shortstop Cal Ripken, Jr. This streak had earned Lou the nickname "the Iron Horse." I have never been particularly in awe of the record. I know that well over three thousand big league players, in the years between Gehrig and Ripken, had at one time or another been placed on the injury list for injuries or illnesses that prevented them from playing for at least two to four weeks. I recognize the self-discipline and grit that go into such a streak, but I also realize the sheer good luck in it. No summer flu. No severe gastroenteritis. None of those diseases that occur by merely being in the wrong place at the wrong time, from tonsillitis to polio to amyotrophic lateral sclerosis. It is the irony of the speed with which the streak of "the

Iron Horse" ended that has contributed to the aura that has always accompanied his record and given it its legendary quality. Gehrig's record run was ended by a disease that killed him a mere twenty-five months later.

Lou Gehrig played first base for the New York Yankees for fifteen seasons from 1925 through 1938 and never missed a game. His streak began in the heyday of Babe Ruth. Ruth hit his sixty home runs in 1927. Gehrig hit forty-seven that season. Yankee second baseman Tony Lazzeri was third in the league with a grand total of eighteen. Only one team other than the Yankees hit more home runs that year than Lou Gehrig did, and that was Connie Mack's Philadelphia Athletics. Gehrig's career ended in the era of Joe DiMaggio, "the Yankee Clipper." DiMaggio was in his rookie year, 1935, when he hit .323 with twenty-nine home runs. Gehrig hit .354 that year with a league-leading forty-nine home runs. The league had caught up to Lou. Every team hit at least forty-nine home runs, and the number two home-run hitter, Cleveland's Hal Trosky, hit forty-two while Boston's Jimmie Foxx, "old double X," was a close third with forty-one.

When Gehrig retired in 1939, only Babe Ruth had amassed more home runs during his career (714 to 493). Of his contemporaries, two players would go on to surpass Lou's total, New York Giants outfielder Mel Ott and Philadelphia-Boston first baseman Jimmie Foxx. Gehrig was thirty-five when he hit his last home run. Ott hit a total of five hundred eleven home runs, but forty-eight of those came after he was thirty-five. Foxx totaled five hundred thirty-four, hitting forty after he was thirty-five and leaving him with one more than Lou before the age of thirty-six. When Hank Aaron turned thirty-six he had hit only five hundred forty-four of his career total of seven hundred fifty-five.

During Gehrig's fourteen full seasons as a Yankee, the team won seven American League pennants and six World Series. In four of these, they swept the National League champions in four straight games. Gehrig batted over .300 in twelve of those fourteen years. The exceptions were his first (1924) and last (1938) seasons. Both years he hit .295, the first as a raw rookie with limited minor league experience and far fewer than 1,500 at bats in professional baseball, and the last as a man already struggling with a fatal neurological disease. He hit 493 home runs and ended up with a lifetime batting average of .340. He led the American League in home runs three times, once in a tie with Babe Ruth. That season (1931) he set the American League record for runs batted in with 184, a record that still stands. In 1934 he won the Triple Crown by leading the league in batting average, home runs, and runs batted in. Only eight American Leaguers have ever won the Triple Crown, four since Lou Gehrig (Ted Williams—twice, Mickey Mantle, Frank Robinson, and Carl Yastrzemski). Only four National Leaguers have done it this century, with the last being Joe Medwick in 1937. Gehrig was twice voted the most valuable player in the American League: in 1927, the year teammate Babe Ruth cracked out sixty home runs, and in 1936. In Gehrig's Triple Crown year, the MVP Award was voted to Mickey Cochrane, the catcher for the pennant-winning Detroit Tigers. From 1931 to 1937, Gehrig was one of the top five vote-getters for this award every single year. His reputation is truly of monumental proportions.

Gehrig came to the Yankees from Columbia University where he played fullback on the football team and was both a pitcher and an outfielder for the baseball team. Like so many young baseball players, he had yet to restrict himself to becoming either a pitcher or a hitter. Since he was still a college kid, he didn't have to choose. He was discovered almost by accident by a Yankee scout named Paul Kichell. Having nothing else to do one fine morning, Kichell watched a game between Rutgers and Columbia. Gehrig was pitching for Columbia. More important, he was hitting.

Gehrig had played both sports at Commerce High School in New York and had been regarded as the best high school baseball prospect in New York. His athletic abilities won him a scholarship to Columbia. He had also been pursued by John McGraw, the manager of the New York Giants, who wanted him to play baseball for the Giants. Lou signed a contract and played a couple of minor league games, but his parents thought that a college degree was far more important than hitting a baseball. His father was a janitor in a fraternity house and his mother a cleaning lady. They knew that a college education was the key to success.

Lou was awarded a sports scholarship to Columbia, but it was threatened because he had played professional baseball. Jim Thorpe had only played semipro ball and had never signed a contract with anyone, and he had been stripped of all his Olympic medals and declared a professional. Fortunately, Columbia and its lawyers intervened and the minor league contract was declared void. Lou had been underage when he signed it. He had his scholarship. His future was assured.

Would this have happened if he, like Thorpe, had been a Native American? If his scholarship had been to Carlisle or another of the "Indian" schools?

Gehrig was six feet one inch tall and weighed about two hundred fifteen pounds. He was the starting fullback on the Columbia football team in the fall and pitched baseball and played outfield in the spring. Columbia was certainly getting its money's worth out of that scholarship.

It was during the spring of Gehrig's sophomore year that Kichell happened to see him play for Columbia. Kichell loved what he saw and called the head of the Yankee organization, Ed Barrow, telling him he had seen "another Babe Ruth." Barrow was not impressed. Future Babe Ruth sightings had become commonplace.

But Kichell was not easily dissuaded. He took in another Columbia game. This time Gehrig hit a home run that left the playing field and landed on the library steps across the street from the baseball diamond. Kichell reported in again and Barrow was now impressed.

Kichell signed Gehrig for a cash bonus of forty-five hundred dollars to play the rest of the season. That was a lot of money in 1923. Gehrig spent most of his first two seasons in organized baseball playing for the Yankee farm club in Hartford in the Eastern League, learning how to play first base. He came up to the Yankees to stay in 1925. The Yankees already had a regular first baseman, Wally Pipp. He'd been a fixture there for a decade and showed no signs of giving up. Gehrig started the year on the bench. On June 1, 1925, he appeared as a pinch hitter. The next day Pipp had a bad headache and asked for the day off. Gehrig replaced him in the lineup and didn't miss another game until 1938.

That was the day amyotrophic lateral sclerosis forced him to call it quits. ALS, like most other slowly progressive neurological diseases, starts almost imperceptibly. When had Lou's muscles become weakened? When had the fatigue of playing every single day become, at the age of thirty-five, greater than normal? When had Lou Gehrig's disease started? When had it begun to affect his ability to play baseball? His ability to hit?

That had to have happened in 1938. It was the first time he hit below .300 since his rookie year, after twelve straight years above .300. It was the first time he had not been voted in the top five for the Most Valuable Player Award. But when in 1938?

Could it have started earlier, say 1937, with subtle changes in his playing? I am not the first baseball enthusiast to wonder about this. It is the perfect baseball question. Baseball is statistics and this is a question that can only be explored by statistics. I am also not the first neurologist to wonder about this problem. And neurologists have a distinct advantage over most other baseball buffs. We have been trained in biostatistical analysis and work in medical centers with biostatisticians. And biostatisticians can do things with numbers that no baseball statistician ever dreamed about. The neurologist that made the single most thorough exploration of the question as to when Lou Gehrig's illness began to alter his performance was Edward Kasarskis of the Albert B. Chandler Medical Center of the University of Kentucky, the only medical center in the world named after a former commissioner of baseball. A. B. "Happy" Chandler had also been governor of Kentucky.

Kasarskis started by using the four seasons of 1932, 1933, 1934, and 1935 as his starting point. The final four years of Gehrig's career were then compared to this baseline. During the

Lou Gehrig taking a practice swing. While his adherence to conditioning compared favorably to Michael Jordan's, his ability to hit long ones was in a league with Babe Ruth's. His career totals (493 home runs and 790 strikeouts) gave him a lifetime ratio of just over one and a half strikeouts per home run. In 1934 and 1936, he hit 49 home runs each season to lead the American League both years, and struck out 31 and 46 times, respectively.

baseline years, Gehrig played 153 games each year, averaging 36.2 home runs each season. His average batting average was .343, with a standard deviation of .013. This means that merely due to random variation or statistical scatter, the odds were that he would continue to hit between .330 and .356 unless something nonrandom happened to him.

Something, however, was happening to him. Or actually two things. He was getting older and he was coming down with ALS. Neither would help his batting skills. If they deteriorated, how could anyone be certain which was responsible?

In order to study the 1936, 1937, and 1938 seasons, Kasarskis computed Gehrig's batting statistics on a weekly basis. This information was then analyzed utilizing a statistical technique called CUSUM, which is short for cumulative sums. This technique is designed to detect any consistent deviations from a reference value, namely, the same analysis for the four baseline seasons. To control for age the same analysis was run on Lou Gehrig's Yankee teammates for the last ten years of each of their careers.

The results showed that nothing bad happened to Lou in 1936 or 1937, whether from ALS or aging. This came as no big surprise. He hit .354 in 1936 and .351 in 1937. A simple look at *The Baseball Encyclopedia* would have revealed that. It was a different story in 1938. He started off more slowly that season and never caught up. In other words, his performance was off from opening day onward. After the first ten weeks, his performance deteriorated even more. His power, as estimated by his home-run production, did not slip until midway through the season. The comparison with the career performances of his teammates showed that Lou Gehrig's severe decline could not have been due to age. The effects of age are slower and more subtle. It had been his ALS from the beginning of 1938.

Why had his batting average declined more than his home-run production during the first half of 1938? Kasarskis would like to attribute this to the fact that the predominate weakness early in his illness was in his legs. This would have altered his speed and allowed opposing infielders to play deeper. In so doing they could be in position to cut off more potential hits before they reached the outfield. Lou's power hits still depended primarily on his less impaired upper extremities.

Is there any other collaborative evidence of this?

In January 1938, Lou Gehrig went to Hollywood and made a western entitled *Rawhide* (not to be confused with the TV series that introduced Clint Eastwood in a supporting role). Gehrig's scenes in the film show no evidence of weakness in his arms or hands, although one scene does suggest that there may have been some atrophy of the small muscles of his hands. Also, his movement in getting out of a chair was not quite normal, either. He had to use his hands to push down on his legs in order to straighten his hip joints. Normally, the leg muscles do this without help, but if those muscles become weak, the patient learns to cope in this characteristic manner. This is called Gower's sign, after the English neurologist who first described it in children with Duchenne's muscular dystrophy. It is usually considered to be evidence of weakness in the thigh muscles.

The 1939 season was a total disaster. Gehrig played in only eight games, batting .143 before he benched himself. A photograph of him in a Yankee uniform taken early that year shows definite atrophy of his hand muscles.

Amyotrophic lateral sclerosis was another of those neurological diseases that was delineated by Charcot and his school. They gave this disease such a perfect descriptive name that it had never become an eponym. *Amyotrophic* refers to the atrophy, or degeneration, of the involved muscles, such as those in Lou Gehrig's hands. As the individual muscles become weak they shrink; as the disease progresses, more and more muscles are affected. But, unlike Duchenne's muscular dystrophy, the atrophy is not due to any disorder of the muscles themselves.

Lateral refers to the lateral columns of the spinal cord, which, when examined microscopically, are shrunken and scarred, or sclerotic. This condition was revealed in the careful microscopic examinations that were done at the Salpêtrière under Charcot's direction. It was here that researchers attempted to correlate their detailed clinical evaluations of patients with the microscopic findings. How could sclerosis of the lateral columns be related to changes in motor function?

The most important and largest structure in each of the two lateral columns (one on either side of the spinal column) is the pyramidal tract, also known as the corticospinal tract. Each column originates as the motor cells of the opposite side of the brain. These motor cells are located in the motor strip at the back of the frontal lobe. They are for the most part large cells with long processes, or axons. These axons pass through the brain stem forming a structure called the pyramid. In the brain stem they give off branches to the collections of the motor nerves that innervate the muscles of the head and neck. They then decussate to reach the opposite sides of the spinal cord, forming the lateral columns. They end up by making contact with the motor cells of the respective anterior horns.

The cells of the anterior horns of the spinal cord that receive their instructions from the corticospinal tract are the very same cells that are injured in polio. When Lou Gehrig took himself out of the lineup, he was evaluated at the Mayo Clinic. A diagnosis of amyotrophic lateral sclerosis was quickly made. This was a rare disease. No one outside of the medical world had any idea what it was. The public was told that Lou had a chronic form of polio, not a bad explanation. The weakness and the atrophy of the muscles in ALS are not caused by the LS, the lateral sclerosis. Disease of the pyramidal tract does not result in muscle weakness or atrophy. It prevents the instructions from getting from the upper motor neuron of the cerebral cortex to the lower motor neurons of the brain stem and spinal cord. This results in spasticity, stiffness, and a lack of voluntary movement—paralysis. But it doesn't cause atrophy. Atrophy is due to death of the lower motor neurons. As these cells die the muscles receive no instructions, so they do not contract. That is what constitutes weakness. But the lower motor neuron does more than send messages to muscle cells to contract. It also serves a trophic, or nutritive, function, keeping the muscles alive and healthy. Once the muscle cell is deprived of motor neuron innervation, it shrinks and becomes atrophic—amyotrophy.

This is the same process that causes weakness and atrophy in polio, but in a far different way—chronically over years, not acutely over days. Also, there is no end to the process, no recovery phase. The disease progresses inexorably, and progress here means death.

The last term in the name, *sclerosis*, means scarring. In ALS, sclerosis refers to the secondary, or reactive, scarring that occurs in the motor pathways following the death of the motor cells and their axons.

On the morning of the ninth game of the season, Lou Gehrig permanently removed himself from the lineup. That was on May 2, 1939, and it was not a fine morning for anyone. A few weeks later, the Yankees held a day for him. Nearly sixty-two thousand fans flocked to Yankee Stadium to honor Lou Gehrig. He stepped to the microphone and said, "Today, I consider myself the luckiest man on the face of the earth." This emotional scene became the centerpiece of the Hollywood movie version of Lou's life story, *The Pride of the Yankees*, starring Gary Cooper.

Lou died on June 2, 1942. He was thirty-eight. It was twenty-five months from the day he told Yankee manager Joe McCarthy, the same man who had once signed him to a New York Yankees contract, that he was going to bench himself since he could no longer help the team.

Teammate Joe DiMaggio is still with us.

Dysfunction of the lower motor neurons is associated with one other clinical phenomenon, rippling of the muscles. These ripples are called fasciculations. As the clinician looks at the weakened and atrophic muscles, these small ripples appear under the skin. Some say they are signs of spontaneous firing of the degenerating nerve cells. Others refer to these fasciculations as the lower motor neurons waving goodbye.

What causes ALS? The short answer is that we don't know. In a very small number of patients, ALS is inherited, a genetic disorder caused by a defective mutant gene. But this is not true for most patients. In most it is sporadic. Unlike Parkinson's, this disease is not restricted solely to humans; other species have ALS or at least hereditary ALS-like diseases.

A number of possible mechanisms have been suggested to play a role in ALS or similar disorders. None of these hypothetical constructs has ever been proved to be important in any disorder. They remain disease mechanisms looking for their own diseases. The most attractive to me is the idea that the death of all of the upper motor neurons collected in the motor strip of the brain and the lower motor neurons scattered in groups from the brain stem to the end of the spinal cord is due to loss of a trophic, or growth-maintaining, factor.

It is the trophic function of the lower motor neurons themselves that gives this theory its appeal. As the lower motor neurons die, the muscle cells that they innervate lose their trophic input and die. Innervation and trophism do not always depend upon each other. Loss of neuronal input to the intestines has no effect on the muscles of the gut. They continue to prosper on their own. This is true of the muscles of the entire autonomic (involuntary) motor system.

The voluntary motor system, however, is a very old system in which the oldest part, the link from the lower motor neuron to the muscle, has a trophic function. Why couldn't the other links in this same system also have the same type of trophic activity? There is no reason why this couldn't be true. There would be a certain phylogenetic logic if they did. Going back to the earliest stages of the descent of all mammalian species, this logic would presuppose that the upper motor neurons would exert the same trophic control over the lower motor neurons that the lower motor neurons exert over the muscles. But what about the upper motor neurons? Why do they become atrophic? Perhaps the neurons of the premotor area, where the concept of any particular movement is set into motion, have a trophic influence on the upper motor neurons. This is all possible. But which comes first? The chicken, in the form of cell death somewhere in the chain, or the egg, in the form of loss of trophic function? And which trophic factor came first? Does that factor even start in the motor system at all? These are all questions to which we have no answers.

But the possibility that a trophic factor is lost is very attractive, for if this is true and that trophic factor can be identified and isolated, treatment with that factor might revolutionize the outlook for patients with Lou Gehrig's disease. As it is now, the outlook remains what it was almost sixty years ago when Lou took his last bow.

Could this disease be caused by a toxin?

Possibly. There is a disease called lathyrism—a form of lateral sclerosis but without amyotrophy. The disease crops up whenever people are forced to use the chickling pea, *Lathyrus sativus*, as their primary source of nutrition. The chickling pea is not the chick pea, or garbanzo, and the two should not be confused. Humans and other animals (for other species under the same circumstances develop the same disease) normally defend themselves from lathyrism by maintaining a varied diet. They don't eat too many chickling peas. After all, many plants contain toxic elements. That is how they survive in a world filled with insects selected by many million years of evolution to eat them as efficiently as possible. The plants, too, have been selected by the same process and just as successfully, for they are still here competing with those insects. Plants often develop toxins to fend off their enemies. Some of these plants are so poisonous that we avoid them altogether. These are rare. Most we handle by eating in modest amounts, so their toxins do us no harm. That is part of the balance of nature.

Then along comes a drought and all that is left to eat are the chickling peas. They become an organism's entire diet, and disease results.

How do we know that lathyrism is due to a toxin? Why couldn't it be due to some deficiency? The change in diet could easily cause a deficiency, a lack of some essential amino acid or some other compound we cannot synthesize ourselves. This part of the riddle was solved by Peter Spencer, a pathologist at Albert Einstein Medical School in New York. Spencer isolated a chemical from chickling peas called BOAA. He gave this chemical to monkeys, who were also given a complete, varied diet. They came down with lathyrism. Since the monkeys were deficient in nothing, lathyrism could not be a deficiency disease.

How does BOAA do its mischief? We believe it causes excessive excitation of nerve cells that triggers a self-destructive process. That's the theory. Perhaps those fasciculations, all that waving goodbye, are a manifestation of such excessive excitation. Possibly, but no such toxin has ever been identified in patients with ALS. There are pockets of lathyrism. Epidemics. The last was in a Nazi concentration camp where the slave laborers were intentionally fed a diet made up almost entirely of chickling peas. No such pockets or epidemics of ALS have ever been described.

Refsum's disease was also recognized during World War II, like the last European epidemic of lathyrism. This, too, was no mere coincidence. Refsum's disease is a genetic disorder. There is a defective gene and a defective gene product, an enzyme. This enzyme normally metabolizes a dietary fatty acid, phytanic acid. Without this enzyme and the omega oxidation that it performs, phytanic acid collects inside the skin, eyes, and nerves, and causes damage. What difference could the war have made? The occupation of Norway by the Nazis was associated with an alteration of the diet of many Norwegians to one that included more and more phytanic acid. Like more chickling peas in the concentration camp diet.

Sigvald Refsum died in 1992, but his disease lives on and so does his name. I remember him for something else, too. As the leading neurologist in Norway, he became the author of a textbook on the neurological examination. This had originally been written by his predecessor, Professor Monrad Krohn. This book is of critical importance because it contains a normal pneumoencephalogram. The pneumoencephalogram was one of the first radiological techniques to supply physicians with an image of the brain. These techniques are no longer done, having been displaced by both CAT and MRI scans, which are far safer and far more detailed and accurate. A pneumoencephalogram was taken by performing a spinal tap on a patient and then replacing some spinal fluid with air. The air enters the cranial cavity and surrounds the brain. An X ray of the skull is then taken. The brain absorbs X rays far more efficiently than the air does. What results is a picture of the air, showing an outline of the brain and its cavities.

One normal pneumoencephalogram contained in Refsum's book is far more than an anachronism. It's not the fact that it is a normal pneumo that is important, but that it is the normal pneumo of Vidkun Quisling, whose name is synonymous with traitor and collaborator all rolled into one. Quisling had formed a fascist party in Norway in 1933. In 1939, he met with Hitler and urged him to invade Norway. After the German invasion, Quisling became a Nazi collaborator and served as the minister-president of the puppet state. When the war was over, Quisling was tried for treason and found guilty. Still, his behavior was totally inexplicable to most Norwegians. There must have been something wrong with him. He was examined neurologically and found to be intact. A pneumo was done. It was normal. There was no evidence of any neurological disease. One fine morning, Vidkun Quisling was taken out and shot.

Such men should also be remembered.

First-Half Jameson

I had seen Dwight Jameson* several times on my television set before I saw him in my office for neurological consultation. He had not been particularly impressive in those few football games that I had half-watched. There was no question about his basic athletic skills. He was about an inch over six feet tall and weighed about one hundred ninety-five pounds. He combined strength and speed, and played free safety with a degree of abandon that had won him some consideration as an All-American pick while in college. But his professional career had never been peppered with such success. During his rookie year he had played on special teams, coming into the games for kick-offs, kickoff returns, and the like. He made the starting defensive lineup in his second year. By the time he arrived in my office, his fifth season had drawn to a close and it appeared that his career was also just about over. He had been back on the special teams for the last half of the season.

The one time I had watched him play that fall, his demotion seemed justified. Not in my mind; I do not pretend to be a judge of professional football talent. That had been the judgment of those ex-players who announced the games and then talked on about the plays and the players between plays, between halves, after the games, ad infinitum, ad nauseam.

*This is not his real name; that is protected by patient-physician confidentiality.

It seems that Dwight Jameson had acquired a bad reputation. He was not a dirty player who tried to hurt key members of the opposing team. This all transpired well over a decade ago when such "punishment" was still considered good form, a part of the macho image of professional football and its practitioners. His reputation was for not making the "big play," especially late in the game. To be more precise, he had developed a talent for letting the big play, invariably a long pass for the winning touchdown, go over his head and into the hands of the opposing team. A few such plays resulting in fourth-quarter losses created his reputation and eventually reduced him to the rank of special team player.

One of the announcers remarked facetiously that Jameson was halfway to being an all-pro.

"Which half?" the straight man of the announcing tandem asked.

"The first half," the ex-linebacker quipped. He then went on to explain that Jameson always looked great in the first half, when the game was not yet on the line. It was toward the end of the game that he fell apart. Good old First-Half Jameson, half of an all-pro. Had he played for a more prominent team his nickname might have rivaled that of Wrong Way Corrigan, the pilot who supposedly took off in New York heading for California and landed instead on the other side of the Atlantic.

The implication was clear. Jameson was not man enough to do what he had to do when the chips were down. In college, he'd had a different nickname; he'd been called Sleepy Jameson. I assumed that had reflected a habit of sleeping through classes.

After the game I gave the comment no further thought. Jameson was little more to me than a bit player in a game I half-slept through on a dreary Sunday afternoon, killing time in between watching the Chicago Bears and having dinner. The kind of day when it was too cold or too wet to hit a bucket of golf balls.

Then Dwight walked into my office. He had been referred to me by his cousin, who had been a resident in internal medicine at our hospital seven or eight years previously and had spent a couple of months learning some neurology with me. The cousin knew enough about medicine and neurology to suspect that something was wrong with Dwight, but couldn't put his finger on it precisely, so referred Dwight to me. It was late in December and his team had lost too many games in the fourth quarter to be in the play-offs.

I did not recognize him. I don't think I would have if he had walked in wearing shoulder pads and a football helmet. I also did not recognize his name when I saw it on his chart and introduced myself to him. Such is fame. As it was, his name did not click in until he told me what he did for a living. He was a safety in the National Football League, he told me.

Dwight Jameson, I thought to myself. Not exactly a household name. He wasn't a free safety anymore. He played only on special teams, but he still thought of himself as a safety and I wasn't one to contradict him. Then the significance of his nickname, First-Half, hit me. And so did the diagnosis. Or at least a possible diagnosis, a disease to be considered, to be eliminated. A prominent part of his differential diagnosis. That disease was myasthenia gravis.

Put simply, myasthenia gravis means grave weakness of the muscles. It is not exactly a diagnosis that conjures up images of happy endings. For the first decade or so of my professional life, happy endings for my patients with myasthenia gravis had been few and far between. Many of those patients had fared quite poorly. Their prognosis had been truly grave and their management had been a nightmare both for them and me. As I recall, I had even taught Dwight's cousin my aphorism on myasthenia, an aphorism designed to help my beleaguered residents learning how to take care of these patients: whenever there is a crisis in a patient who has myasthenia gravis, no matter what you decide to do, the chances are greater than fifty-fifty that the patient will get worse. No matter what you do, the odds are against you. That is the nature of the disease.

In my residency, I had been taught another rule. If there is a neurologist you really dislike, refer all your myasthenic patients to him. Let him make all of those bad decisions.

Myasthenia gravis is a disease of the neuromuscular junction. The neuromuscular junction is the crossroads at which the motor nerve innervates the muscle. This junction is also known as the motor end plate and is a highly specialized structure that is surprisingly constant in both structure and function throughout most of the animal kingdom. The motor end plate evolved as a good way to convey orders from the nervous system to the effector organ, the muscles. It developed long ago and has undergone only minor evolutionary changes in the last several hundred million years. The neuromuscular junction should be seen as a very old structure carrying out a very old set of functions. This junction relays messages from one cell to another, one of the key problems to be solved by complex, multicellular organisms. In a way it is very much a modified synapse. The synapse is the specialized structure by which neurons communicate with each other. In a motor end plate a motor neuron communicates with a muscle cell. The neuronal structure makes up the presynaptic portion, which is separated from the muscular part, the postsynaptic receptor membrane, by a space. This space is called the synaptic cleft.

The job of a motor nerve is to convey messages from the central nervous system to the muscles. The message travels as an electrical impulse down the axon of the nerve leading from the cell body to the nerve terminal. Once the terminal is reached, the cleft between nerve and muscle must be crossed. This is not breached by electricity but by a specific chemical agent, acetylcholine, which is released by the nerve ending. This chemical neurotransmitter then crosses the synaptic cleft and interacts with the postsynaptic receptors generating another electrical impulse or action potential, and initiating that series of chemical reactions that produce contraction of the muscle. This is what happens in humans, what happens in eels, and what happens in all the species between the two. It is a solution to the problem of delivering the right message to the right place at the right time. It was such a good solution that no better one has yet to evolve despite millions of year of descent along a variety of separate lines.

Why all this complicated electrochemical stuff? Wouldn't simple electrical transmission be easier? Perhaps, but chemical transmission has its advantages. With it, messages can only cross the synapse in one direction, from the presynaptic nerve terminal that releases the chemical to the postsynaptic receptor that binds with it. There is no back talk. Besides, chemical transmission came first. Cell membranes of primitive organisms without specialized nerve cells or muscle cells respond to chemicals and have developed specific structures designed to respond to specific chemicals.

Two variations on this primitive sequence have evolved and continue to function in all complex animals, including humans. One is the endocrine system; the other is the nervous system. The entire endocrine system is based on chemical transmission of messages. Hormones are released and travel throughout the entire body, and are only taken up and act on those cells that have specialized membrane receptors for that hormone. Specificity of the message depends on two factors: the chemical structure of the messenger and the pattern of cells with receptors that respond to that message. The pituitary gland releases a specific polypeptide to increase production of steroids by the adrenal glands. That polypeptide goes everywhere in the body. Most cells are oblivious to it and their membranes have no receptors for it. Not so the adrenal gland; here the polypeptide is taken up and does its job. That is the essence of the endocrine system at work. In asking the question of which came first, the nerve or the receptor, the answer is the receptor and the chemical.

In the endocrine system, the message carrier is called a hormone; in the nervous system, a neurotransmitter. In the latter system, the transmitter is not set loose upon the entire body to find the right receptor; it is delivered to the correct place by the correct nerve. That allows every nerve to use the same transmitter for only one muscle cell to receive each specific message. The neuromuscular junction is one of the oldest of these delivery systems. The same neurotransmitter chemical, acetylcholine, carries out that same function in every human muscle, and in every muscle throughout most of the animal kingdom.

Once acetylcholine has hit the postsynaptic receptor and triggered the ensuing process in the muscle, it has to get out of the receptor. It is the initial interaction between acetylcholine and its receptor that initiates the process of muscle contraction. Remaining there initiates nothing more. In fact, it prevents new interactions and as a result causes weakness and paralysis. This is how the poison curare works. It enters the bloodstream, like a hormone, is distributed to the body's neuromuscular junctions, and once there binds to the postsynaptic receptor—and stays there. Acetylcholine can no longer get in. That means no new interaction, no initiation of muscle contractions. The result is paralysis leading to respiratory failure and death. All from a little chemical that slips into the acetylcholine receptor and won't get out. Curare's uniformly deadly effects demonstrate the unity of this system throughout the animal kingdom and also point out the most vulnerable part of the entire system.

Once the process is triggered, the acetylcholine is released from the receptor. This allows the next molecule to enter the receptor so that the muscle can be stimulated to contract again. That process is where many natural poisons work. Evolution got started devising these poisons long, long ago, and the acetylcholine receptor has been the target for many of them. Many snake poisons, such as bungaro toxin, the toxin of the deadly bungarus snake, function in the same fashion and are just as deadly. This knowledge is not new. Claude Bernard, the greatest of all experimental neurophysiologists, studied curare in the 1850s and localized its site of action to the neuromuscular junction.

Life then depends on the next molecule of acetylcholine being able to get into that receptor. The previous molecule has to go. And go it does. Acetylcholine is destroyed by an enzyme called acetylcholine esterase. This enzyme cleaves acetylcholine into two small molecules and reopens the receptor. The neuromuscular junction is back in business again. It is ready for the next jolt of acetylcholine.

The acetylcholine that acts on the motor end plate seems to carry out two separate functions. This process has been discussed already in this book in relation to two other diseases: the poliomyelitis of Wilma Rudolph (Chapter 11) and Lou Gehrig's motor neuron disease (Chapter 15). Acetylcholine both initiates contraction of the muscle and performs a trophic, or growth-stimulating, function that keeps the muscle alive and well. Wilma Rudolph wore braces because polio had injured some of her motor neurons so severely that they lost their trophic capabilities and the muscles of her leg became wasted. As a result, her leg was crooked for years until recovery occurred and the muscles were stimulated to grow back. Lou Gehrig's nerves died off, one nerve cell at a time, day after day after day, and his muscles became weaker and weaker. Deprived of all trophic input, they also became more and more shrunken, in a disease that became graver than grave.

Myasthenia is far different in other ways, however, from either polio or amyotrophic lateral sclerosis, or any other disease for that matter. It does not begin by causing permanent weakness that progresses. It may not ever progress in the usual sense. It fluctuates. The symptoms come and go. Sometimes they are there. Sometimes they aren't. Sometimes the acetylcholine can get its message through. Sometimes it just can't. The major factor in this intermittent function is often the influence of exercise, or muscular activity. The more a muscle is exercised, the more likely it is to become weak—conditioning in reverse.

The patient feels fine in the morning. He is strong. There is no evidence of any weakness. He looks, feels, and acts as if he is normal. And he is. All of his muscles are reacting quite normally to the messages being relayed to them. He goes to work. He feels fine. He works a couple of hours. He is still okay; but then the system begins to fail. Not everywhere at once. It is not a matter of generalized weakness either slowly or suddenly appearing. It is usually just one or two muscles that become weak. Often it is the eyes that go first. One eyelid begins to droop. Sometimes even both do. In neurological circles this drooping is called ptosis. Ptosis is caused by weakness of the muscle that elevates the upper eyelid. This is one of the few muscles that is at work almost one hundred percent of the time

during the waking day. Ptosis on one side can make the patient
look as if he has something wrong with one eye. The drooping of
both eyelids, of course, can give the patient a sleepy appearance.

Bingo times two! I may be slow on the uptake sometimes,
but this I recalled. Dwight had had another nickname, "Sleepy,"
and it hadn't come from sleeping in class.

Ptosis merely resembles sleepiness because of the patient's
inability to keep his eyes open. It is not normal sleepiness. The
patient is not tired; his eyelids are weak. There is a big difference.
The weakness does not end there. The muscles that control eye
movements and keep the two eyes looking at the same place at
the same time are also working constantly. If their balance
becomes upset, the two eyes no longer track identically. The
entire visual-motor system is designed to get the same image to
the same place at the same time so the brain can see one image.
If the messages from the two eyes do not get to the same visual
cells at the same time what is delivered is no longer interpreted
as a single image but as two images. Two images means that
there are two objects out there. Every line on a printed page
becomes two. That long pass heading for the end zone becomes
two footballs arcing down the field. Double vision, also known
as diplopia.

I asked Dwight Jameson why he had so much trouble in
those fourth quarters.

"You sure don't beat around the bush," he replied.

I persisted.

"I see too many footballs," he finally admitted.

"How many is too many?" I asked.

"Two," he said softly.

"That's one too many," I agreed.

Dwight saw two footballs late in the game when he and his
body were becoming fatigued.

But only on long passes," he insisted. That was not much of
a consolation to his coaches or teammates or the fans. Getting
beat on long passes was precisely what was not supposed to
happen to a free safety. No long bombs. It was also precisely the
result myasthenia would produce. Tracking a fast-moving object

requires precise, continuous firing of the muscles that move the eyes. Continuous acetylcholine receptor interactions in rapid succession. Any failure at all would mean diplopia. Two footballs. Six points for the other side.

Back to special teams.

I looked at Dwight's face, at his eyes. He looked normal. They looked normal. There was no ptosis. Both eyes were in perfect alignment. I instructed him to follow the tip of my pen and then moved my pen back and forth. His eyes followed it perfectly. Minute after minute.

"After a game," I inquired, already anticipating the answer, "do your eyelids droop?"

He looked at me curiously. Maybe I wasn't such a fan. "That's why I was called Sleepy, because I look sleepy after a game. I'm no more sleepy than anyone else, I just look more tired. My eyes droop."

"And the next day your eyes look fine."

"They look fine by the time I have dinner and relax for a while. I don't even have to go to sleep. I just close my eyes for a few minutes."

Weakness and recovery. The hallmark of myasthenia gravis.

"Have you always been called Sleepy?" I asked. Was this a lifelong condition or something new?

He said the drooping had begun in college, during his senior year.

"Onset during his senior year in college," I wrote in his chart.

Intermittent weakness, weakness followed by recovery, is the key characteristic of myasthenia gravis. Recovery occurs when the muscle relaxes, when fast rates of firing are no longer required. Sleepy Jameson clearly had a history of weakness brought on by exercise and relieved by rest.

Myasthenia, of course, is not a new disease. Its peculiar intermittency has allowed modern physicians to diagnose it in retrospect in the writings of physicians from previous eras. The first description is usually credited to the English physician and anatomist Thomas Willis, who also described the circle of blood vessels at the base of the human brain that now carries his name, the circle of Willis. He called the disorder *paralysia spuria non habitualis,* paralysis that was spurious and not fixed or habitual. His description, written in 1683, includes the following details: "The patients are able at their first rising in the morning to walk, move their arms, or to lift up a weight with strength but before noon . . . they are scarce able to move hand or foot. . . . I have now a prudent and honest woman in cure, who for many years has been obnoxious to this kind of bastard palsy, not only in the limbs, but likewise in the tongue. This person for some time speaks freely and readily enough, but after long hasty or laborious speaking, presently she becomes as mute as a fish, and cannot bring forth a word, and does not recover the use of her voice till after an hour or two. . . ." Shades of Dwight Jameson.

There is another case of some historical interest that comes down to us from the nonmedical literature, and the subject has become known as the first American with myasthenia. This patient was a Native American chief named Opechankanough. When he was over seventy, he became incapacitated by severe weakness and had to be carried about on a litter. More to the point, his eyelids were so weak that his attendants had to hold his eyes open in order for him to see. The chief had both generalized weakness and ptosis.

In the nineteenth and early twentieth centuries, clinical literature exploded with descriptions of patients with various neurological maladies. Most of the diseases we see and diagnose today were first described in the hundred years following James Parkinson's 1817 essay on the disease that now bears his name. Many clinical tales of patients with fluctuating paralysis were reported. They presented a major challenge to nineteenth-century neurologists and pathologists. The patients were weak, but their weakness came and went. Their muscles were rarely atrophied. That meant that the messages got through often enough to prevent atrophy. When the patients died, examination of their brains revealed nothing out of the ordinary. That was a problem. If the muscles were still there to respond, then it had to be the nervous system that was at fault. It could no longer generate its orders, just as it couldn't in polio or amyotrophic lateral sclerosis.

Even the great Charcot could not figure out this disease. In 1892 Charcot described the case of a sixty-year-old medical inspector whom he had seen two years earlier. The patient had complained of diplopia and bilateral ptosis, but said all these symptoms disappeared after sleep (rather reminiscent of my patient). Weakness of the fingers and arms followed later. Charcot noted the fluctuation of the ptosis and also noted weakness in chewing. He made the diagnosis of polioencephalitis.

But polio does not fluctuate. Sleep is of no avail with polio. The muscles that are weak stay weak even after a very good night's sleep. More than that, the muscles, deprived of acetylcholine input to the receptors, become wasted and atrophied. Sleepy Jameson would have been misdiagnosed by Jean Martin Charcot. It is very humbling to read these clinical notes by one of the greatest neurologists and clinicians in the history of medicine, and wonder what future generations will make of my diagnoses. For one, I will be quite pleased if my clinical batting average is in the same league as Charcot's, even with the advantage of all our technical advances.

In 1895, three years later, a German neurologist named Jolly solved part of the riddle in the same publication in which he gave the disease its name. He used electrical current to stimulate the motor nerve and cause a muscle contraction in a patient with myasthenia gravis. The muscle contracted. That meant that the nerve responded normally to an electrical impulse and so did the muscle. No wonder the nervous system looked normal and there was no atrophy of the muscles. But things didn't remain normal. After repeated stimulations, a normal muscle keeps on contracting. But not in myasthenia gravis. Here, continuous electrical impulses lead to a weaker and weaker response. The longer Jolly stimulated the nerve, the weaker the response became. It was as if exercise caused weakness, which, of course, was just what happened clinically to patients like the one Jolly had studied.

The first impulse releases acetylcholine and the muscle responds as it should. But the neuromuscular junction is not normal, it can't recover normally, and its lack of recovery results in less response the next time and successively less with each stimulus—until late in the game two balls go flying over outstretched hands that just can't reach as high as they could a mere two hours earlier.

Myasthenia gravis also has one other unique characteristic as a disease. It is the only disease that is defined by its response to a drug. This characteristic became well defined in the years leading up to World War II and goes back to the nature of the neuromuscular junction defect.

The initial breakthrough in our understanding of this disorder came when Mary Walker, a resident in St. Alfege's Hospital, near London, had the idea that it would be worthwhile to try to use physostigmine, "a partial antidote to curare," on a patient with myasthenia gravis "in the hope that it would counteract the effect of the unknown substance which might be exerting a curare-like effect on the myoneural junctions." It seems that an American neurologist, Derek Denny-Brown, had visited London that year, had lectured on myasthenia gravis, and had discussed the resemblance between myasthenia and curare poisoning. Physostigmine (or eserine) was known to act as an antidote to curare. Denny-Brown was one of the most respected neurologists of his generation, an insightful clinician and inventive researcher. He understood the relationship between myasthenia and curare. It never occurred to him to give physostigmine to a myasthenic. There was no "eureka" for him.

Mary Walker remembered Denny-Brown's comments the next time she saw a patient with myasthenia. If physostigmine worked in curare poisoning, it was worth a try in myasthenia. She gave her fifty-six-year-old patient an injection of physostigmine salicylate. The patient's weakness improved. Dr. Walker tried again with similar success. And yet again. The physostigmine worked. No one injection improved all of the patient's symptoms, and sometimes the injection failed to produce any obvious benefit. But overall the benefit was clear. Controlled injections of a wide variety of other substances had no effect on the weakness.

The history of physostigmine is interesting. It is the active substance of the esere beans of Calabar, a district in what is now Nigeria and a center of slave trade in West Africa. The people who lived there had the custom of forcing anyone who was accused of witchcraft to undergo trial by poison. The poison they used was derived from poisonous seeds of the esere plant. Anyone suspected of witchcraft was given eight of the beans in water. The accused's mouth would shake and mucus would come from his nose if he were guilty. If he vomited, he was declared innocent. Both of these responses are pharmacological effects of esere, which became known as both eserine and physostigmine.

In another report Mary Walker reported the same improvement from a related medication called prostigmine, which could be taken orally. Walker's two reports, both published in the late 1930s, revolutionized our entire approach to myasthenia. This disease could now be diagnosed accurately and then treated successfully.

Physostigmine improves the weakness in myasthenia the same way that it reverses the blockade of the neuromuscular junction caused by curare. Physostigmine blocks acetylcholinesterase, the enzyme that destroys acetylcholine. Blockage of this enzyme increases the life of acetylcholine so more remains in the synaptic cleft. There is more opportunity for that acetylcholine to reach the partially blocked receptor, and once it does the receptor responds.

Acetylcholinesterase inhibitors quickly became the standard form of treatment of myasthenia and the gold standard for diagnosis of myasthenia. The diagnostic test now defines the disease. Injection of physostigmine or any other acetylcholinesterase inhibitor will reverse the weakness. Today these injections are done with a fast-acting analogue known as Tensilon. Such tests are so specific that myasthenia is often defined as muscular weakness reversed by the use of an acetylcholinesterase inhibitor.

I was itching to give Dwight Jameson an injection of Tensilon but I had nothing to test. He was normal. I could detect no weakness on examining him. If there was no weakness, there would be nothing that Tensilon could improve.

According to Dwight's history, his weakness appeared with exercise. I told him to exercise. Our offices were on the ninth floor. I had Dwight run up and down the stairs. Once. Twice. Three times. I examined him after three round-trips. I thought I noted some ptosis, especially in the right eye. When I asked him to count from one to twenty, the last two or three numbers seemed to be slightly slurred. There was something there but not quite enough to study or test.

Back to the stairs. A fourth time. Then a fifth. He was getting tired and I was getting tired of waiting for him. By now he knew something was wrong. He was seeing double. He had severe ptosis bilaterally. His eyes did not track normally. By the time he counted back to twelve, he was slurring his words. "Twelfth, eff-lef-thens. . . ."

I gave him the Tensilon and waited, but didn't have to for very long. Less than a minute. Dwight's eyelids lifted up. The ptosis was gone. His eyes straightened out. They now moved in conjunction with each other. His speech became crystal clear. There was no slurring at all. Dwight Jameson had a positive Tensilon test. By our definition of the disease, Dwight Jameson, First-Half Jameson, Sleepy Jameson had myasthenia gravis.

I told him what was wrong. He asked me what I could do to help him. One option was the use of medications much like the Tensilon I had just given him. "That sure helped," he observed.

It clearly had helped him, but such medicines are not unmixed blessings. They themselves are toxins. That is why crisis management in myasthenia always seems to go wrong. No matter what decision you make, the odds are against you. Insufficient amounts of acetylcholine at the receptors cause weakness, but so does too much. The right amount is a narrow range that is hard to obtain and even harder to maintain.

"Isn't there anything elthes you can do?" he slurred. The Tensilon had worn off by then. He was again slurring his speech and looking very sleepy. His natural recovery would take more time.

Fortunately, there was more that could be done. The reason I had more to offer Sleepy Jameson, more than mere variants on the medications introduced by Mary Walker fifty years earlier, was that we now had a far better understanding of the disease. We now know why myasthenia is an immune disease. It is, in fact, an autoimmune disease. Autoimmune diseases are a group of disorders in which the patient produces antibodies against one or more proteins of his own body. If that antibody interacts with a normal antigen of the thyroid, a disease called Hashimoto's thyroiditis results. In myasthenia, the abnormal antibody reacts with the motor end plate, more specifically, with the protein of the acetylcholine receptor of the end plate. These antibodies can be measured in the bloodstream of patients with myasthenia gravis. The circulation of these antibodies is one of the reasons exercise causes weakness. Exercise causes more blood to be pumped to the active muscles. More blood means exposure to more antibodies. This creates more chances for antibodies to latch on to receptor site antigens and block the synapses; and more blockage means more weakness. Exercise also stresses the reserve capacity of the motor end plates.

I told Dwight that we would do a blood test to measure his level of acetylcholine receptor antibodies. He wanted more than just the results of some esoteric blood tests.

Does this antibody produce the disease? It seems to. If purified acetylcholine receptors from electric eels are injected into rabbits, the rabbits produce antibodies to these foreign antigens. These antibodies then react with the rabbit's own acetylcholine receptors. The rabbits also become weak. In fact, the disease in rabbits has so many clinical features in common with myasthenia gravis that it is called experimental autoimmune myasthenia gravis. These antibodies can be measured in the sera from these rabbits by the same method we used to measure them in

Dwight. The similarity of this antigen, from electric eels to humans, is impressive. It could almost make a person believe in evolution.

It seems that the basic defect in myasthenia gravis is caused by a loss of acetylcholine receptor protein from the postsynaptic membrane. The antibody-antigen reaction reduces the available number of receptors, and this causes the weakness that is so damn grave. But the reaction is not the cause of the disease. It is the mechanism by which the weakness occurs. But how does this entire process become triggered? Why would Dwight Jameson have suddenly started making antibodies to attack his own body?

The production of specific antibodies, like neuronal learning, could be the result of either instruction or selection—the same age-old question that has perplexed scientists and philosophers since at least the time of Socrates. The traditional scientific view has considered this to be a perfect example of instructive learning on the part of the immune system.

Immunologists have pointed out for years that the body is capable of manufacturing an antibody for almost any foreign substance, or antigen, introduced into the body. The huge number and variety of potential antigens and subsequent antigen-induced antibodies make the notion of instruction very attractive. This attractiveness had been furthered by the observation that the body also manufactures antibodies to artificial substances that have been newly synthesized and had never before existed in nature.

What process other than instruction could possibly explain this? Looks can, however, be very deceiving. The power of the process of selection should never be underestimated.

When a foreign substance enters the body, a preexisting cell immediately recognizes the intruder and, in order to defend the body from it, begins to multiply and manufacture a range of proteins—including within that range the one protein (antibody) that neutralizes the chemical intruder. As the preexisting cell multiplies, there can be minor mutations (genetic drift) that can, in turn, make other proteins that are even more effective against the intruder. What once looked like an instruction process, with the body developing a new molecule in response to the environment, has turned out to be a selection process.

In this selection process the foreign element selects a preexisting cell within the body (or is selected by that cell) and that cell produces the range of antibodies that it can produce. No more and no less. This range of antibody responses wards off the intruding antigen. It is all a matter of selection.

Selection is nothing terribly new. In 1943, Nobel Prize winners Salvador Luria and Max Delbrück studied the problem of bacterial adaptation to antibiotics. They discovered that bacteria do not really adapt to the antibiotic in their environment. Entirely new strains of antibiotic-resistant bacteria do not spontaneously generate. The process is one of selection.

In this selection process, preexisting alternative forms of bacteria flourish, not entirely new bacteria. Most bacteria faced with the bacteriocidal environment died off. A few survived. Those that survived did so for a reason. Survival wasn't a random event. The bacteria had some capability that had allowed them to become the only bacteria still surviving in that environment. In effect, survival of those that were fittest to meet the challenge. The so-called adaptive enzymes that are responsible for today's explosion of antibiotic-resistant bacteria are produced by genes that were already present in a small number of bacteria. The problem has not been new bacteria so much as the widespread extension of the altered environment, so that those few that were resistant were given the opportunity to become the most fit and survive. Selection, not mutation or instruction.

Socrates may have been right after all. He taught that all learning was nothing more than being reminded of what was already in the brain. He never explained why learning often remains so darn difficult.

What does this process of selection have to do with First-Half Jameson? He possessed within his body the immune cells that were capable of producing antiacetylcholine receptor antibodies. Many of us probably do. Normally we don't produce that or any other antibody to our own antigens. Then in Dwight this cell was selected into action. But why? How?

Most likely the selection was spurred by some trivial, unrelated event. Perhaps it was a viral infection or some other foreign substance that somehow entered into the body and then selected the right cell to produce antibodies to its antigens, but the wrong cell as far as Dwight was concerned. That cell was selected into activity and produced a range of antibodies to a number of antigens. One of these antibodies was Dwight's own acetylcholine receptor protein. The result was the disease we call myasthenia gravis.

The overlap of this selection and response system is not always a bad thing. In fact, the overlap can be helpful. It explains why smallpox now survives only in a few laboratories around the world, even though during the sixteenth and seventeenth centuries one out of three Europeans who survived infancy died of the disease. Edward Jenner, an eighteenth-century British physician, realized that milkmaids who had had cowpox, a mild infection of the hands that was an occupational hazard of milkmaids, never developed smallpox. Jennerian vaccination consists of intentionally spreading cowpox in order to prevent smallpox. It works because the antibodies induced by the virus of cowpox also interact with the antigens on the smallpox virus. It has worked so well that smallpox has become a veritable "endangered species."

"Where do those antibodies come from?" Dwight asked me.

"The thymus gland," I replied.

That was the key to what we might do to help Dwight Jameson and perhaps even cure him. It had been known for years that the thymus gland may be enlarged in some patients with myasthenia. At times there can even be a tumor in the thymus, a thymoma. Such tumors, like all tumors, require treatment. As early as the 1930s, it was known that surgical removal of the thymus gland with its tumor was sometimes followed by improvement in the patient's myasthenia. Interest in thymectomy as a treatment for myasthenia stems from the observations of an English surgeon named Alfred Blaylock. In 1936, Blaylock removed a cystic thymic tumor from a young woman with progressively severe myasthenia gravis. This tumor had been irradiated previously without effect on either the tumor or the myasthenia. Blaylock reported the beneficial effect of the operation three years later, when the patient's myasthenia was considerably improved. This documented success initiated the somewhat illogical decision to remove thymus glands without tumors from other myasthenics. It took almost forty years to realize how frequently this procedure helped the patients. By the time I saw Dwight, thymectomy had become a cornerstone in the treatment of myasthenia and was usually combined with the use of medications that decreased the production of antibodies, immune suppressors of various types.

"So what's the plan?" he persisted.

We measured his level of acetylcholine receptor antibodies. It was elevated. Just what we had expected. We did an MRI scan of his chest. His thymus gland was enlarged, another nonsurprise. After a couple of weeks of immunosuppressive treatment, a chest surgeon removed Dwight's thymus gland. Dwight stayed on immunosuppressant therapy until the next summer when training camp started.

Jameson went on to have a very good preseason, and he won back his job as free safety. He then had a good season, playing as well in the second half as he did in the first half. He was not an all-pro. He never had been. He did, however, play another four years and then became a defensive coach at the college where he'd been mentioned as a possible All-American candidate.

Dwight never lost the nickname Sleepy, but no one ever called him First-Half again. To this day his myasthenia has not recurred.

Not everyone who receives immunosuppressive therapy does as well as Dwight Jameson did. Our modern use of immunosuppression dates back to 1965 and a report by a group of Swedish physicians. They used the pituitary hormone that stimulates the adrenal gland, adrenocorticotrophic hormone (ACTH), or corticotrophin. It increases the production of steroids by the adrenal glands. These steroids, in turn, suppress immune responses. The Swedish group studied patients in severe myasthenic crises, often on respirators. After an initial period of deterioration, the patients who had been given ACTH improved to the point where they no longer needed respiratory support. On average it took about ten days to go from being dependent on a ventilator to being free. That was progress. One of the patients in this report was identified by his initials, H.G.

H.G. was Hjalmar Gullberg, an outstanding Swedish poet and a member of the Swedish Academy. At the age of fifty-nine, H.G. developed myasthenia gravis. His condition deteriorated rapidly. Prostigmine treatment only temporarily restored his strength. The poet's myasthenia had struck him while he was working on a book of poems inspired by Dante. His illness gave the last poem in this collection an aura of imminent death. After a brief remission, a dramatic exacerbation followed. The poet became bedridden once again. A tracheostomy was performed and he was placed on artificial ventilation.

In the era before widespread thymectomy and aggressive immunosuppression, respiratory support was the key to preserving life. Even while on the respirator, Gullberg was able to write, and he began his last volume of poems, *Eyes, Lips,* a work that is intensely personal and moving.

He was given another course of corticotrophin, which resulted in a dramatic change in his condition. His friends regarded this latest remission as miraculous. He had apparently been brought back to life. But during the treatment that saved his life, he had been through three tracheostomies. The corticotrophin courses had added months to his life, but H.G. soon realized that the myasthenic symptoms were returning. He once again became unable to talk or swallow. He wrote to his friends that he would not go through a fourth tracheostomy or suffer through another ordeal on a respirator. He preferred to die. The next morning, he walked down to a lake near his home. One of the poems he had written in his youth became his epitaph:

there is a lake
thereafter—nothing more.

chapter 17

Saving the Best for Last:
Babe Didrikson Zaharias

IN 1950 THE ASSOCIATED PRESS organized a poll of American sportswriters to choose the greatest athlete of the first half of the twentieth century. That honor went to Jim Thorpe. Thorpe had won international fame by winning both the pentathlon and decathlon at the 1912 Olympics and later played both professional football and major league baseball. He remains the favorite to win any similar poll for the entire century, especially since legends tend to grow with time.

My personal vote for both honors would go to Mildred "Babe" Didrikson Zaharias. In the 1950 poll, she received no votes for best overall athlete and in 2000 she will again get no such votes. True, she was chosen by the 1950 Associated Press poll of the same sportswriters as the outstanding female athlete of the first half of the twentieth century, and like Jim Thorpe is likely to win again when the poll for the entire century is taken. A very good argument, however, can be made to consider her to have been the greatest athlete of this century—period. The great

American sportswriter Grantland Rice said of her: "She is beyond all belief until you see her perform. Then you finally understand that you are looking at the most flawless selection of muscle harmony, of complete mental and physical coordination, that the world has ever seen."

But Babe was more than just a very gifted athlete. She excelled at so many different athletic endeavors over such a prolonged period of time that her career raises some questions about the nature and implications of human windows of opportunity and how these different individual abilities can be maximized.

Mildred was born in Port Arthur, Texas, in 1911 and grew up in Beaumont, Texas. Her parents were Norwegian immigrants. The family name was Didriksen, but Babe changed hers to Didrikson. She got her start in athletics working out in their backyard using homemade gymnastic and weight-lifting equipment. No one ever worked harder or at more different activities. She quickly got a reputation as a tomboy, a girl who preferred the sports that boys played to the games that girls played. As a young teenager, she played softball with the boys and hit the ball farther and more frequently than anyone else, earning her the nickname Babe. Or at least that is how her legend begins.

Because of her success as a high school basketball player, Babe was hired to play semiprofessional basketball for a company-sponsored, industrial basketball team. She was officially hired to be a typist for Employers Casualty Insurance Company of Dallas. In reality, she played basketball. The coach of the ECIC team had scouted and recruited her, not the office manager. In those years, such teams served many of the functions that have now been taken over almost completely by college basketball. The ECIC team on which Babe starred competed in an organized league of similar teams. The league itself was one of many that flourished across the country at the time. All of these leagues were under the auspices of the Amateur Athletic Union. The AAU had been organized in 1888 to regulate and govern amateur athletics. In the 1930s it was still the dominant ruling body of amateur athletics in this country.

Babe Didrikson, not yet Zaharias, running away from the field in the hurdles. She is the only Olympic Gold Medal winner in track of either sex to go on to become a stellar professional golfer.

During the first half of this century, participating in college sports as a student-athlete was not the only alternative open to talented athletes like Babe Didrikson. Athletes of either sex did not have to go to college in order to compete or to develop their talents. The most important alternatives were the industrial leagues, supported by local businesses, that competed on local, regional, and national levels under the banner and regulations of the AAU. The AAU had sponsored its first national basketball championship for men in 1915. The first NCAA men's basketball tournament was not held until 1939. Needless to say, there was no NCAA woman's basketball tournament in the thirties.

In the amateur system then in operation, athletes were given jobs and responsibility, working for the sponsoring business and playing for the company's teams. Jobs were not that easy to come by. The country was in the midst of the Great Depression. This was a pathway that worked for many great and not so great athletes, especially women athletes, since college sports did not offer them equal opportunities.

This system also meant that success at the highest level of professional sports was not the only reward available to most young athletes. Industrial sports were not only a path to success; they *were* success. This situation long outlasted the depression. In the mid-1940s, Bob Kurland of Oklahoma State was one of the two important men who helped to change the history of basketball and the way the entire game was played. The other was DePaul University's George Mikan. Mikan went on to play professional basketball and help establish the NBA. Kurland opted to play industrial basketball. In Kurland's mind, the future in AAU basketball, with a good job thrown in, was far more attractive and stable than professional basketball, where the leagues seemed to come and go with remarkable frequency.

Babe took the same path as did Kurland. During her three years of AAU basketball, Babe was chosen as an All-American every year. During her second season, in 1931, she led the company basketball team to the AAU National Championship and was named female athlete of the year by the Associated Press, the first of six times that she would win that honor.

It was in the next year, 1932, that Babe Didrikson achieved both national and international fame, not in basketball but in track and field. Employers Casualty Insurance Company of Dallas sent a team to compete in the AAU track and field championships. Babe was the entire team. She won five titles outright: the shotput, the baseball throw, the long jump, the eighty meter hurdles, and the javelin throw. She tied with Jean Shiley for first place in a sixth event, the high jump. All in all, Babe garnered thirty points and won the team championship for her employer all by herself. The second-place team was the University of Illinois. Illinois' twenty-two-woman team won a very respectable twenty-two points. Along the way, Babe had set world records in the javelin throw, the eighty meter hurdles, the baseball throw, and the high jump. Jean Shiley, of course, shared the high jump record with her. In a single afternoon Babe had set four world records. The victories had taken her not much more than three hours, and they remain the greatest feat ever accomplished in one afternoon by any athlete of any sex. It would have been a great way to end the track and field season, but the year was far from over.

The 1932 Olympics were held in Los Angeles, the first time the United States had played host to the games. As always, Babe set her goals quite high. "I am," she proclaimed, "out to beat everybody in sight, and that's just what I'm going to do." In those quaint days, a delicate female athlete could only compete in three events. Under today's rules she would have been able to compete in all six events that she won in the AAU championships, since the AAU competition served as the Olympic trials.

Babe competed in three of the events in which she held world records. She set a new Olympic record on her first attempt in the javelin throw and won her first gold medal. She then set a new world record in winning the eighty-meter hurdles in 11.7 seconds. Two events, two records, two gold medals. Her third event was the high jump and among her competitors was Jean Shiley, with whom in she shared the world record. The two of them tied once again. They both cleared five feet five and one-quarter inches, a new world record. The bar was then set at five feet five and three-quarter inches. Both women sailed over it cleanly. Everyone there thought they had just witnessed another tie at a world record level. They were wrong; the officials disqualified Babe. It seems that her head went over the bar before the rest of her body. That apparently violated some peculiar rule of etiquette. Babe was given the silver medal.

One wonders what these ultraconservative officials would have done with Dick Fosbury. He won the high jump in the 1968 Mexico City Olympic Games with a radical technique that came to be called "the Fosbury flop." In this move the jumper goes over the bar headfirst with his back down instead of the traditional position. Fosbury developed this approach and became the first man to jump over seven feet. By 1980, all but three of the sixteen Olympic finalists used "the Fosbury flop"—and none was disqualified.

Following her Olympic triumphs, Babe was once again voted the outstanding woman athlete of the year, but before the year was over she was suspended by the AAU for allowing her picture to appear in an advertisement for cars. Horror of horrors. Sports officialdom had gone beyond being either quaint or ultraconservative. It had become an anachronism, out of step with reality. This was the 1930s. Most people were worried if they would have a job next month and these guys were still acting as if amateur athletics was the natural domain of the rich, who could afford to play golf and lawn tennis and not worry about their next meal. It was almost as if someone who had to work for a living just wasn't "clean" enough to compete on the same field. It is not surprising that in the long run rulings such as this helped to undermine the public's view of the AAU.

For the next few years, Babe survived as best she could. She barnstormed around the United States with her own basketball team. She took up golf, playing as an amateur. The AAU had nothing to do with administering amateur golf. As part of her self-created mythology, Babe claimed that she had never before played golf. This is not true. She had played some golf in high school as a member of the girls' golf team. She had never played the game very seriously and first applied herself to it when she was in her twenties. In 1935 she won the Texas Women's Championship. She also played baseball with the House of David baseball team and even pitched an exhibition game for the Philadelphia Athletics* She was later stripped of her standing as an amateur golfer. Having few alternatives left, she toured the

---

*The House of David was a so-called Israelite religious sect from Benton Harbor, Michigan, that sponsored semipro basketball and baseball teams. These teams barnstormed around the United States playing all comers. The baseball team often played teams from the various Negro Leagues, industrial teams, and even teams made up of major league players trying to make a few extra dollars during the off-season. This was not a bad level of competition for a woman who started playing baseball seriously in her mid-twenties.

country with professional male golfer Gene Sarazen. This was almost as professional as anyone could get, since one of the main objectives of the tour was to sell Babe Didrikson golf clubs. If she couldn't endorse someone else's cars, she could at least endorse her own clubs. In 1938, she married professional wrestler George Zaharias and became Babe Didrikson Zaharias.

In 1943, her life in sports finally turned around. She was reinstated as an amateur in golf. Since there was no well-organized professional women's golf tour at that time, it is unclear what her precise status had been. Some sort of golf limbo, if not purgatory. In the next four seasons, Babe won forty golf tournaments. In one stretch, in 1946 and 1947, she won seventeen consecutive amateur tournaments. This all but inconceivable streak included both the 1946 U.S. Women's Amateur Championship and the 1947 British Ladies Amateur Championship. She then turned professional and helped found the Ladies' Professional Golf Association. She and Patty Berg became the first LPGA stars and were instrumental in establishing the LPGA tour. In 1948 and 1950, she won the U.S. Women's Open titles. In 1953 she underwent a colostomy for cancer of the bowel and then came back to win the Women's Open for a third time in 1954. She eventually lost her battle with cancer and died in 1956.

Babe had been named by the Associated Press as woman athlete of the year a total of six different times, over three decades: the thirties, the forties, and the fifties. No other athlete of either sex has been voted such an honor so many times, over such a long span of time. Starting in 1956, the winner of the Associated Press's woman athlete of the year award has been given the Babe Zaharias Trophy. Babe had been the overwhelming choice as woman athlete of the half century and has been elected to five different halls of fame.* Paul Gallico, a sportswriter before he became a successful novelist, called her "the most talented athlete, male or female, ever developed in our country."

---

*These are the International Women's Sports Hall of Fame, the National Track and Field Hall of Fame, the LPGA Hall of Fame, the Olympic Hall of Fame, and the World Golf Hall of Fame.

It is impossible to name another athlete who succeeded at so many endeavors over such a prolonged period of time. She took up golf several years later in life then any man who ever competed successfully on the professional tour, yet she dominated the competition for several years. She also took up baseball relatively late, although her level of actual accomplishment in baseball is much harder to judge.

Babe had played some golf in high school, already a relatively late age to get started. Her record at the sport then was undistinguished. She was a star in basketball and in track and field. Yet she became the best female golfer in the world. Though in her middle twenties and even later, she obviously hadn't been too old to learn and perfect her golf game. Why not? This is not a trivial question that only has implications for the world of sports. It raises issues of broad significance, questions that we cannot answer completely. The most obvious of these is whether windows of opportunity are identical in men and women. Do these windows open and close for both sexes at the same time? We just do not know. They may well not be identical. As far as I know, no one has seriously addressed this issue.

How can it be that such basic brain functions differ between the sexes? Such differences in basic neurophysiological function are a part of everyday life. Growth rates are not the same in men and women. Most boys have their adolescent growth spurt at an age when most girls have long stopped adding on height. Puberty also starts later in most boys and, of course, ends later. Both growth and puberty are thought of as endocrinologically controlled activities; however, endocrinological control is only the last step. In reality, these growth stages are neuroendocrine activities directed by the brain and its interaction with the environment. There are clear-cut differences between the two sexes for these activities and also among individuals of either sex. So it is quite possible that the timing and range of various windows of opportunity are different not just in different individuals but also between the sexes. If we judge by Babe Didrikson Zaharias, women may well have a definite advantage, a longer window of opportunity for acquiring at least some skills. It is difficult to generalize, however, since there are such individual differences within each sex. It is possible, after all, that Babe was a statistical "outrider" among women.

Not only do Babe's accomplishments raise questions as to when those windows close, they also serve to remind us that, given the right environmental circumstances, closure is not an absolute dead end. Appropriate early exposure may be the factor that makes acquisition and development of skills during later periods of life possible. Babe had played some golf in high school. She had also played softball as an adolescent, and then in her twenties was able to apply herself and learn to play baseball well enough to play for the House of David. Could she have learned to hit major league baseball? Could she have done what Michael Jordan wanted to do? Could she have made it to the majors? In all likelihood, she could not have. If Michael Jordan had merely wanted to play semiprofessional baseball, he might well have reached that goal. But he wanted to play baseball at the toughest level of competition. Success in most of life's endeavors does not depend upon reaching the level of skill that is needed to hit major league pitching. At any one time, there are no more than five hundred men who can actually hit major league pitching well enough to make a living in that way. And some of them don't even hit that well, although they often get paid as if they could.

These neurological principles apply to almost every aspect of our lives. The window of opportunity for hitting is not that different from the window of opportunity for language, for reading, for education in general. What Babe and her lifetime of increasing achievements suggest is that early exposure to and acquisition of a skill are the necessary prerequisites for later-life acquisition and development of analogous skills. As a teenager, Babe hit a softball well enough to earn her nickname. A decade later, she adapted that same skill to playing baseball.

The neurological realities of human anatomy present both limitations and opportunities that have obvious implications for education in general. We are often very dissatisfied with many of our school systems, especially with the failure of our high schools, which often graduate students who seem to lack the ability to read and write at an acceptable level. But it is not the high schools that have failed us and are continuing to fail us. The problem occurs far earlier in our educational system. The problem is with the primary schools. The window of opportunity for language closes quite early. Remedial reading should not be a college course. Ideally, it should not even be a high school course.

Every effort must be made to pry open the windows of language as early as possible and keep them open for as long as possible. The Head Start program. Early childhood enrichment. A curriculum in primary school that stresses language. Often the present system seems bent on teaching facts and attitudes instead of processes and skills. Children are asked to learn a set of facts, not to understand them, and then to regurgitate them on some multiple-choice test. In order to produce educated individuals, we should go back to basics. Back to the three R's— reading, reading, and reading. Prying open the window of language and reading later in life, for a second time, just will not work if it was never adequately opened at the right time. Reopening it or expanding on what is already there will work. It is not quite like learning to ride a bicycle—once learned, never forgotten—but it is a lot closer than we would like to believe.

Once the basic skills are acquired at the right age, later expansion of these skills is possible. And not just in sports. The great English novelist and short story writer Joseph Conrad was born in 1857 in Russian-dominated Ukraine. His parents were Polish. Originally named Teodor Józef Konrad Korzeniowski, Conrad grew up speaking and reading Polish and Russian. At the age of seventeen he ran off to Marseilles and began life as a seaman on a French ship. Later he switched to English ships, learned English, and became a British subject. In 1894, he settled in England to become a writer and wrote in English, which was neither his first nor his second language. His first novel, *Almayer's Folly*, was published the next year and was followed by such masterpieces as *Lord Jim* (1900), *Heart of Darkness* (1902), *Chance* (1913), and *Victory* (1915).

For Conrad, English was at best a third language; yet he mastered it as few other writers ever have. This was only possible because he had learned two other languages so well early in his life. In his thirties he became one of the greatest writers in the history of the English language. Babe Didrikson Zaharias did not start out as a golfer. She started out as an all-around athlete who used all of her skills and never let them wither. Later in life she applied all of these skills to golf. Very few individuals can develop into either a Babe Didrikson Zaharias or a Joseph Conrad. But if neither of these important figures had been given the right exposure to their respective fields early in their lives, neither of them would have developed his or her great potential. Fortunately for the rest of us, they enriched our lives as well as their own.

Suggestions for Further Reading

(and Viewing)

1] *Why Michael Jordan Couldn't Hit a Baseball*

The process of selective rather than instructive development of the brain (human and otherwise) is discussed in many places. I have found Michael Gazzaniga's *Nature's Mind* (Basic Books, 1992) to be the best starting place. Questions about acquisition of speech and handedness are well presented in Michael Corballis's *The Lopsided Brain* (Oxford University Press, 1991). An elegant description of behavioral maturation of the brain can be found in Eric H. Lenneberg's *Biological Foundations of Language* (Wiley, 1967). The study by Richard Schulz and his colleagues, "The Relationship Between Age and Major League Baseball Performance: Implications for Development," was published in *Psychology and Aging* in 1994.

A far more detailed presentation of the tragic story of "Genie" can be found in Russ Rymer's *Genie: A Scientific Tragedy* (Harper Collins, 1994).

Stephen Jay Gould is both a baseball aficionado or addict and a paleontologist. His view of Darwinian logic is part of all of his writings. The "Prologue" to his first book of essays, *Ever Since Darwin* (Norton, 1977), may be the best summary I have ever read. None of the biographical books on M.J. even entertain the notion that his failure to hit minor league pitching was evidence that he was merely human.

2] *Primo Carnera: The Bigger They Are*

The only readily available source in English for the life of Primo Carnera is *Primo, the Story of "Man Mountain" Carnera* (Robson, 1991). The story of the Roman emperor Maximinus can be found in "The Acromegaly of Maximinus" in my book *Toscanini's Fumble*

(Contemporary Books, 1988). Budd Schulberg's *The Harder They Fall* (Random House, 1947) was out of print the last time I looked. The movie version directed by Philip Yordan can be obtained as a classic at your neighborhood video store. A sign of the times. It was Bogart's last film.

4] The Seventh Inning Stretch: Michael Jordan and Wayne Gretzky
The physics of hitting a baseball is discussed in William F. Allman's "The Art and Science of Hitting a Baseball," in *Newton at the Bat*, edited by Eric W. Schrier and William F. Allman (Scribner, 1984).

5] The Bantam: Ben Hogan
There are two interesting surveys on the "yips" as a form of action-induced, occupational dystonia. One is K. D. McDaniel, J. L. Cummings, and S. Shain, "The 'yips.' A Focal Dystonia of Golfers," *Neurology* 39 (1985): 192–195. The other is P. Sachdev, "Golfer's Cramp: Clinical Characteristics and Evidence Against It Being an Anxiety Disorder," *Movement Disorders* 7 (1992): 326–332.

The older neurological literature is generally useless, spending far too much time debating the nature of such maladies. I have written about dystonic writer's cramp once before in "The Twenty-five Cent Cure," which appeared in *Newton's Madness* (HarperCollins, 1990).

Donald Hall's meditation on work is called *Life Work* (Beacon Press, 1993). There is a movie of Ben Hogan's life story, made in 1951 before Hogan's yips had started. Entitled *Follow the Sun*, it stars Glenn Ford, Anne Baxter, and June Havoc, and centers around Hogan's stirring comeback from his near-fatal crash to winning the U.S. Open. The most interesting part of this venture, Hollywood's first movie about golf, is that pro golfers Sammy Snead, Jimmy Demaret, and Dr. Cary Middlecoff all made brief appearances in it.

6] The Nineteenth Hole: Wolfgang Amadeus Mozart
Music and the Brain (Heinemann, 1977), edited by Macdonald Critchley and Richard A. Henson, has been an endless source of both scientific concepts and delight. Critchley's own contribution, "Occupational Palsies in Musical Performers," and "The Development of Early Musical Talent in Famous Composers: A Biographical Review," by Donald Scott and Adrienne Moffett, are both particularly relevant.

7] Muhammad Ali's Brain
William Langston, the neurologist who led much of the initial work on MPTP-induced parkinsonism, has coauthored a book that tells the

entire story, *The Case of the Frozen Addicts* by J. William Langston and Jon Palfreman (Pantheon, 1995). Parkinson's disease and many forms of parkinsonism can be successfully treated for many years in most patients. Ali has been one of these patients. Information on these disorders and their treatments can be obtained from the United Parkinson Foundation, 833 West Washington Boulevard, Chicago, IL 60607.

I have written about other aspects of Parkinson's disease before. The tale "The Man Who Would Save the World," in *Toscanini's Fumble*, describes the scientific basis for the treatment of Parkinson's disease in detail, while "Such Is Fame," from *Life, Death, and in Between* (Paragon House, 1992), shows how we learned to tell the difference between parkinsonism and Parkinson's disease.

Of the various biographies of Ali, I like *Muhammad Ali, A View from the Corner* by Ferdie "the Fight Doctor" Pacheco, M.D. (Birch Lane Press, 1992), but then I tend to be prejudiced in favor of books written by physicians. Budd Schulberg's *The Loser and Still Champion: Muhammad Ali* is, unfortunately, out of print. Alice Wexler's book *Mapping Fate* (Times Books, 1995) tells the story of the hunt for the gene for Huntington's chorea, from the point of view of a member of a family who carries the gene.

9] The Men with the Not-So-Golden Arms: J. R. Richard and Whitey Ford
The medical presentation of J. R. Richard's clinical tale is W. S. Fields, N. A. Lemak, and Y. Ben-Menachem, "Thoracic Outlet Syndrome: Review and Reference to Stroke in a Major League Pitcher," *American Journal of Neuroradiology* 7 (1986): 73–78.

Whitey Ford's story is hidden away in H. S. Tullos, W. D. Erwin, W. Woods, D. C. Wukasch, D. A. Cooley, and J. W. King, "Unusual Lesions of the Pitching Arm," *Clinical Orthopedics and Related Research* 88 (1972): 169–183.

10] The Tenth Inning: Bruce Sutter
The saga of Bruce Sutter, as compiled by Steven P. Ringel et al., was published in the article "Suprascapular Neuropathy in Pitchers," *American Journal of Sports Medicine* 18 (1990): 80–86. It is replete with radiographs, tables, drawings, and illustrations, but no patients are named. However, the names of every physician who helped treat the anonymous pitcher (who coauthored the paper) and ever wrote a paper on the subject (or even on a remotely related subject) *are* mentioned. I guess they figured that Sutter already had far more than his allotted fifteen minutes of fame.

11] Flying Like a Butterfly: Wilma Rudolph
Piecing together the details of Wilma Rudolph's struggle with polio
was more difficult than I had imagined. Most sketches of her life and
obituaries describe her weakened left leg. In her biography, *The Story of
Wilma Rudolph* (Bantam, 1977), Wilma said that it was her right leg that
was crooked. Since I have no reason to suspect that she had any difficulty with right-left discrimination, I have tended to resolve the confu-
sion by taking her word for it.

    In this story and all of the other tales told here, non-sports-
related deaths have been ignored unless I could see any relevance in
the medical details. Since poverty relates to exposure to disease and
access to medical care, it is clearly relevant. The aspects of this story
that have to do more with polio than Wilma Rudolph can be pursued
in John R. Paul's *A History of Poliomyelitis* (Yale University Press, 1971).

12] The Four-Minute Neurologist: Roger Bannister
The fortieth anniversary edition of Roger Bannister's story of his
achievement, *The Four-Minute Mile* (Lyons & Buford, 1994), remains the
most detailed recitation of the attainment of that goal. Stephen Jay
Gould's *The Flamingo's Smile* (Norton, 1985), like all of his other books,
remains in print.

14] Just Right: Mahmoud Abdul-Rauf
Oliver Sacks's insightful look at a surgeon with Tourette's syndrome,
"A Surgeon's Life," can be found in his collection of clinical tales *An
Anthropologist on Mars* (Knopf, 1995). It is at least as good as his other
collections and I can think of no higher praise. In this tale, Sacks
describes the absorbedness of surgery and its effect on the surgeon and
his tics far better than anything else I have ever read.

    Bill Brashler's *The Bingo Long Traveling All-Stars & Motor Kings*
is available both in its original form (University of Illinois Press, 1992)
and in the movie version starring James Earl Jones, Richard Pryor, and
Billy Dee Williams. Although the movie is certainly quite good, if you
have to choose, leave the VCR off for an evening or two.

    A recent biography of Charcot, *Charcot, Constructing Neurology*
(Oxford University Press, 1995), by Christopher G. Goetz, Michel
Bonduelle, and Toby Gelfand, puts Charcot's accomplishments and his
influence on the development of neurology into perspective far better
than anything else I have ever read. It also gives the reader a picture of
how our understanding of the nervous system in health and disease
got started.

15] *One Fine Morning: Lou Gehrig*
The Pride of the Yankees can be found at your local video store. The film
was released in 1942 and starred Gary Cooper as Lou Gehrig, along
with Teresa Wright as his wife, Walter Brennan, Dan Duryea, and others. These others included Babe Ruth, who played himself. The film
was nominated for eleven Academy Awards including best picture,
best actor, best actress, best original story (by ex-sportswriter Paul
Gallico), and best screenplay, but only won for best editing (Daniell
Mandell). Lou Gehrig's acting debut in the 1938 western, *Rawhide*, is
not that much more difficult to locate, but it is far less worth viewing.
In this fifty-eight-minute, black-and-white epic, Lou played a rancher.
Ex-bandleader Smith Ballew had the lead role. Miss it if you possibly
can. Ray Robinson's biography of Lou Gehrig, *The Iron Horse, Lou
Gehrig in His Time* (Harper, 1991), can be found, however, and is worth
finding.

The story of Wapniarka, the Nazi concentration camp where
the prisoners were forced to subsist on a diet of chickling peas and
developed lathyrism, was told in my book *Toscanini's Fumble*
(Contemporary Books, 1988).

A biostatistical analysis of the medical impact of ALS on Lou
Gehrig, "When Did Lou Gehrig's Personal Illness Begin?" by Edward
J. Kasaraskis and Mary Winslow, can be found in *Neurology* 49 (1989):
1243–1247.

16] *First-Half Jameson*
The article by Von Reis, "Results with ACTH and Spironolactone in
Severe Cases of Myasthenia Gravis," can be found in *Acta Neurologica
Scandinavica* 41 (1965). The best historical introductions to myasthenia
are the ones by J. I. Arli, "History of Myasthenia Gravis," in *Historical
Aspects of the Neurosciences*, edited by F. Clifford Rose and W. F Bynum
(Raven Press, 1981); and G. L. Keynes, "The History of Myasthenia
Gravis," *Medical History*, 1961. The former includes the immunological
part of the tale as well as the details on the identity, disease, and death
of H.G.

17] *Saving the Best for Last: Babe Didrikson Zaharias*
Babe Zaharias wrote a rather self-serving autobiography, *This Life I've
Led*. It is no longer in print. Susan E. Cayleff's recently published biographical study, *Babe, the Life and Legend of Babe Didrikson Zaharias*
(University of Illinois Press, 1995), presents her athletic career, accomplishments, and legacy in a fabric that also includes her personal life
and the roles she played in athletics, feminism, and lesbianism. It is

well worth reading. There is, of course, a movie, simply titled *Babe*. Released in 1975, it features Susan Clark as Babe and ex-football great Alex Karras as George Zaharias. It cannot be recommended either as biography or entertainment. It may be easier to locate, however, than Babe's autobiography. The film based on Paul Gallico's novel *The Poseidon Adventure* is also easier to find than a copy of the novel. The novels of Joseph Conrad all remain in print, although their availability does increase whenever another one is made into a movie.

Author's Note

In view of the paucity of books in comparison to the number of videos available on the athletes, to say nothing of the ease with which the videos can be obtained, I may have started this book with the wrong question. The real issue may be why a neurologist would write any book at all, let alone a book on sports. By now I hope the answer is obvious. If not, rent the videos.

Index